T0087747

Desierto

ALSO BY CHARLES BOWDEN

Killing the Hidden Waters (1977)

Street Signs Chicago: Neighborhood and Other Illusions of Big-City Life,
with Lewis Kreinberg and Richard Younker (1981)

Blue Desert (1986)

Frog Mountain Blues, with Jack W. Dykinga (1987)

Trust Me: Charles Keating and the Missing Billions,
with Michael Binstein (1988)

Mezcal (1988)

Red Line (1989)

The Sonoran Desert, with Jack W. Dykinga (1992)

The Secret Forest, with Jack W. Dykinga and Paul S. Martin (1993)

Seasons of the Coyote: The Legend and Lore of an American Icon,
with Philip L. Harrison (1994)

Blood Orchid: An Unnatural History of America (1995)

Chihuahua: Pictures from the Edge, with Virgil Hancock (1996)

Stone Canyons of the Colorado Plateau, with Jack W. Dykinga (1996)

Juárez: The Laboratory of Our Future,
with Noam Chomsky and Eduardo Galeano (1998)

Eugene Richards, with Eugene Richards (2001)

Down by the River: Drugs, Money, Murder, and Family (2002)

Blues for Cannibals: The Notes from Underground (2002)

A Shadow in the City:
Confessions of an Undercover Drug Warrior (2005)

Inferno, with Michael P. Berman (2006)

Exodus/Éxodo, with Julián Cardona (2008)

Some of the Dead Are Still Breathing: Living in the Future (2009)

Trinity, with Michael P. Berman (2009)

Murder City: Ciudad Juárez and the
Global Economy's New Killing Fields (2010)

Dreamland: The Way Out of Juárez, with Alice Leora Briggs (2010)

The Charles Bowden Reader (2010)

El Sicario: The Autobiography of a Mexican Assassin,
Molly Molloy, co-editor (2011)

The Red Caddy: Into the Unknown with Edward Abbey (2018)

CHARLES BOWDEN

Desierto

Memories of the Future

FOREWORD BY

William deBuys

UNIVERSITY OF TEXAS PRESS · AUSTIN

Lannan
CHARLES BOWDEN PUBLISHING PROJECT

Copyright © 1991 by Charles Bowden
The Charles Clyde Bowden Literary Trust
Mary Martha Miles, Trustee
Foreword copyright © 2018 by William deBuys
All rights reserved
Printed in the United States of America
Photography: Mark Klett. Gun Found In Drifting Sand, Kelso, CA, 1/22/87
Book design: Dustin Kilgore
The first edition of *Desierto* was published by W. W. Norton & Company.
Excerpts from *Beyond the Wall* by Edward Abbey. Copyright © 1971, 1976, 1977, 1979, 1984 by Edward Abbey. Reprinted by permission of Henry Holt and Company. All rights reserved. Reprinted by permission of Henry Holt & Company and Don Congdon Associates, Inc. © 1984 by Edward Abbey. Excerpt from *Desert Solitaire* by Edward Abbey ("I have never heard a mountain lion . . ."). Reprinted by permission of Don Congdon Associates, Inc. © 1968 by Edward Abbey, renewed 1996 by Clarke C. Abbey.

Requests for permission to reproduce material from this work should be sent to:

Permissions
University of Texas Press
P.O. Box 7819
Austin, TX 78713-7819
utpress.utexas.edu/rp-form

♾ The paper used in this book meets the minimum requirements of ANSI/NISO Z39.48-1992 (R1997) (Permanence of Paper).

Library of Congress Cataloging-in-Publication Data

Names: Bowden, Charles, 1945–2014, author.
Title: Desierto : memories of the future / Charles Bowden.
Description: Austin : University of Texas Press, 2018. | The first edition of Desierto was published in 1991 by W. W. Norton & Company.
Identifiers: LCCN 2017048495
  ISBN 978-1-4773-1658-0 (pbk. : alk. paper)
  ISBN 978-1-4773-1659-7 (library e-book)
  ISBN 978-1-4773-1660-3 (non-library e-book)
Subjects: LCSH: Sonoran Desert—Social conditions—20th century. Capitalists and financiers—Sonoran Desert. | Drug dealers—Mexican-American Border Region. | Sonoran Desert—History. | Capitalism—Moral and ethical aspects—Sonoran Desert.
Classification: LCC F787 .B678 2018 | DDC 972/.17083—dc23
LC record available at https://lccn.loc.gov/2017048495

FOREWORD

WILLIAM DEBUYS

You might think, as Charles Bowden did, that the world is a down-spiraling mess, but that's not a reason to read him. The important thing to Bowden was not so much the direction of the spiral as the intensity of its motion. He wanted to feel the gyre. He wanted to see it, taste it, and report it in all its brutality and paradoxical beauty. He was a connoisseur of the actual mess we've made of our world, and he described its flavors meticulously. That's why for almost a generation people have been reading Bowden with amazement (*Desierto: Memories of the Future* came out in 1991), and that's why people will still want to read him today. The wine hasn't changed. It's just aged a little. And the taste is even richer.

Bowden's writing gives off heat. It's the heat of the desert, the heat of sex, the heat of argument. He interrogated everything, following the evidence, hoping to "locate some kind of heartbeat beneath the modern world I live in." He was born in Illinois in 1945, moved to Tucson while still a kid, and was based for most of his life in southern Arizona. The desert that became Bowden's natural habitat was not the ecological desert described as Sonoran or Chihuahuan but the cultural place straddling the life-warping division of the international border, a place inhabited by campesinos, artists, drug runners, fat cats, hunters, and hustlers: *el desierto*. The place got into him. Bowden became the most *mexicano* of gringos. He was a big, bluff white guy, but the spirit of the Day of the Dead, that weird Indo-Iberian decoction of morbidity and ecstatic celebration, sloshed back and forth inside him like a tide.

I asked a mutual friend to describe him. The friend said, "He had an element of confrontation." While other gringos poked around south of the border finding seams in the landscape where they could move safely and unobtrusively, "Bowden would ask, 'Who's the most fucked-up person here? I gotta go talk to him.'" And that's what he did, hazards be damned. One of the ironies of his life is that, after decades of asking questions where a lot of well-armed, hard-eyed people thought he didn't belong, he died in his sleep in 2014, having moved to Las Cruces, New Mexico, to probe the anarchy and carnage of Ciudad Juárez.

Bowden was drawn mothlike to the darkest flames, not just to feel the burn, but to tell the story of their kindling, the light they gave, and the ashes they left behind. His problem, as his friend explained, was the problem of the artist: "How do you get people to see what's there? It's nearly impossible."

But it becomes more possible in the dreamscape of *Desierto*. Bowden gives no chapter headings, no hints of structure, only a collage of stories that mysteriously compound upon each other into a hyperreality of longing, fatalism, and apocalypse, of *la problema*, the violent nihilism of the drug trade, of the surreal greed and egotism of Charles Keating, impresario of one of the greatest financial calamities of recent history, of the mystical yet practical Seri Indians, listening to deer talk one minute and carving junk for American tourists the next. Who is sane? Who is not? The boundaries blur. Cruelty and loss abide. Joy, fleeting, has to be tackled and held.

Follow the money: Americans import drugs, and in exchange they export anarchy, corruption, guns, and terror, not intentionally, at least not most of the time, but as a by-product of their appetites and careless wealth. That's one trail Bowden follows through the desert, an environment that sometimes "is just happenstance, a platform where looting takes place." Other times, the desert is a thing to be obliterated with acres of swimming pools, negated by twining fairways, and denied by an unlimited stream of BTUs chilling palaces clad in Italian marble for the Medicis of today. The present continually quotes the past. So will the days ahead, producing in Bowden's phrase "memories of the future." This is true also of *la problema*: there was always *una problema*. People have always died in the desert for no good reason. People always will.

The money trail is not the only one that Bowden follows; it's not even the main one. He writes, "I have a need for visiting the battlefields of love." The people of *Desierto* twitch with desire, they thirst and lust. Bowden watches them. He understands. He sees life through their eyes. "The whole world is sexual to us, down to the very last stone." Because of which, sometimes they kill, which means that many crime scenes conceal love stories and some of the most savage acts originate, far away, in moments of vulnerability and innocent naked hunger, in moments of tenderness.

It is the tenderness that keeps me turning Bowden's pages. Maybe I have grown inured to the unending brutality of the borderlands, which is meted out casually in government policies no less than in fits of individual rage. What gets to me is the tenderness Bowden finds among the iron-bar realities of *el desierto*. I read him with a pencil in hand, so I can mark the moments:

> No one remembers the reasons for his murder. That was years and years ago and the shrine now looks naked in the desert and wants paint and the visit of a fistful of paper flowers.

An image such as that one—and there are many in *Desierto*—halts me in my tracks. I read it again, looking for its magic: *the visit of a fistful of paper flowers.* The tone is exact, the cadence complete, every word necessary. It had to be a visit—something temporary, which time will erase. It had to be a fistful, not a bunch or a handful, because of the slightly sweaty tension in the closed fist, the objection it embodies to letting go of the flowers, to accepting that death is death. A fist is also a weapon. It expresses defiance, if not to the will of God or to fate, then to the sunlight that still touches the face of the bastard who did this deed. And of course the flowers are paper, whether their bearers are rich or poor but especially if they are poor, because nothing else blooms in this desert of loss or retains its beauty under the punishing sun. Paper lasts longer, but not long. A dusty wind blows over the brokenhearted gift. I can see the red crepe flutter.

Bowden reminds me of one of the least appreciated giants of American letters, a writer with an appetite for telling analogous stories from a similarly personal point of view. Like Bowden, this writer worked as a reporter, but was more than a reporter. He styled himself a spy traveling undercover in unsafe territory, and he wrote long, edgy, booze-fueled riffs that brimmed with wild insight and sensuous detail. He disdained the conventions of literary structure and refused to be contained by the standards of so-called journalism because he felt compelled to tell a deeper, wilder, and yes more sexual story about the workings of the world and the fragile, faulted people in it. His masterpiece was not the lyrical novel for which he was awarded the Pulitzer Prize but the sprawling, inspired, rampant creation that dumbfounded critics when it first appeared. *Let Us Now Praise Famous Men* is the *Moby-Dick* of American nonfiction, both in its history of initial rejection and ultimate canonization and in its qualities of omnivory as to subject matter and sheer brilliance of expression. Of course I am speaking of James Agee, and I have no idea if Chuck Bowden ever read him, let alone liked him, but in the end they are cousins in style and appetite.

Their subject is the union of opposites, the angels and devils joined at the hip, the beauty married to the beastliness of life. Agee said *Famous Men* was "an independent inquiry into certain normal predicaments of human divinity." Bowden might reject a word such as *divinity*, but not too fast. Like Agee, he saw the holiness of the quotidian, the hunger for transcendence and mercy, the pathos implicit in just carrying on:

> There are similar fiestas everywhere in Mexico for different
> Virgins, for various saints. They exist because people hurt,
> because work is hard, because women are desirable, because
> miracles are necessary, because few can stay sober without
> sometimes being drunk.

Agee would have extolled such observations. He understood the effort and openness, the compassion and years of seasoning required to make them. He was a critic as well as a writer, and his film commentary is as penetrating as his reportage. He died too young to see *Chinatown*, but he would have loved it, especially the final gut-wrenching denouement, when Jack Nicholson interrogates Faye Dunaway about a girl she's been protecting. Nicholson is slapping Dunaway, trying to get the long-hidden truth out of her, and Dunaway, at the edge of incoherence, her head whipping left and right with each slap, is sobbing back at him, "She's my sister, she's my daughter, she's my sister. . . ."

I see Bowden, under similar questioning, admitting another incestuous unity: "It's the hunger, it's the horror, it's the hunger, it's the horror."

In *Desierto* Bowden ultimately confesses the paradox at the source of his fascination, the spark that ignites his fire, the two siblings that make a whole, each also parent to the other. And Agee would understand him, would make the same profound admission: "I am watching ruin, and yet savoring life. I am complete."

FOR EDWARD ABBEY

R. I. P.

BUT I DOUBT IT.

A NOTE ON THE TEXT

Sometimes the people and places in this book have been given fictitious names. This has been done to protect the privacy of individuals and the peace and calm of places or because of the hazards of the drug world. The facts have not been altered.

The Yaqui songs quoted in Chapter 4 are from Larry Evers and Felipe S. Molina, *Yaqui Deer Songs, Maso Bwikam: A Native American Poetry* (University of Arizona Press, 1987). Earlier versions of some of the material in this book have appeared in *Smart, City Magazine, Buzzworm, Witness,* and *Phoenix.*

Desierto

1

I turn the pages of the transcript and hear the singsong voice of an old Indian woman. The date is so exact, all the words passing before my eyes were spoken into a tape recorder just two months ago and then carefully written out in longhand by another Indian woman on white sheets of paper. I have a file case full of such interviews, all part of a desire on my part to locate some kind of heartbeat beneath the modern world I live in. Behind my head a piano solo seeps from the speakers, a mesquite log smolders in the fireplace, now and then a quiet flame licking the wood. In an hour or two, it will be dawn. This is a favorite time for me, a pause when the clocks cease to convince me and the fantasies come easily. The old woman in the transcript remembers a morning, a sunrise with no date given, that occurred perhaps eighty or a hundred years ago. She is not seeking fantasy. A child is lost and the people go and search for him in the desert. He is found safe. With the deer. This happened west of me, somewhere a hundred miles off in the *desierto*.

Then, it is later, sometime later, and two Indian women are making tortillas. One says she is hungry, and the other tells the man to kill something for meat. The man whose boy was lost gets up and takes his gun and goes off into the desert. Soon, the women hear a shot, and they think, good, we will have meat. The man returns, sits down, and does not speak. He looks sad. Finally an old man, a gnarled figure who has been buried in silence in

1

some corner of the hut, gets up and goes to him. He asks if he shot something for meat. The man who went out with the gun says that, yes, he took a shot. But something bad happened.

The man continues his telling. Soon after leaving the hut he saw a deer, fired and hit it, and then the deer went over the mountain. He followed. He found a small cave, and before the mouth of the cave a woman sat weeping. Her hair was long and she clutched her side and blood poured from the wound. Crying painfully, she looked up at the man. The man left and came back to the hut where he sat silent and ill at ease. Where the women waited.

And then the man says nothing more and there is no meat for the tortillas.

I stop reading and lose myself in the fire. I believe this story, which may never have happened. I am sure I believe in many things that may not have happened, and I do not believe in many things that have happened. For example, I have very little belief in the last several decades. In my world, a dry bone of desert that takes up vast amounts of ground in the United States and Mexico, the past twenty or thirty years have seen by many yardsticks an enormous amount of change. Small cities have become big cities, small towns have become empty ghosts, factories and power plants have defied the cloudless skies and dead rivers, millions have claimed as home ground tracts on which no one can even grow food. Most people I know traverse huge portions of this desert regularly, driving very fast in fine automobiles, do this even though they could not cover thirty miles of this ground on foot if their life depended on it. Sometimes when their life does depend on it, they show up as small items in the newspapers, as bodies found twisted under the sun because a machine failed them or their sense of direction went bad, and, given those circumstances and left on foot, they have perished, their dried lips pulled back to reveal the snarl of their teeth.

Such things can be briefly sensed and then the waves of daily life drag me back down to the comforting numbness that is our lot. I live in a time when the imagination is dead and everything is memories. We call these memories the future. We have developed new religions to pursue this faith and to win converts. The future will be clean, the loins carefully sterile, the trash neatly sorted into proper piles of plastics, paper, and metal, the food pure, always there will be honey, never white sugar, the underarms unshaven yet fresh with herbal aromas. It will all be memory of course, memory of a white American before the Latins, the blues, the Asians who work too hard and score too well on all the tests. In this memory, we speak Ecology the sacred tongue, we park washed Volvos outside log A-frames, pluck succulent vegetables from the black soil of our gardens, read non-sexist books to each other in the glow of the evening. The rapacity of industrialism will be chastened by our biodegradable ethics, the floor under our feet will be tile, the basic commodity of life will be information, which will explode around us like starbursts. It will be like the sunny days of the early Republic, except we now know better, and we do not practice slavery, we do not deny women their rights, we do not endorse weapons, we do not slaughter Indians but rather cherish them as simple children of the forests, plains, and deserts. We have learned from our sins and from the sins of our fathers and of our fathers' fathers and it would not be just for our punishment to continue. We listen to songs of humpbacked whales, we are a new people.

Religion has failed us because long ago it separated us from Nature, which we now call Our Mother, and made us worship things. History has failed us because long ago it convinced us that by reason we could absent ourselves from the pain of life and reach harmony, peace, and plenty. Science has failed us because it bedded down with wealth, became technocracy, and made so many things that clutter up our lives. We have nothing left but this Ecology. However, all around us people are committing heinous acts, and heresy, and turning a deaf ear to the call of this new god. The darker races are raping the earth, killing the creatures of the sea, slaying the last forests, sleeping with their women too often and having too many offspring. They are trying to poison us with their drugs, taking the rare species of the forest, cooking them down into vile potions which now flow like acid through the veins of our lives. It may be too late for them, they may have gone too far, sinned too much.

We can imagine nothing, not a single thing. We reach instead for memories, memories of our future. Instead of going west, we will escape to the moon, the planets, safety beyond the farthest star. Instead of liberal social legislation we will have liberal environmental legislation, a little tinkering with landfills, a ban on disposable everything, car pools, passive solar design in housing, abundant devices for contraception, mass tree plantings. We will not question our world, but polish its edges. We will use our memories. And crawl toward our future. And live in this great barren.

I know very few people who agree with me on this matter. Most of the people I know believe in the future while I seem to merely remember it. I think of these notions often in the hours before dawn when no one is out and about to question my instincts.

Because of the time in which I live, and the forces loose upon the land now, I may be fated to spending my entire life remembering the future. I hope not, but it could be. I will witness cities built where there is no long-term basis for them, watch families and friends proliferate in a place where there will never be enough food for them, and watch the earth underneath all this activity grow weary, sag with fatigue, and slip into a coma that smacks of death. Sitting here, the fire crackling, I quietly watch the past flowing into a future that cannot accommodate it, or stop its intrusion.

At such moments I often go to ground, literally. I seek some dues and solace in plants, animals, swirls of soil. I begin to believe the Indian story of the man with the deer. I dread the feeling of killing that which sustains me, and yet my finger inches toward the trigger. I think I am reaching for a flower but I come up with gore on my face.

I remember stumbling on a woman weeping, blood pouring out of a gaping wound. Her blood was sticky and I dabbed my finger in it and placed some on my tongue. I will not tell you what it tastes like. Some things you must do on your own.

This is all true. Or so I believe in the hours just before dawn. The rest of the time, I am more or less just like you.

* * *

About nine in the evening, the truck got stuck in a dry wash. The air was hot with the breath of May, and the sand sucking at the tires refused to give back the machine. We were sixteen miles from a highway and had to catch a plane at dawn, the by-the-clock embrace of modern life. We had two quarts of water and no food. I looked up and bats flew just above my head and the only light was the stars. We were in a huge patch of desert, a couple of thousand square miles, where no one lived, a hot pan divided into various bombing ranges, gunnery ranges, Organ Pipe Cactus National Monument, and the Cabeza Prieta National Wildlife Refuge. Our presence was illegal, another little tick of modern life. To the south, twenty miles or more, lay El Camino del Diablo, the Devil's Road, a dry spinal cord that helped organize this piece of ground in the mind. For centuries, travelers had loosely followed its path and many had died. No one knows how many, so everyone enjoys imagining the numbers of swollen tongues, rasping voices, blank eyes not blinking in the noonday sun as the flies flickered over the quickly mummifying flesh.

Ironwood and palo verde trees stood like skeletons above the wash, and scattered saguaros poked up at the night. We began to walk fast and in four hours hit the hamlet of Tacna on the Interstate. All the way there, military aircraft flew over our heads, red lights and flares splashing war games against the blackness. Once in a while we would hit barren ground, the earth flat and empty of life, cold fragments of steel implanted in the center of a target.

The restaurant was closed but we saw a light in the kitchen, knocked, and two Basque women came out. They were not afraid, but they were curious. Their faces were blank, voices flat. I said I was hungry and they handed me a bag of M&Ms, which I ripped open clumsily spilling the contents onto the hot dirt. I got down on my hands and knees and grubbed for them in the night. Later, I told a friend of mine of this moment and she said, "You should never admit to such things." I asked why and she said, "You just shouldn't." She was perfectly groomed, her blond hair a flame in the night of a parking lot as she spoke this advice to me.

Standing in the dark behind the closed restaurant, one of the Basque women asked, "Where have you come from?" We had the look of drifters wandering down the Interstate. When we motioned toward the south, she said with surprise, "That's the forbidden zone."

Precisely. For years, I'd pored over the maps, taken sidelong glances from the car as I'd skirted its edges, dreamed about what fantastic forms, beasts, night thoughts, and fears filled its emptiness. I would talk with friends about it. Books, I read the scant books, dusty texts of strange people who had wandered in and still gotten out. Once I was in a state office in the capital and there spreading across the wall like a brown mold was a sixty-year-old map of the area. The man behind the gray steel desk looked up and his eyes gleamed. The forbidden zone. Eventually, I was living in a studio apartment with small sectionals of this area taped against the block wall. My neighbors were all divorced or anxious to get married so they could get divorced. I would sit on the floor with my drink, tracing my imaginary journeys across the contour lines, blobs of red and brown, little dabs of green. I would rehearse long walks through the map, my legs tightening on the rises, my ears alert to the sound of a rattlesnake in the summer's darkness. When visitors would look at me strangely, I would get up and pour them a drink and then continue tracing with my finger through the dust of the maps.

Finally I went into it. First, in a jeep. Later on foot. There were no footprints, no sounds. I found others who shared the same passion, secret lovers who were loathe to talk about the place. Ed Abbey would cross it on foot and then when he wrote up his walk, he would fake the geography, give false directions, invent place names. He said this was necessary to protect the place—to protect any place in our life and times. Once we were walking down an arroyo near his house and listening to the birds sing and I remember him hammering me on this point. He was kind of hunched over in his jacket, his head nicely chiseled like a candidate for Mount Rushmore, his voice flat as the plains and very quiet.

I didn't agree with him.

I don't think silence lends protection any longer. I don't think anything lends protection any longer. And I'm not sure protection is as important as knowledge at this date. It is time to know because soon it may be too late to learn. All space is now temporary as the vise grip of our appetites tightens against it.

As for that time when the truck got stuck, we finally found a rancher in the dark of the night, a man living in a trailer on the edge of this big empty, who was willing to take us back into the big blank and help pull the truck out. He was a lean-boned man, and his dreams lay in cultivating thousands of acres of jojoba, a desert shrub whose seed produces a light oil akin in properties to that of a sperm whale. We crawled into the cab and went bumping off into the darkness. His hands tightened on the steering wheel, the green dash lights glowed off his face, and once in a while he'd ask if it was still farther and we would say yes. Finally, he said that he'd never been down here before, never been south of the big Interstate road that his fields sprawled along. The forbidden zone.

We slapped a chain on the stuck truck, ripped it from the silent sand, and then rumbled back slowly on non-roads to the highway. We thanked him and he just shook his head.

For a while, every time I was in the hamlet I would go to the Basque restaurant. They had a bar and I got to know the owner, the paterfamilias of the clan. He'd come over from the old country and been a shepherd to flocks up in the Rim country to the north. He cooked a lot then and based the restaurant on his recipes—a lot of ways to cook ewe. The design came from no blueprint—he told me he'd carried it all in his head from his memories of home and he cut out the boards and beams from the whole building in his front yard with the help of some Mexican wetbacks. He never went south into the desert. He ran the bar, he explained. One day, his daughter, one of the women who had watched me grovel in the dirt for food that night, won the state lottery for hundreds of thousands of dollars. But even this did not change life at the restaurant.

A couple of months after the truck got stuck, we left a case of imported beer on the steps of the rancher's trailer. All around the metal building tufts of jojoba poked up hungrily from the sand.

That's how I came into the country. But everyone has a different story. Abbey had his. For the same country.

On the bus my seatmate was an old black man from Houston, Texas, bound for Oakland, California. Looking out our big window at the desert, he said, "Ain't nothin' much out there."

I was looking too. Somewhere about thirty, forty miles to the north, beyond the foreground of cactus, creosote bush and sand, lay the route I planned to follow back.

"Ain't nothing at all out there," I said. I wanted to reinforce his opinion. "Nothing but nothing."

He nodded, smiling.

In the double seat in front of us was a black woman and her four children. A little girl with her hair braided in cornrows, with an elaborate set of strings and beads attached—like Cleopatra—looked back at us, smiling at my ridiculous beard. She said, "Where you goin'?" I said, "Home."

—Edward Abbey, *Beyond the Wall*

Deserts can be very specific places for a botanist or zoologist. But not for most of us. We tend to see deserts as a quality more than a place. To go off into the desert in our language means not to visit a locale, but a state of mind. And so if we consider a very specific desert, the Sonoran, and a very specific place, El Camino del Diablo, we still cannot really contain ourselves with bundles of the specifics—checklists of plants, and animals, weather reports of startling June days and cold January nights. That is why when we read the Christian Bible, a very early collection of desert writings, we feel an eerie kinship with the wandering Hebrews. Not in the promised land. Not in Egypt. Not in Babylon. But in the Sinai. Every one of us, regardless of where we are sitting on this planet, no matter what the birds are trilling in the green forest outside our window, every one of us snaps alert with a clear sense of the ground when the Hebrews enter Sinai and begin their long trial by God in the desert. We can feel the night air coming off the plains of hot stones, feel the soft swishing of the fabric in the tents, catch the bloom of the blood spraying from the sheep's throat unto the barren ground.

The desert. We now have many photographs that we use to fog that simple word. The days tumble together, the sun at noon annoys with light and flattens everything the eye sees into boredom. The ground boils with the goings of large ants, and every plant seems to rake the flesh with a lust for blood. If a careful tabulation is kept of good moments, they turn out to be very few. A half hour riding the cusp of dawn, a few minutes as the sun melts below the horizon. The seconds in the middle of the night when the body turns, the eyes briefly open, and the cold sky burns with white stars. That's about it.

And yet we go. We say, "We're going into the desert." We seldom say quite where because it does not matter. And besides, everyone knows where we are going. Into the desert.

> Sex has been of no great consequence to me, and the celibacy
> of desert life left me untroubled. Marriage would certainly have
> been a crippling handicap. I have therefore been able to lead
> the life of my choice with no sense of deprivation. Existence in
> the desert had a simplicity that I found wholly satisfying; there,
> everything not a necessity was an encumbrance. It was those
> three months in the Sahara in 1938 that taught me to appreciate
> things that most Europeans are able to take for granted: clean
> water to drink; meat to eat; a warm fire on a cold night; shelter
> from rain; above all, tired surrender to sleep.
> —Wilfred Thesiger, *The Life of My Choice*

> Oh, how many times did I set out in the desert, in that vast
> solitude parched with the fires of the sun that offers a dread
> abiding to the monk, how often did I think myself back in the
> old Roman enchantments. There I sat solitary, full of bitterness;
> my disfigured limbs shuddered away from the sackcloth, my
> dirty skin was taking on the hue of the Ethiopian's flesh: every
> day tears, every day sighing; and if in spite of my struggles sleep
> would tower over and sink upon me, my battered body ached on
> the naked earth. Of food and drink I say nothing, since even a

sick monk uses only cold water, and to take anything cooked is a wanton luxury. Yet that same I, who for fear of hell condemned himself to such a prison, I, the comrade of scorpions and wild beasts, was there, watching the maidens in their dances; my face haggard with fasting, my mind burnt with desire in my frigid body, and the fires of lust alone leaped before a man prematurely dead. So destitute of all aid, I used to lie at the feet of Christ, watering them with my tears, wiping them with my hair, struggling to subdue my rebellious flesh with seven days' fasting. . . .

I grew to dread even my cell, with its knowledge of my imaginings; and grim and angry with myself, would set out solitary to explore the desert. . . .

—St. Jerome

I asked, "Why are the Indians afraid of the ocean?"

"Because the ocean will curse people who do not honor the ocean's mother. The ocean is treacherous. It will curse." Some of my mother's relatives, who also lived in these huts, talk real fast, they sound like they are crying when they are talking.

—Martha Celaya, Hea'Ced O'otham Clan, interviewed by
Fillomen Bell, September 27, 1989

Sixty soldiers on foot, 1,500 head of stock, more than two hundred men on horseback, a thousand friendly Indians, all going north from Culiacán in Sinaloa. It is March of 1540, and Francisco Vásquez de Coronado is marching toward personal ruin and a page in dusty books of history because of a tale from the twelfth century. Around 1150 when the Moors swallowed Spain, seven bishops were rumored to have departed into the big sea to the west. And so in 1536, when Cabeza de Vaca and three companions emerged from the blankness of North America near Culiacán and fell into the arms of Spanish slavers, their faint tale of cities of wealth somewhere to the north fed an old flame of seven fabled cities of gold.

Part of the desert, wherever it may be found, is a landscape so plain and abstract that it beckons from the mind a belief in things that cannot seem to take hold as easily in wetter, denser places. The desert is so empty to us that it has a place for everything. The real estate operator of the twentieth century is blood brother to the conquistador of the sixteenth century. Cortés sensed this of his companions when he wrote his king, "[They] are not pleased with some of them [the rules], in particular with those which bind them to strike root in the land; for all, or most, of them intend to deal with these lands as they did with the Islands first populated, namely, to exhaust them, to destroy them, then to leave them." The exhaustion and the leaving continue to this very second. So does the hunger, a feeling of emptiness in the belly. Cortés is huddled on the coast wondering what lies inland in the world called Mexico when the king of these lands sends Teudilli to question the white strangers. We know of this very moment because years later Cortés's secretary Gómara writes it down on a paper with a quill so that the world will always possess a life of his great master. The clerk notes, "Teudilli sent a message to Moctezuma in Mexico describing everything he had seen and heard, and asking for gold to give the captain of the strangers, who had asked him whether Moctezuma had any gold, and Teudilli had answered yes. So Cortés said: 'Send me some of it, because I and my companions suffer from a disease of the heart which can be cured only with gold.'" Of course, the great captain lied. Not about the disease, but about the cure. He would never be cured. Centuries later, we will sit in the desert and thumb through books and scorn him and his words and his life while we continue to live them. We will worship the desert, stare at huge photographs of its expanse, images cunningly taken by lovers who carefully edit out of their frames all evidence of our own existence in this place. We will be the first people here to shift our gaze from our works to the places we have not worked. Human beings who come after us will be amazed at our actions and write long dull essays about what they imagine to be our self-hatred or failure of will or decadence. They will note that we always studied these beautiful photographs in well-constructed rooms kept at a pleasant temperature, rooms from which only by straining our necks we catch the barest glimpse of the desert we professed to worship. God's mercy, which we are told is infinite, will be displayed in the fact that we will die before we ever have to read these essays.

The conquistadors of our moment do not carry swords but computer passwords. The room is sterile, the air fed by a machine, the drawings, plans, photographs all huge and lining the walls as people in white shirts and red ties scurry around the office plotting new towns and cities on the brown face of the desert. A private helicopter waits at the airport to ferry inves- tors, the woman bringing that cup of coffee is quietly dressed, her skin a faint musk. On the walls, too, are soft pastel paintings of Indians wrapped in blankets, and the Indians never blink as the computer screens flash up international markets before their eyes. Anything can be out there in the raw land, millions of dol- lars, flipped deals, new cars, a night of love in a good hotel on the coast. She steps out of the steaming water, her young body firm, and dreams of the dinner with candlelight that she will savor after he is done with her. I am listening to a woman when she whips out a photograph: she is on a yacht off San Diego, he has gotten her on the boat, and she is wearing a captain's hat in the small color print, her firm bare breasts gleaming in the sun with the sea at her back. It is all possible here, because, because, we tell ourselves there is nothing here now, nothing but a void, a hot breath full of death and perdition and vile with the odor of Satan. We are called by our God, by banks in New York, by the price of

gold on the Singapore exchange this very morning, by the sur-
plus of yen pushing at the walls of vaults in Tokyo, by our greed,
our vows, our memory of our mouth tugging at our mother's
breast—the hot flow of milk dribbling onto our lips—by something so deep we cannot name it, something so black we cannot
face it, something so strong, we cannot overcome it, something
so sweet we will kill ourselves and everyone else for one more hit
of it.

I am sitting in an office atop a tower, the desk is wood, the
walls green, the windows giant eyes staring out at the empty valley of desert. A brass telescope points south into the raw land.
And I imagine. The pen scratches—a gold-tipped Parker that is
an exact replica of a model half a century old—the fax machine
whirrs, the phone is never still, the warm flow of air onto the
receiver, the seven cities, they are out there, we all know that,
we just must look, we must be hard, we must not give into our
weakness, we must not surrender to faint memories of mercy.
We want to be winners, we want the woman on our terms, we
want to crush others with our power. We want our God to love
us so that we can stop this fear that lies on our tongue like bile
every morning in that bad, lonely moment when we awaken just
before the sun roars over the mountain and makes the emptiness
real estate again.

Sixty soldiers afoot, two hundred men on horseback, 1,500
head of bawling stock, a thousand Indians with skin smeared
with grease, their eyes black, the tips of the spears stone, their
feet like iron, all moving north into the main chance. Seven cities
of gold.

Forget history as a record of discovery. Forget exact facts. Forget the botany, the fine checklists of birds, the interesting notes
on granite, the fascination with volcanic intrusions, the cry of the
dove, the scream of the lion in the night. Stop this insistence on

putting the thing in a box with a label. Listen to voices, centuries of voices, and notice that they ignore the desert. It is the thing to cross, the place to violate, the way to the Seven Cities. Come, the voices say, we will go to Mecca, we will go to Cíbola, we will go to Xanadu where Kubla Khan a stately pleasure dome decreed. By the time I get to Phoenix, you'll be rising. We will go because this is one place we cannot be stopped because there is no stopping place. The desert, dry winds, bad water, bones bleaching white by our trail. No stopping.

Coronado says march. The enterprise is huge, he will wind up in Kansas chasing the Seven Cities through black clots of buffalo. But for now, he sends off a spur of his army into the desert, a small squad led by a man named Melchior Díaz. Díaz is to team up with ships that are fighting their way north up the Sea of Cortez, the supply arm of this caravan of greed. The geography, of course, is all wrong, Coronado is off in New Mexico terrorizing Pueblo Indians, the ships are straggling up the Colorado River near Yuma, Arizona, separated from their commander by four hundred miles of hard ground. The plan will fall apart. But Díaz does not know this. He is the good soldier sweeping off into the dry ground. He will be injured by his own lance, his bladder will be torn, and he will die slowly and painfully. His eyes are our first eyes. What he sees we will keep seeing forever, only names will change and the claims we make to our God.

> Captain Melchior Díaz took twenty-five picked men and set out with guides in search of the seacoast between north and west. After traveling 150 leagues Díaz came to a province inhabited by people like giants, exceedingly tall and muscular. They were, however, naked and lived in huts of long straw built underground like caves, and with only the straw rising above the ground. They entered these at one end, without stooping,

and came out at the opposite end. More than one hundred
persons, large and small, slept in one hut. When transporting
burdens they carried on their heads more than three and four
hundred pounds. It once happened that when our men wanted
to bring a log for the fire and six of them could not carry it, one
of the Indians picked it up in his arms, put it on his head all by
himself, and carried it quite easily.

These Indians eat corn bread, as large as the big loaves of
Castile, baked by the heat of ashes. When they travel about
from place to place they carry, on account of the intense cold,
a firebrand with which they warm their hands and body by
changing it from time to time. For this reason the large river
that flows through that land is called Tizón [Firebrand] river.

These natives were planning to attack our men and were
looking for an opportune occasion. When they saw that our
men wanted to cross the river, they rushed to build the rafts
with much diligence and speed. Thus they hoped to catch them
on the water and drown them, or find them divided so that they
could not support and aid one another.

During this time, while the rafts were being built, a soldier
who had gone foraging in the country saw a large number of
armed men cross a mountain. They were waiting for our men to
cross the river. He reported this, and an Indian was locked up
secretly in order to learn the truth from him. As they tortured
him he told of the whole plan the Indians had arranged for
the moment when the soldiers should cross. After learning
of their plans the captain ordered that the Indian who had
confessed the plot should be killed in secret, and they tossed
him into the river that night with a heavy weight in order that
the Indians should not know that they were suspected. The
next day, sensing that our men suspected them, they came to
a warlike mood, shooting showers of arrows. However, as the

horsemen began to overtake them and the lances cut them down mercilessly and the harquebusiers also were taking fine shots, they had to abandon the field and take to the mountains, until not a man was to be seen.

—"Castañeda's History of the Expedition," in *Narratives of the Coronado Expedition 1540–1542*

Melchior Díaz . . . turned back because he did not find water or grass, but many sand dunes. On the way back he had some skirmishes at the river district, because the natives wanted to waylay them while they were crossing the river. During this return, Melchior Díaz died from an accident. He killed himself when hurling a lance at a dog.

—*Relación del Sucesos*, "Relation of the Events on the Expedition that Francisco Vásquez Made to the Discovery of Cíbola"

We are still cavaliers, and we enter this ground with an air of bravado. It is the only safe way for us to do it. Those with piety, with caution rippling through their anxious hides, we believe that these the road eats, these the Devil waits for. Diablo, what a lovely sound, and so we go toward the sound. We tell people the Devil's Road is pitiless, remorseless, heartless, harsh, dry, vicious, ugly, evil. The trees are stunted, the ground hard, the ants hungry. Once, some Salvadoran refugees went down in this country, the water gone, the pain heavy, and nothing left but the dying. As some sprawled there too weak to move, small desert rats began to nibble at their bodies. This we know from survivors who could still remember those faint tugs at their flesh.

And those of us who go now, we are mainly men, and in our dreams and the accounts we scribble down, we go womanless. The Devil's Road is always a hundred miles of white light, no soft breasts for a pillow, and if you get out, the dream of a whore at the other end. She will wear satin and smell strongly of perfume and her tongue will flick against her teeth. Every night as you lie there alone you will think of her and so she is part of the road, always. When you get out you will admit this to no one. You will go to mass or go to your wife, but you will not admit the real fact. But the proof of what has happened is everywhere—the desert is crowded with tales of strange women coming out of the dunes, the bosques, the cactus. Virgins with auras glowing around their saintly faces, weeping women who beckon but whose sockets are empty of eyes. So we go womanless and dream of women. That is part of the desert, and a lot of the heavy traffic on the Devil's Road.

> . . . when they were boys, a beautiful white woman carrying a
> cross came to their lands with a cloth and a veil. She spoke to
> them, shouted, and harangued them in a language which they
> did not understand. The tribes of the Río Colorado shot her with
> arrows and twice left her for dead. But, coming to life, she left by
> the air. . . . A few days later she returned many times to harangue
> them. . . . Since these people repeat the same story, and the
> places are so far apart, we surmised that perhaps the visitor was
> the Venerable María de Jesús de Agreda. It says in the account
> of her life that about the year 1630 she preached to the heathen
> Indians of North America and the borders of New Mexico.
> And sixty-eight years having passed since then, to the present
> year in which we are told this story by the old men, it would be
> possible for them to remember it. . . . We only note the addition
> that they did not understand her. Now God, who performed the
> greater miracle by which she was conducted to these regions
> from Spain, and who does not do things imperfectly, would have
> given her the gift of tongues so that she might be understood.
> But as the accessory follows the principal, it must have been
> she. And . . . since they then were boys, they would have little
> understanding of what she was teaching them. Or else Satan,

chaos of confusion, afterward confounded them, erasing it from their memories.

—Juan Matheo Manje, 1699

Marching on, north, I follow this condemned jeep road as it meanders toward the mountains. Why do I *do* this sort of thing? I don't know. I've been doing this sort of thing for thirty-five years and still don't know why. Don't even care why. It's not logical—it's pathological. We go on and on, our whole lives, never changing, repeating ourselves with minor variations. We do not change. Bruckner spent his life writing the same symphony nine times, trying to get it just right. Seeking perfection, Mozart wrote his single symphony forty-eight times. We cannot change. Saul on the road to Damascus, struck by the lightning of revelation, turns his coat inside out, drops the S and adds the P, and goes right on. Right on fantasizing. And here I am on the old devil's road. . . . Under a clear sky. Marching. Singing. Marching. . . .

Delirium. Walking along, I realize I've forgotten to button my fly. My prick is hanging out, dangling like a banner in defeat. Like the nose cone of a possum. Like the pseudopod of an uncircumcised amoeba. . . . But what the hell—it looks so nice out today I think I'll leave it out all afternoon. . . .

—Edward Abbey, *Beyond the Wall*

Dreams take up most of the space. The giant cactus, the mountains, the big valleys, the coyote drifting on the edge of the eye, the fierce light pounding the senses, all these things are swept into a small corner and dreams squeeze every living thing and every dead thing for space. Gold mines take up enormous amounts of room. As do missions where God will be in his glory. Phantom cities squat like beasts everywhere. Dreams take up so much space that no one seems to actually be here in this specific place with real ground under real feet.

It is eight o'clock at night and the cafe calls itself Sweetwater. Everyone has had too much to drink. The lawyer lives in this desert: he has lost money backing dirty movies. The other lawyer has just lost a big drug trial. The real estate man, he is flat also, times are slow. A jazz group is warming up in the corner when the fourth man speaks. He is very drunk, his fat face swollen with booze, and he shows me photographs of fly fishing. His guide, he explains, asked him if he knew of Edward Abbey, and he obliged this shred of curiosity by unleashing a rolling thunder of denunciation. He tells me this with pleasure, knowing we were friends. But then, the man who is very drunk has known me for some time and we have shared many drinks and stories. The music from the jazz trio begins to curl around us in the air; the color photographs lie still on the table. There is a feeling in the air of emptiness. No one will ever be fed. The menu will prove too scant because, alas, money is not enough, although it is very necessary and a good thing to have. A blond woman stops by, is embraced. She is buxom, the men's eyes dart with a new keenness. The water table is sinking slowly under our feet, the drinks magically reappear, and I am technically in the Great American Desert. But the music makes the ground very difficult to hear, the fat man's jokes and tales distract me, and the lawyer keeps returning to the finances of pornographic films. The dreams simply take up too much space.

The facts tell very little here. A saguaro can survive thirty-six hours below thirty-two degrees Fahrenheit; a saguaro can cast down 200 million seeds in its frenzy to replace itself; no one knows how long the giant cactus can live. Three facts, all so tidy in a row.

It is sometime in the nineteenth century, there is no telling exactly now. The heat of early summer is in the air and two Pima women gather the fruit of the saguaro. The year has no number. They are not alert, that is the way the story has come down the

decades, and two Apaches jump them. They rape them. When
it is over, the women walk slowly back to the village. The older
woman begins to cry.

"Don't cry," the younger woman says. "It could have been
worse. They could have killed us. As it was, they only raped us."

The older woman answers.

"I'm not crying about that, I'm crying because I'm lonesome
for my dead husband."

... Making a drawing of the country on a piece of paper, on
which he indicated many nations of people so monstrous,
that I will make bold to affirm them with no little fear of being
discredited. . . . Of a nation of people who had ears so large that
they dragged on the ground and big enough to shelter five or
six persons under each one. . . . There was another nation with
only one foot who lived on the banks of a lake in which they
slept every night, entirely under the water. These people were
the ones who wore handcuffs and bracelets of the yellow metal.
. . . The monstrosities of another nation . . . did not stop here,
for they sustained themselves solely on the odor of their food,
prepared for this purpose, not eating it at all. . . . It appears to
me doubtful that there should be so many monstrosities in so
short a distance, and so near us. . . . But even though there might
be still greater doubt of all these matters, it seems yet more
doubtful to remain silent about things which, if discovered,
could result, I believe, in glory to God and in service to the King
our Lord. Moreover, although the things in themselves may be
so rare and may never before have been seen, to anyone who
will consider the wonders which God constantly performs in
the world, it will be easy to believe that since He is able to create
them He may have done so.
—Herbert Eugene Bolton, "Father Escobar's Relation [1604] of
the Oñate Expedition to California," *Catholic Historical Review*

Move, just keep moving, because to stop is to die, to lose one's mind, to succumb to the forces of Satan. The desert is full of stories of murderous treks, of people who keep going for days and when they arrive cannot speak, their tongues swollen, their eyes crazed, their minds vanished into some place no one wants to consider. Get through it, put it behind, escape. Centuries of escape by visitors moving on in a panic so that they will not be late for their long-sought and desired petty deaths at desks or in beds.

It is 1858, and Raphael Pumpelly walks from the mine in the Santa Ritas. A friend has been gone for half an hour and night has fallen as he looks for him. A house cat breaks from cover, and meows. He picks it up, the animal's eyes stare ahead, the nose twitches. Pumpelly grows wary.

He finds his friend's head in a pool of blood, the body naked, the flesh probed by many lances. He bends down and touches— the skin is still warm. He sees a warrior briefly silhouetted, then a crouching form slipping away. The nervous cat has saved Pumpelly's life. Back at the mine headquarters no one is aware of danger. The American is making bread, the Mexican fast asleep when Pumpelly returns. He listens at the door: Apaches call in the night. The flesh rots, bones turn white under the moon.

Pumpelly flees the Apaches and crosses the hard ground to the west. He hooks up with a man eager to break out to the coast. They are in the baked flats a hundred miles east of Yuma, a miserable village on the Gila. His companion dismounts to spit on the grave of an enemy.

Pumpelly asks, "Why did you kill the poor devil?"

"An old grudge," his companion explains, "about a Mexican woman."

The man has ridden with some hard men. The bravos are noted for killing a priest and using his robes for a saddle blanket.

They ride on through the heat. Pumpelly finds the rack of a

desert bighorn that weighs thirty pounds. They reach Yuma, cross the river, and head into the country of dunes. The companion sets up an ambush with a friend. But Pumpelly senses something and his companion suddenly faces a cocked gun. The man laughs and says, "You're sharper by a damn sight than I thought you was. You'll do for the border."

Move, goddammit, move.

. . . to really tell about this whole extraordinary culture—in Texas and the Southwest, all the way to California—of aimless wandering, this mobile, uprooted life: the seven-mile-long trailer parks, the motorcycles, the campers, the people who have no addresses or even last names.

—Truman Capote, 1974, in *Capote: A Biography*

Among those we passed between the Colorado and the Tinajas Altas was a party composed of one woman and three men, on foot, a pack-horse in wretched condition carrying their all. The men had given up from pure exhaustion and laid down to die; but the woman, animated by love and sympathy, had plodded on over the long road until she reached water, then clamboring up the side of the mountain to the highest tinaja, she filled her bota (a sort of leather flask), and scarcely stopping to take rest, started back to resuscitate her dying companions. When we met them, she was striding along in advance of the men, animating them by her example.

—Report of Lieutenant Michler, 1856, Emory,
United States and Mexican Boundary Survey

I felt like a polluter from another planet. Even the dead were clean.

—Richard Trench, *Forbidden Sands: A Search in the Sahara*

In the end, I think that Plato may be right—the only reality lies in ideas. That is why so few people who go into the desert will speak of ideas. There are too many of them out there and they whisper in our ears and frighten us. We retreat into terse entries of leagues or miles made that day, of the weather, the scum on the surface of the water when we finally make it to camp in the dark of the night with our animals faltering and terror filling our bellies with poison.

I remember once walking a valley thirty miles long and filled with creosote bushes each seeming to be evenly spaced from the other. I noted a handful of cactus in the long march and the rest was this deadening vista of little green shrubs with glistening tiny leaves. I outlined an entire book in my head as I walked and then kept writing and rewriting it. When I would pause and throw my pack down on the ground for five minutes' rest, I wrote and rewrote the outline of that book in a tiny notebook. This went on for a day and a half. In the middle of this orderly delirium, I looked down and saw a round stone ball by my left foot, an object clearly the work of another human being and left here by design or accident centuries before. I picked it up and put it in my pack. The following day I reached water at a place called Charlie Bell's well. A stout steel fence blocked access to the tank from any rogue steers that had wandered into the country and their bones lay scattered around the perimeter. I could hear their bawling in my mind. Late that night, I reached a mining camp on the edge of this empty desert and slept by the road. The next day I caught a ride home and when I unpacked discovered that the stone ball had rolled free from a pocket in my knapsack while I dreamed. I drove back a hundred and fifty miles and found it. It has stayed put on my bookshelf for years now.

I never wrote the book I outlined so obsessively. But I remember it clearly. I just will not write. Instead, I will tell people about the heat or the glare or tales of the Devil's Road, or about rare species encountered or fragments of pottery that cluttered the ground near my bedroll. I am not alone in this action.

Or inaction.

I suppose I should say something like it makes you wonder. But it doesn't. It doesn't make me wonder at all.

Sometimes late at night I will take the round stone ball down from the shelf and hold it in my hand for a while. Then I put it back.

What does a man think of, alone at night, marching forward, dreaming backward? Only of conventional things: the women I have known and loved; my three superior children (superior to their father); the children of my mind and notebooks, both those born and those still paring fetal fingernails in the limbo of creation.

They give me something to look forward to. A future even better, from my personal viewpoint, than the past. The worse the world appears to become, with our industrial civilization sinking deeper into its misery and squalor, drifting toward the universal civil war, the better and happier my personal life becomes. . . .

I dream of black helicopters but sleep like a baby. . . .

I'm a half mile from the road when I hear the rhythmic beat of a helicopter, the rapid shudder of rotating wings. At once, instinctively, without looking up or around, I step off a cutbank and drop into the deep shade of an ironwood tree. I lie quite still. The sound of the machine comes from the direction of Pozo Viejo, approaching swiftly. Then I see it, flying low above the road, following my route, a huge dark military helicopter of the type known as a "Huey," bearing on its fuselage the markings of the United States Air Force. It passes by, vanishing north. . . . Looking for me? Not likely. But possible. I wait. In fifteen minutes, the dragon returns, still following the road, and disappears back into the west. The vibrations fade quickly into

nothing, into nothingness, into the basic absurdity from which
the monster came.

—Edward Abbey, *Beyond the Wall*

An execution took place among the Cuchanos [Yumas] whilst
we were in their neighborhood, which created great sorrow
among us all. An Indian boy named "Bill" was in the habit
of going up and down the river on board the steamboat, and
frequently visited the post and our camp. Being very smart and
good natured, he became a great favorite; and speaking some
little English and Spanish, could act as interpreter. He was
secretly accused and tried before the council "for being under
the influence of evil spirits"—the evidence going to show, that
for the sake of frightening a little child he had forewarned it of
its death on the following day, which in reality accidentally took
place. He was convicted and sentenced to be executed. Whilst
seated on the ground with three others of his tribe, laughing,
talking, and playing cards, the executioner walked up behind
him and struck him three blows upon the forehead and each
temple, killing him instantly.

—Report of Lieutenant Michler, 1856, Emory, *United States and
Mexican Boundary Survey*

I have a friend who roamed the deserts with me when we
were boys. Now his hair is a disheveled mass like that of a crazed
prophet, his beard long and tangled. Sometimes now he has
spells of madness. But when we were boys, his eyes were keener
than mine in the desert, his head and heart would disappear
into the Yaqui villages during the dances, fly at night through
the country of the Tohono O'odham. One afternoon recently he
stopped by my house. He had been drinking for days, apparently,
and rushing from spot to spot. In Bisbee they refused to serve me

any longer in the bars. In Nogales, Sonora, he wound up in the *zona rosa* and outside a brothel saw a woman standing before a taxicab and screaming at the car's hood, "Eat me." He said he fell down in the dirt and wept at that sight. Then he looked up and a giant catfish was magically swimming up the *calle*, the mouth huge and open, the long whiskers lashing like whips against the gaudy facades of houses. We are sitting out in the sun and he is shaking now at the memory. He announces with some vehemence, "I do not want to live in a biological desert." He sketches for me a world in decline, a place eating its own entrails and spiraling down toward pollution, plague, general ruin. And then he is gone. He says in parting, "Don't call me unless you want to drink whiskey."

I am taken by his images—the woman raging at the grill of the cab, the giant catfish moving down the street—but feel none of the force of his despair. Díaz falling on his lance as he charges after that dog, Padre Kino founding missions and staring through the desert toward richer pastures, the developers I know slicing it up like a Christmas goose—a long strand of efforts to slaughter the place, or, at least, get past it. These things are part of our desert and I accept them. So did Abbey, I suspect, on that last trip, his body wrapped in a sleeping bag with ice as the truck rumbled out into the hot ground. There is really nothing out there except our claims, drowning in the blast of the afternoon winds.

I can remember the last few weeks. Abbey says he wants to go camping, nothing complicated, just go out and sit under some saguaros for a few days and barely move. We are sitting in a cafe, the tables around us crowded with college girls, and as he talks his eyes wander. He will be dead in three weeks.

He smiles and tells me that a few years ago he wrote this essay and noted that no one in his family ever dies. Then suddenly his brother died. Then his mother was run over by a truck. Now he's got this medical problem. He just keeps up with that little smile, and his eyes keep wandering. I look down at the remains of a greasy hamburger on my plate.

We go out in the parking lot and he leans against his battered truck, the blue front all punched in. Once I was waiting for him in some joint and finally he rolled in late because he'd just had a head-on collision with a car. A plastic flower on the hood now graces the truck's wound from that adventure. He hands me a copy of his new novel and I say, no, no, I've already bought a copy, so keep it, I'm willing to pay. He shrugs and explains that he wants to sign it and, consider this point, this here copy is the only one in this parking lot. I cave in before such ratiocination. So he signs it and hands it over and I never look at what he has written. I am not keen on such messages.

Two weeks later he calls late at night about our trip to sit under saguaros and I say I cannot go, I have a light fever, I want to sleep. He says that is no problem, we will do nothing out there, just sit and tell lies. But I persist, I must give in to my fatigue. The next day he begins to bleed, that night he's on the table and the knives are flashing. Four days later the phone rings, his wife says he is dead. They put him in his sleeping bag and go far away and bury him that day. I sit in my yard and drink red wine while the city birds sing around me. Late that night, I am on my second half gallon when I pull his novel off the shelf and read what he scribbled that day in the parking lot.

> —fellow traveler in this fool's journey out of the dark, through the light, and into the unknown. . . .
> —Ed Abbey, Tucson, February 1989

I never asked where he is buried. People call and ask me, call long distance with the line sometimes fading in and out and their voices warm with a kind of yearning for the location of the fabled grave. Finally, somebody told me. But still I do not go there. It is a place I know well, but this new fact has not changed the old, familiar ground. Just made it that much older. I suppose I take some comfort in knowing the actual ground, sitting in my city house at midnight and sensing the moon brushing against the rock out there. But I cannot find any particular importance in where the hole lies.

For me, Abbey is in the traffic roaring down the Devil's Road, a place that has become a vague metaphor because most of us like the sound of the name. We crave the splendor that a whiff of hell gives us, we want a sacred drama so that our crabbed lives can share the power we sense in the ground around us. That's understandable. And surely beside the point. The name itself is recent, a tag pinned to the route in the past century or so, and one that will drift away and be forgotten eventually. It is like the name of a dog; the beast will answer to the sound we assign it but the sound tells us nothing about the beast. This is our custom. We purse our lips and say "Desert," and the thing is done, contained. We have been at this practice for centuries and I cannot see us stopping now. It has helped us avoid the place we live.

Otherwise, we might open the door and face that June afternoon.

*   *   *

The slides spash color against the white wall as we sit in chairs, drinks in hand, and look at the photographer's shoot. I'm pretty drunk but I'm not the only one. The way to the viewing has been long and pleasant. Smoke curling off the fire, flowers promising spring, the meat searing and crackling out by the ramada. We have had roasted chickens drenched in marinade and cooked over mesquite, fish caught in Glacier Bay and perfectly filleted, rice propped up with garlic and pepper. In the midst of the cooking, a run had to be made to the liquor store. The evening paced itself with pleasures. Out the door, the penstemons are about to bloom, and the furnace breath of summer comes closer.

And then came the moment that night had spiraled toward. The boxes of slides are placed on a small table, the projector ignites its blank eye, the chairs are scattered about the unfinished den of raw wood and new smells. The photographer is nervous, the weeks of work, the hope of a vision, all this goes on the line now. I am ill at ease at what will come. The desert is a faint world, but the images will assert that they are truly the flesh on all the dry bones rattling against each other within the small world. I worry that I will recoil from the photographers, that I will not recognize my life in the clean frames of the lens. I look up and on the wall is a photograph of Edward Abbey. We all knew him, and we like to drink too. He is sitting on a rock in the desert, a hat on his head, his bearded face serious with thought, and he is scribbling notes about something or other.

I take no photographs; I am the ignorant guest at a professional gathering. The images are perfect, the colors very bright and they scream past my eyes in fiery clots: the cardón big by the sea, the boobies clustered in their nests, sea lions touching noses, an old mission in the sierra lonely with its stone, a face, my God, finally the human face of an old woman who is the caretaker of some church no one prays in much anymore. Then come Roman legions of boojums twisting against the sky, palmchoked lagoons brilliant with color, islands in the sea, a pile of trash left by careless tourists, landscapes as fresh as the day Adam desired a companion to be named Eve. The photographer clicks off one by one. A church blooms on the wall, one ancient with stone and brooding, over that one he lingers. The problem, he explains, is the sign, the huge beer sign right next to the church. He had to climb a hill and very carefully frame the shot to crop out the offending beer sign. The images will all be a book about the desert, there is no doubt of this fact.

All this, I'm sure, helps keep away the loud notes, the garbage cans out in the alley banging away like rats in heat. I'll give you an example of this clatter from the newspaper, Section F, page 7:

SHOOTING DEATH DETAILED

A naked Apache Junction man, bristling with cactus spines, charged at a Pinal County deputy sheriff and could not be stopped with a nightstick or two superficial gunshot wounds, according to an official report.

Wayne Roux, 31, finally was killed by a gunshot wound to the chest fired by a Pinal County sheriff's deputy near Apache Junction Sept. 19, but not before an early morning, hour-long rampage that included the sexual assault of a woman and injuring another deputy with a large rock, the report says.

I am grateful for the drink in my hand as the last slide dies on the wall and the lights come up again. Then comes the talk. A woman mentions a recent book on the desert, one where a wanderer treks beaches, finds a bottle of scotch that has washed up, throws down his eighty-pound pack, and has himself a drink. She asks, "Why would they publish an account by an alcoholic who lives off litter?" I think of William Mulholland, one of the real forebears of the fantasy expressed in the movie *Chinatown*. On the day he successfully achieved his theft of water from the Owens River, snaked the treasure across the Mojave Desert into the Los Angeles basin and unleashed his booty on the city, they made a public occasion of it. As the spillway gushed with the flow, he stood up to give a speech and said to the assembled crowd, "There it is. Take it." Everywhere I go, I can see that they did; every time I see the photographs the crime has been erased.

Finally, I leave and drive down city streets under the overhead lights. I pour a drink in the kitchen and go out and sit on a railroad tie, the night sulking over my head with heavy clouds as I wait for rain, a glass of wine in my hand. There was one shot in the slide show that was not part of the show, just a casual image snapped by a guy who was camped on the coast in Baja. A gray whale was beaching itself, the surf spuming around the massive hulk, that big eye staring out with some understanding the camera could not fathom, the flippers lashing the air. And a small child in a red dress raced into the surf, the one running foot suspended in the air, raced to touch the giant who had suddenly punched into the safe world of the shore. Whales do not belong on beaches, we all know that. But these things happen. There is talk about the picture later, it is thought that it was a female aborting a hard birth, a soul locked in a death dance and come to ground for relief from the sea and the long dying. But then, what does belong in a place, a location, a time? What should be in the picture? *Landscape* seems a word that is swept clean by a new broom before it can be witnessed, an image refined and smoothed, all the edges gone, all the sea lions rubbing their noses, all of our kind exiled from the sacred ground. Based on what we write about the land and the photographs we take of the land, we cannot face ourselves in the mirror.

*　*　*

The deer under the fig tree stares with dark glazed eyes, the antlers are in velvet, the fur is something I yearn to touch. The pen is very small, and half the space has been taken by the huge hills of the *mochomos,* leaf-cutting ants. Down under my feet lie the caverns with leaves dangling from the ceilings and the fungus growing from them is the crop of this insect garden. Sometimes the *mochomos* get under old houses, they love the loose soil,

and they toil for years on their gardens, the caverns constantly
expanding. Then one day a corner of the house will collapse as
the insects' vaults give way. The problem is that one cannot really
see what is going on. There are clues, of course, the endless lines
of ants flowing past with each insect waving a piece of green leaf
in its mandibles, the big hills of dark brown earth blooming in
the yard. But much remains hidden from view and at best one
can only sense the dimensions of what is going on in the earth.
The deer seems unconcerned by the anthills or the people standing around drinking beer. It is a pet in a place where few reach
that wonderful status in life.

A few miles to the north lies Culiacán, a booming Mexican
city in the state of Sinaloa surrounded by irrigated fields and
lanced by rivers. Just to the east the rock face of Sierra Madres
begins, and ten miles to the west the Sea of Cortez laps against
the shore. This is a tropical place and the deer is encircled by
orange and grapefruit orchards. The house is nearby, a simple
cement building with a *sala* cut through the middle to catch a
breeze on the hot days. The woman is eighteen or twenty and
about to give birth. Her face has the glow of someone carrying life and her belly has begun to drop. Soon she will go to Los
Angeles so that the child will be born an American citizen, a
kind of life insurance policy for the family. A few yards from the
house is a round cement ramada with a grill for those meals of
carne asada and beans in the cool of the evening when friends
gather and share happiness and hopes. The new pickup is parked
behind the house, the paint red, the seats bucket, the stereo a
maze of buttons, equalizer adjustment tabs, and power switches
for secreted amplifiers. Behind it is the swimming pool, empty at
the moment but surely a joy when summer bakes the land. The
orange trees are very near and the scent of the citrus produces a
sense of gratitude that such a thing can grow on this earth, the
leaves shiny as if some spirits emerged in the night and delicately

polished each and every one of them. Last night, the owner was here and hosted a party. He is only twenty-five and was born very poor in a rough barrio of Culiacán. But he has worked very hard and now he has this rancho, and a grand city house in Culiacán in the very best neighborhood and another house in Tucson with another woman. As the meat seared last night the men drank and then the owner brought out a gun and they took turns shooting oranges off the trees. The stars danced overhead and no one could doubt that life was a good thing to have, especially with the woman hovering nearby so big with child.

The technical border of the desert is a hundred miles to the north. Culiacán has long functioned as a fist striking blows against the desert, the beginning of a road that burns north into the heart of the heat and thorns. Like the *mochomos* busy with their caverns underground, the desert has more to it than the rich color photographs of saguaro forests and dunes and mountains and sunsets acknowledge. That is why Culiacán does not appear on maps of the desert but is a vital element in its actual life. A Spaniard named Guzman, a savage rival of Hernán Cortés, founded Culiacán in the early sixteenth century. And then he hurled his men and their lances north on slaving raids into the *desierto*. After that came soldiers and miners looking for precious metals, which in due time were discovered. In 1683, on the southern edge of Sonora, a huge strike was made near what became the pueblo of Alamos. These riches fueled the Jesuit fathers who stormed farther north spreading cattle, wheat, the Holy Faith, and Our Lady. The name of the state of Sonora came from Señora, Our Lady, who by the miracle of a virgin birth gave us Jesus Christ. Later, near the current United States / Mexico border, silver was found lying on the ground in pure plates at a spot called Arizonac, in Tohono O'odham the "place of the small spring," a name that Americans splashed across an entire state. So on the maps, Our Lady faces the place of little water.

The man who is hosting this gathering near the fine orchard by the pet deer is a drug dealer. The house holds a room full of AK-47s and hand grenades. He has killed two men in my own city of Tucson. He is related to Rafael Caro Quintero, the reputed boss of bosses in media presentations of the drug war. These facts are sharp obsidian edges slicing against my calm and if I dwell on them, it leads to the thoughts darker than the blackness of the soft night whispering against my skin. In the face of the land and the sky, they hardly matter, they are just a temporary burst of pain in a long song that sings of the joy of life. They shrivel up, the flesh disintegrating like sun-rotten cloth, and then collapsing into dust whenever I look over at the serenity of the woman carrying the child in her huge belly, her breasts swollen in anticipation of the start of yet one more life.

I'd better come clean. I cannot contain the word *desert* inside tidy borders. The sound rolls out of my mouth and a blur of images and feelings floods me—the lips full on a woman walking her high heels to work, the scent rising off the nape of her neck, the anxiety in an old man's eyes as he scurries across four lanes of traffic, people shitting, wincing, smiling, laughing, people are everywhere when I hear the word. We cannot imagine this land without people but for decades now we have recorded the land with our cameras and carefully cropped from our photographs signs of our own kind. And yet this land has not existed without human beings for at least twenty thousand years, perhaps much longer if the scholars ever finish their vicious, sectarian arguments on the issue. We seem to hate our own face.

I have tried to research this matter in a casual way. I go to the Center of Creative Photography in Tucson, a major repository for snapshots. I am in this huge room, the air has a strange stench of chemicals, some element has been injected into the atmosphere to protect the photographic prints from time. There are no windows, the desert cannot stare in at this record of its skin. I look down at my hands and see them encased in the delicate white gloves of a dandy. The help moves silently as if they are members of a religious order, their faces pale and empty of passion. I walk down the aisles and the shelves are piled high with archival boxes of prints. All around me are the bones of the work of Edward Weston, Ansel Adams, Frederic Sommers, W. Eugene Smith—the chemical footprints of decades of shutterbugs.

They bring the boxes to my table, a staff member delicately lifts out each photograph and lays it before me on a fine wooden table. I am not allowed to touch, my gloves are not enough. The room is exquisitely quiet, the staff member's face reverent, the photographs themselves as sterile as the loins of a mule. The composition is there, the tonal scale is under control, the printmaking perfect, all the white dots have been carefully removed. The moon, she rises over Hernandez, New Mexico, the dunes of the Mojave roll like a woman on wet sheets in a cheap hotel. This goes on for hours, the bank of fluorescent lights humming a blues over my head.

I wander off, go down corridors in the huge building, and find the archive for written materials, for those scribblings of photographers, those daybooks of Weston, those notes on composition, those angry letters of clients who have not yet paid up. Against one wall of the stacks stand two footlockers, beaten, old metal things, and next to them is a ratty stuffed chair. The chair was where Gene Smith spent years drinking himself to death and popping those bennies. I keep one of his ravings on my refrigerator at home, they howl in big bold type—

Stretcher bearers standing by—stretch my strength, stretch it, stretch it mighty more than man. John Henry, give me back your hammer. I am the storm and I war with eternity, and there is no goddess as prize and I would protect the emptiness from

the fiery dragons. St. George, second floor, inside room—and a
bottle of gin.

. . . Camera, camera, what do you do—and I damn your eye,
damn your wink, damn your memory—for with all of that you
still can't think.
   —W. Eugene Smith to John Morris of Magnum,
    Thanksgiving Day, 1955

The footlockers are covered with felt-tip messages, things
scratched out like belligerent tattoos and the rhythm section
of the messages always seems to ride on the word *fuck.* The big
room for the documents is almost silent, nothing but the breath
of the air conditioning licking the linoleum floors. The chair
waits there reeking, a thing drenched with burgundy, Tokay,
Mad Dog 20 / 20. The throne of a proper wino. Everything is safe
now, the son-of-a-bitch is dead, the photographs in the boxes
are immortal as they lurk in the magic air; the desert, the desert
is framed and suitable for the claws of curators. Hear the mat
silently being pressed against the paper, the exhibits going up on
the white walls, the world made clean.

    I leave and outside the auto exhaust off the city streets tastes
as sweet as honey, the roar of the machines is music, and I pray
for a bag lady. I remember how down in Culiacán, on the corner
of a similar street, an Indian boy did cartwheels between the line
of waiting cars, and then pounded on the windows begging for
money. I watched this from a hot dog stand with a young drug
dealer for company. I asked him if the town had any fire eaters, the kids who fill their mouths with kerosene then spit it out
against a match and produce an arc of flame. After a while the
fuel eats at their brains and they spend the rest of their short
lives as very simple-minded fire eaters. Ah, he said, yes, they are

usually around. Then we went to the market and brought amulets from a *curendera*.

Pass the bottle, find the desert. Years ago, I was covering a copper strike in a small desert town. A striking miner, a man of about fifty, became so agitated in explaining to me his hatred of scabs that he wheeled around in his small trailer and finally grabbed a sawed-off shotgun from a cabinet. He was a very intelligent man who had not had a drink in five years. Outside the sun beat against the siding and the light was blinding. Down the road the pit stared up from the ground like a blind eye, and spilling out of it were the pus and drippings called tailings, lifeless streams lapping against the desert of saguaro and ironwood. As the man talked, the barrel of the shotgun flashed in the trailer and his man's voice kept rising and rising, and finally cracked in a spasm of his anger. I imagined the snakes curled up in the trailer's shade under our feet. To the west of his trailer, not a human being lived for at least one hundred miles, and the desert out there is found in many fine books of photographs. Then the guy calmed down and told me of a fellow who lived outside of town when he was a boy. They called him John the Baptist, his hair hung very long, his beard ran wild. No one knew quite what had happened to him, something back in the Spanish-American War. The soldier's pension check came regularly. He lived in a dugout with his wife, the whole burrow filled with stacks of technical magazines. Then his wife died and John the Baptist took to wearing her dresses, bras, and panties. Once a game ranger came by and this thing came struggling up from the earth, an apparition waving a gun with a bent barrel, the dust swirling around his dress. When he died, they buried him proper. Then local people sacked his dugout looking for buried treasure. There was a fire, the magazines became ash and blew away in the wind. The striking miner is very relaxed now; the memory of the crazy old hermit seems to have had a calming effect.

Imagine something with the specific gravity of lead and yet the lightness of a feather and that is the desert. I am driving and it is 110 degrees and the radiator continues to boil over. The truck steams in the shade of coconut palms near the Rio Yaqui, the Mexicans walking by politely say *"Buenos tardes"* as the metal hisses and groans. In the language of botany, I am in a mesquite bosque assemblage, in the jargon of geography the Sonoran Desert, in the political hype of Mexican politics an irrigation district built by the Party of the Institutional Revolution, and on the map I am in Ciudad Obregón, a city named after a dead general and president cut down by the bullet of a devout Catholic assassin in 1928 while the general dined in a Mexico City restaurant. In my mind I am in a kind of blur. I live as if I once took some dose of a very powerful drug and can no longer control the flashes that explode from the concise packages called ideas. It seems that giant fire storms, warm my heart, the tongues of flame licking against my brain as it rides so smugly in a fluid container I am told is my skull.

I'll give you an example: the day the radiator boiled over in Ciudad Obregón. Steam, hot water squirting from the metal, the girl over there at the stand selling coconuts, her skin so smooth, the hair black and trailing, the shine on her smile. We ride into town, find the radiator shop, the man puts down a beer, cigarette dangling from his lip, and never smiles. On the wall is a poster of a woman with huge breasts, a strip of aluminized duct tape blocking out her apparently useless face. The man's torch hits the hole in the radiator and while we wait, we look for some beers, finally finding them down the street in a cantina selling six-packs. The bar is full of gay Mexicans listening to jazz with dark mascara around their eyes. Alvaro Obregón built this town around his cartel controlling garbanzos, and he made a killing after the revolution shipping these chick-peas to New York because there are on this complicated earth little pockets of people who

lust after the finest garbanzos. The town's name changed from
Cajeme to his own, the maps were redone, and a new history was
scratched onto the small city by the Rio Yaqui. What I remember
as I drink a beer is a moment from a fiesta. To the south a few
miles is the pueblo where a girl lives who served me menudo at
the fiesta for the Virgin, her body leaning over the rickety table
with the steaming bowl in hand, her smile so rich, her eyes so
hungry. Here, she says to my friend, is my address, come to me in
Pueblo Viejo. The farm town stares up from her eyes like a cata-
ract she would like removed. As she talks pilgrims inch past on
the cobblestones toward the shrine. They are seeking absolution
for a thousand nights of illicit pleasures, Holy Mother forgive us
because the sap rises in the spring.

Then the radiator is fixed. Once I start driving again, everything falls back into its proper place and disappears.

It is the party in Culiacán with the pet deer nearby in its pen,
and the meat searing on the grill. The man hosting the party, he
is very tense, he must send a thousand pounds of cocaine north
on the road in the next week. Also, he is reactivating a pig farm
out back, and considering restoring the poultry barns. There is
blood on the ground eight hundred miles north where his pistol
pumped bullets into the bodies of men. The bananas are hanging
ripe in Culiacán, the saguaro will not flower for five months in
Arizona, and photographs keep coming with polarized lenses
coaxing the sunset into soft glowing colors. I can hear the mandibles of the *mochomos* grinding underneath my feet, the secret
gardens expanding. The woman is like a flower soon to open, her
face serene as a pellet from the gun rips into the soft pulp of the
orange dangling from the tree in the clean whisper of the night.

The deer is sitting in the safe shade in its pen; the weeping
woman is out of sight and mind for the moment.

2

Now it is summer, the hot, dry winds come, the air boils up to a hundred degrees and then keeps right on rising. At night I can hear the steam coming off, the flesh sizzling as people lay on the sheets in the darkness across my city and wait for the meaning of their lives to be made plain. Everything in the night is rich with scent, the flowers choke the town, and I want to hold a woman as the sweat rolls off me.

There is no place in the desert where the heat does not seem to penetrate. Sometimes in the afternoon, it'll be 105, 110 degrees, or more, and I'll sit out in the sun for hours, drinking water, cold water, and my skin blackens, the air is like napalm, the birds hide in the trees and refuse to stir.

Nothing stops, the pounding of the sun does not slow it down, the messages keep coming, the solicitations, requests. Temptations. The voices tell me this is the Sunbelt, the new world beyond earlier imaginations, the place where houses erupt from the earth, roads unwind and whip across the passive ground, glass towers shoot their cold shafts into the sky, bankers lick their fingertips and count. The sunglasses this year are a passionate pink, convertibles flourish in the auto market, and the eyes, all the young eyes are pleasingly blank and ride on milk-fed faces. Also, a lot of people are earnestly recycling their trash. None of this interferes with my self-appointed task.

I have habits I must kick, but I am failing in all my efforts.

When I was editing a magazine a friend came by with two photo albums belonging to a fence and sometime drug dealer who operated on the south side of town. The shots went back more than two decades and faithfully recorded every prostitute that had worked the avenue. Many of the faces were blank from a recent fix, some were hard, most were long dead. I wanted to publish them with brief anecdotes of the long-gone women. But this was not really possible. The faces were mainly brown and black and that is not a good sell. The women were whores and that touches some rim of darkness no one, I was told repeatedly, needs to wallow in. I could not argue against any of this; after all, I know my own country. I kept the albums for weeks and looked at them from time to time and then gave them back. Finally, I quit the magazine and retreated to my house. I thought maybe everyone was right, maybe I should check what others called my appetite for darkness. I would take a self-designed cure, one based on plants in the yard, birds at the feeder, a ringing telephone that was never picked up. Then my friend stopped by again and this time he told me of one of the women in the albums. I remember her photograph, the eyes glazed, the face lovely yet dissolving from drugs, the breasts large, nipples dark, her body sprawling backward in a bare chair as the fix took hold. She was a very good-looking whore. When I looked into her face, I wanted her. He told me that the day before he had been in a room when the decision was made to kill her. The woman was part of a rip-off, and somehow during the robbery of a drug dealer, she was identified. She and her partners had made off with $150,000, and she must pay. Underlings quite naturally offered to take care of this matter for the boss, but the *patron*, he said, no, this one he wanted to handle himself. Now I watch the hours slide by. The morning paper will come, today, a week from today, a month, a body will magically appear, the paper saying that no identification was found, the causes of the death at present unknown.

Then she will be tossed in a hole and life will continue. And I will remember her. I have to kick this habit.

Naturally, I find images to kill this experience, fantasy to cage these sensations. In my mind, it looks as if huge tectonic plates are grinding me up into a fine powder. One plate is a cold metal slab of machined steel, fine bearings, every facet precisely milled, and the entire surface is crowded with American factories, banks, malls, and cities erupting like chancres from the land. Pus drips from these swellings and the whole is laced with lines of cocaine, the frosting on the cake. I call this plate home and vote in the elections. The second plate is mud, the edges jagged and handmade, the noise is intolerable, the radios never go off, the buses lack mufflers, the exhaust is black, the faces brown, the feet sandaled, babies are everywhere, the desert besotted with disposable diapers, the breasts bared to hungry young mouths, the sierra's green humps dotted with secret fields of marijuana and poppies, the whole behemoth graced with smiles and the light in a woman's eyes. No matter how harsh the grinding as the two plates rub against each other, I cannot hop onto one plate and abandon the other. I stand in the desert, the light white and painful, the deer creeping down the arroyos, their eyes blazing with fear. Before I can raise my gun, the plates have at me, and the grinding never ceases. The whore with the lovely face and the glazed eyes as the fix slams in, the whore should not have stolen the money. Now her breasts are cold forever.

The phone rings and it is Alfonso, who lives in a barrio in this old tumble-down house and his neighbors are largely Sonorans who have come north to make money and hide from *la migra*. When he gets excited, he speaks very deliberately, his voice utterly clear, but his feelings are always given away by the rise and fall of his words. At such times, he often laughs to mask the churning inside him. The laugh is quick and very short at the tail end of his sentence, like a flag snapping in the wind.

Now Alfonso is talking to me over the telephone about *tortugas*, desert tortoises, and I can imagine his head tilting forward into the receiver, a well-shaped head with short black curly hair, the face with just a daub of a mustache. He is so eager to tell this story, he says, because he cannot tell it to other people. If he did that, they would use it against him, they would tell him he was racist or fascist or sick. He is certain they would do that. There are enemies everywhere.

But he tells me anyway. He has this neighbor in the barrio, Manny, and one day Manny went out to the Indian reservation west of town and he was walking along an arroyo when suddenly he saw tortoises everywhere in the desert. He had a sack and he scooped up seventeen of them and took them home to the barrio. There, he made a big fire and let it burn down to hot coals and then he placed all the tortoises, still alive, on their backs amid the coals. When they had cooked, he busted them out of their shells and scraped out the meat and had a hell of a meal.

Alfonso went over there and saw all the carnage, the heap of shells on the brown ground. Manny said, "Al, come over here," and he showed him a small tortoise, the seventeenth one as it happened. He said, "He's so small I'm going to keep him for a pet."

I listen to him pour this tale through the phone with that quick crack of a laugh at the end. I think idly to myself of the dull facts: that in Arizona all tortoises are protected, and that more are held captive as pets than exist free in the desert, that diseases are spreading from my world to their world and knocking them off wholesale. They are also swiftly being exterminated by cattle, off-road vehicle enthusiasts, and general goodwill. Finally, I mumble, "Well, you know cruelty is an idea and a word wherever you go. But it's a thing that always has a border and this border varies from place to place." I go on in this vein explaining away a small mountain of tortoises roasted alive.

Alfonso listens, there is a pause, and then he said, "Try and tell that to other people. You'll see what happens."

There is another story told me by a friend of mine named David. He once mentioned that he had eaten desert tortoise while running around with the Seris along the coast of Sonora, and he had found the meat dry and not very good. I reacted with mock horror since tortoises have always been beasts that bring a child-like pleasure to my eyes and heart. David can be a very deliberate person, and he patiently explained to me that cultures, well, they're different and that people in different places see the same thing with new and strange eyes. His meal happened this way. He was out in the desert, that hard desert that bakes right next to the Sea of Cortez, with some Seri guys and he announced that he'd like to see a tortoise. They told him he must think a song and then sing it and the tortoise would appear. So he relaxed for a few minutes and a tune came into his mind, and he began to sing it. He walked through the desert and within three minutes he looked down and there was a desert tortoise.

The Seri guys came over and scooped the animal up. David's tune wilted in the heat of the day. The Indians found a hollow in the rock and made a fire with dead wood, and then wedged the tortoise in there alive and cooked it. And that is when David ate desert tortoise.

I try to construct a theory on how a moral person should live in these circumstances, and how such a person should love. Actually, this begins as a dream, one of my very few: I am in the desert, a tortoise moves slowly at my feet, and I am very secure. The time of day or night is very unclear in this dream, but an enormous peace floods my body. I move through the mesquite and ironwood trees along a dry wash, and suddenly I see a black car, a very large vehicle with tinted windows. Men are standing around it with automatic weapons, a deal is going down. In the dream—this part baffles me—I cut them all down in a single magic burst. They are violating my place. I never speak, just fire. Then I leave. Highways take over, cheap motels, the bathrooms smelling of strong chemicals, the sun blocked by heavy drapes. I wind up in Mexico at a fiesta for the Virgin, the penitents crawling on their knees toward Our Lady. I join the procession, the Indians are kissing Her image. I lean forward with hungry lips, but for me the image is ice cold.

Then I wake up and the dream goes away. I move without a plan or outline. I waver, retreat, then lunge. I am a coward who fears sleeping in the same bed twice. I find myself in a hotel room in Culiacán, Sinaloa, and my companion, a drug dealer, is standing by the television doing a line of cocaine. He is getting his nerve up because we are going to meet his supplier so that he can arrange that shipment to Tucson. My companion is in his twenties and was raised on the streets of Culiacán, His name is tattooed across his back, his English is very slight, his face a constant smile. Last night, he was out until 3 A.M. getting ripped on coke with his brother. He brought his brother up to the room to show him such a fine place. He plans to bring his father up for a tour also. He also bought a fifteen- or sixteen-year-old, fucked her twice. He says he had to teach her how to give head, that at first she was very clumsy about the matter of her teeth.

He has two small children, a wife, a house, and a $20,000 car. He has clawed his way out of poverty, gone north, violated our immigration laws, made a living selling drugs, and found a kind of happiness. In the bathroom rests his kit—two hair sprays and a canister of mousse. I am always attracted to people with hunger despite what I may think of their appetites. He finishes two lines and we go.

When we get back to the hotel, my friend is past the charge of his coke hits and sinking in the warm embrace of alcohol. His deal is in motion, there is just the wear and tear of getting the drugs across the border. He becomes pensive and says he has had enough. It is too rough, there are too many cops, he wants to get out. So far he has no record, he is clean. He will get a job, settle down. Man, he can do body work, he's still got his tools. Of course, first he is going to trade his $20,000 car because he has found this cherry truck, man it is perfect, the stereo system pumping five thousand watts. Of course, he must deal a couple more loads to bankroll his new life. His face is soft, round, and full of good feelings. I look out the hotel window at the river that winds through town. Clouds of white egrets stream down it toward the sea as the sun fades.

Christ, get out of here, the voices shout.

A few weeks later I am back in Tucson at a dinner. I order off the menu, the room is very chaste with Mexican decorations, the restaurant an old house in a historical district. My companions believe in nature, the environment, the death of industrialism, the good fight for a sick planet. They pull at me with stout ropes, pull me back into a world that is green, logical, scholarly, passionate. One is facing felony charges because the FBI does not approve of his politics. Another pioneered acts of terrorism now called monkey-wrenching. This is the real world, they say, save the whales.

I go home and I am sitting in a soft chair in my house in Tucson reading a thick book about the Russian czars when the doorbell rings. It is a friend from the West Coast. He speaks very rapidly, he always does, and he has this offer. We will sail in three months out into the blue Pacific. The voyage will take forty days. The Japanese trawlers have been setting huge drift nets, the things trail off for miles and kill everything that swims in the sea. We are going to take them out. Not the nets, the ships themselves. Sink the bastards. He takes me out to his truck. Here, he says, look at this. He unwraps a new AK-47 with a banana clip sticking out its bottom like a perfect black tooth. He picks up a black belt and straps it on, six extra clips of shells dangling around him.

We are going to board the trawlers, he explains, we are going to finish this business. He is tired of being idle while the planet dies. Then he shows me his black helmet with visor, his flak jacket. Are you going? he asks. I can feel the stirrings within me. They are undeniable. They are the same ones I feel in Culiacán as I listen to the words and watch the faces of the *pobres* who take rather than be taken. The huge plates keep grinding.

Every day of my life I have talked to plants. And now I go to them for comfort. They never answer back. It is hard to stay with the trees, or stay with the cactus, or stay in the hot flats. There are many things of which I feel I must warn people. The landscape is a trick to make us miss our lives. Toward evening, avoid the sunsets—the colors are too rich and they always lie. Beware, too, of the photographs, especially the ones where the cactus is silhouetted, backlit, and the spines glow. Ignore the animals. Believe me, they should be ignored. They hate us and our cities. They hate the way we smell. I have seen their noses twitching with disgust and horror. I try to pretend that all of this is quite wrong, that I am hopelessly mistaken. I deliberately go outside with a drink in my hand and make myself watch the sunset. The next day I tell other people about the sunset I witnessed and how fine it was. And then on my way home, a coyote darts across the road and my body snaps alert. For almost an hour I try to hold the excitement in my mouth, savoring the moment, rolling my tongue against the rich fur of the coyote's back. That night I dream of the flowing tail, a plume brushing your lips.

Go back south into Mexico, I think, it will be safer, simpler. The people there, I am told, have more soul. One afternoon I am in the sierra with some friends miles and miles down a rutted track. The last village has a peasant who sells soda pop which he keeps cool in a tub of wet sand by a bed made of tree limbs and strips of steer hide, with the hair on. An olla dangles from the roof beams, a hollow gourd with rabbit-skin straps functions as his canteen, chickens peck at the dirt floor of the house, and a line of children waits politely to watch me pour a Pepsi down my gringo throat. The roof is thatch and flowers glow in painted tin cans near the door. There are no walls. This is not a good village to linger in. The *federales* sometimes burst out of the green and ask very hard questions. A man named Chalo lives somewhere out here, a paid killer of the drug world, a man widely feared. I never see him, he is like a lion, a floating presence. We push on until the river plows into the solid rock of a gorge and there we scramble to gather specimens of those wild orchids that cling to the cliffs and put out small yellow flowers. We are sitting in the sand by the river drinking small bottles of cold beer when we hear rocks tumbling down the hillside. Two peasants appear carrying machetes. We hand one guy some beers. He pops one in his mouth and pulls the cap off with his teeth without ever skipping a beat. The world is beautiful and alive and throbbing with desires and dreams. I believe totally for the moment in flowers. Back in town, down off the sierra, two Mexican government helicopters whirr about the countryside officially looking for drugs. I look up at them. They are fired upon.

I do not seek such tales. I ask no questions. But they come, like tortoises answering a song. I am sitting on a sofa against a wall in this Tucson office drinking a beer. The man who is my host here runs tours, adventure travel they are called, and something happened on his last trip. There is this river that has intrigued him and when the summer rains came and brought the water up, he went into the back country with a friend and two women. Here, he will show me, and he gets up from his chair and pops a cassette into the machine and images light up on a monitor. They are unloading a small plane in a meadow, then Indians appear and pile everything onto nine mules. The tape has sound and I can hear their voices, the grunting of the animals, the occasional buzz of a fly. The women are young and laughing. They ride for a day and a half to get to the bottom of the deep canyon. The walls are stone with a green forest dripping down, the river brown with flood. Now they are in the raft, white water roars ahead and the microphone picks up this beckoning sound. They laugh, plunge in. A waterfall, and they are standing under it, the women in small bikinis, the water very silver as it pours over them. Their hips are white and soft against the dark rock. Suddenly, a cave swings by on the shore with people living in it, limbs recently cut from trees lean against the entrance to soften the weather. The man sitting by me as the tape rolls says that the people in the caves along the canyon looked displaced, looked as if they had not been in their residences very long. He could spy from time to time marijuana and opium poppy fields on the slopes, the poppies white and lush with blooms.

Now the camera pans a village. The church is ancient but the yard in front of it overgrown with weeds. The weeds should be kept cut by men wielding machetes. Ah, something is wrong here. The buildings are adobes, the roofs thatched. There is no one in the village, not one soul. The camera moves inside a hut, it noses around corners and stares at some kind of shrine. A big cross is nailed to the white stuccoed wall. The camera moves closer, the focus becomes sharp, the image huge, and then I see someone has drawn the outlines of helicopter gunships on the walls. For a hundred miles along the river, the camera finds nothing but abandoned villages. When they get out there are whispers from other villagers. The gunships came, people say, fifty, sixty, perhaps more people were killed. Survivors were taken out with ropes tied around their necks. Those who could not walk, or those who stumbled, such people were shot out of hand. Those who survived the walk are said to have been dispatched to prisons. The tape ends, just like that. The river turned out to be very good, well worth booking as a tour next year. But these other matters trouble him. We stand outside his office under a mesquite tree as traffic roars past on a nearby road. The sun is very hot and red ants scramble on the ground around our feet. I ask, "What do you want me to do?" He stubs his bare foot into the ground and draws a circle, and sighs.

The trick is very simple, I think, the trick is to love. To know and still to love.

But it is not easy for me to sigh. Someone takes five men into a shed around Easter. The cops allow that it smacks of a drug killing. A friend of mine slips into the morgue and views the bodies. The head on one hangs loose and is barely held by a single flap of skin. A second corpse is more interesting. The back shows evidence of spine tickling, little jabs up and down the huge nerve with something sharp, perhaps an ice pick. The front of the guy has thirty-seven stab wounds between the waist and the throat. The head itself is kind of a mess, the fine bones rearranged by repeated blows with a pipe. The dying must have been very slow and well orchestrated. Multiply by five and that is the afternoon in the shed. Outside the killing ground the desert is creosote, a plant that can live more than ten thousand years and yet will tell us nothing. The nearby hills are black basalt from an ancient volcanic eruption. The men are in their twenties. The air is still and warm.

Thirteen more are cut down in Agua Prieta, Sonora, just across the fence, the men and women put down a well or buried in a septic field with lime splashed across their faces. *Las drogas,* the drugs, have done all this work between Good Friday and Ascension morning. "That report, that it was over three hundred pounds of marijuana," a friend tells me over a drink, "well, that's wrong." I look up at her bright young face as she continues, "It was two hundred forty kilos of cocaine that were ripped off. They say they did the women first, cut them open and wrapped the intestines around their bodies. They thought it would make the men more likely to talk." I nod. When they found the killing field in Agua Prieta, the fingers of the women were scattered about the ground like flower petals. They could tell the sex from the bright red nail polish. They used a hook to fish bodies out of the well and thought they were finished when suddenly another rotting corpse bobbed up to the surface. They say the odor was very strong. A man is sought. He is known locally as Mr. Tombstone. In a few weeks they catch him holed up in a trailer outside of Tucson. He is found building model airplanes.

After all, such people are not so different from you and I, although we wish this were not so. I meet this guy in Tucson. He is a short solid man with a thick neck and strong arms. His English is very poor, his eyes hard. He laughs often. He takes me to his guest house and proudly shows me the ancient beams in the ceiling, things he stole from an old adobe the city once hired him to restore. He jabs me in the side, the smile curls off his lips, the eyes sparkle, and he laughs about stealing those beams. He is a happy man with deep desert roots. His mother is a witch, and the demons and herbs of the dry ground waft through the rooms. Of course, he will not speak until she touches me and nods that it is okay.

He wanted the big marriage so he invited the guys he dealt with in from Miami, and asked the local talent too. One photo from the gala shows the dour face of a contract killer, the thin mustache, dead eyes, pale bloodless skin. After the ceremony, he and his new bride got in the rented Rolls-Royce for the ride to the reception. Everything had to be just perfect. Even in the life, the drug life, a man still has his dreams. She is dressed in white, he is wearing his tuxedo and snap-brim hat. As the chauffeur looks back in the rearview mirror, he sees a cocked .45 automatic being held against her skull. The driver hears the man saying, "If you ever leave me, I'll kill you." The Rolls-Royce screeches to a halt, the chauffeur takes off panic stricken into the desert, dodging the creosote and mesquite. The man with the pistol runs him down and reassures him that he is not going to die. So they all continue on to the reception in the big hotel where the fountain bubbles with champagne and the hired photographers circle and capture a record of the event. The man who staged this wondrous wedding once refused to leave his house for a business matter because he saw a dog in his yard and he knew, he truly knew, death was waiting. He seldom makes a move without consulting his mother the *bruja*. He is leaving on a trip now, he tells me, and I ask where. He smiles and says, Texas, California. Bolivia.

A jagged scar snakes down his chest from open-heart surgery after the drug bust. They caught him with thirty pounds of cocaine, the very last crumbs of the big shipment. But he does not wish to speak of those matters. He wants to be known for his art. The family abandoned him when he was ten, he arrived in Tucson as a teenager and slept under the bridges. Now he is fifty, he cannot read or write, and he has created the room. Three women have left him because of his devotion to this chamber. The Madonna sitting in the chapel—stolen from the gravestone of a major Mexican dealer. The gold flowers and leaves scrolling across the walls, all cut by his hand. And over the door a heraldic image with the words *Imperio Realm*—The Imperial World.

He will dream about the room, then lock himself in it for days and weeks executing that dream. He hires artists to paint murals—but so often they disappoint him. The gilt frames on the walls enclose paintings cut out of books and pasted in. This is not a project. This is a dream.

He tells me all this. Many men have tried to kill him. The authorities have stalked him also. No matter. The room. The dream. He insists.

"This idea, I have always had the idea, up here, in my head. Sometimes I stand here by the bar and the ceiling lifts thirty feet in my mind, the room is big like a cathedral, and I look out and see ladies dancing, they are dressed very fancy. I was born with this in my mind. This picture here, of the conquistador, there is a story behind this picture. My friend is at a swap meet and sees this mirror, and it's cracked and he buys it, and then he takes the glass off and behind the mirror is this picture. And he says this belongs to me, so he brings it here."

He reaches under the bar and brings up a maroon book. The pages contain thousands of entries of human beings with the same surname—a computer-generated listing of the nation's directories. Inside is a Xerox sheet with a drawing of a knight in armor, each piece of the suit explained. The man, who does not read, watches me read.

Another volume appears, white-covered, the wedding album. He is dressed in a black suit, a hat cocked on his head. His bride is beautiful and in white: they look into each other's eyes, they cut the huge cake, toast with champagne, they ride in the white Rolls-Royce. He never smiles in these pictures. She is very lovely, the white-trimmed flat hat tipped over her serene face. She is one of the women who has left him because of the room.

The room, he sighs, only expresses maybe twenty percent of what is in his mind. He has had earlier lives, he has seen the room somewhere before. He hires an artist to paint the mural on the ceiling, and look at it, look at it, it is not right, it is like a fucking tattoo. It is not what he sees in his mind, what he sees there is beautiful. He wants to express beauty.

He is not a bad man, he says, he does good things. Sure, he is in some illegitimate businesses, but he is also in some legitimate businesses. This does not concern him. But he has the room, he has made the room. So far he has worked more than two years rendering it properly. There still remain rubies to place in the gold rosettes that dot the walls. The fountain must be finished. Things appear, as if beckoned, things that belong in the room.

He leads the way to the enclosed porch. Now I am in the jungle, a riot of tropical birds swirls before the eye, a green swatch of palms dances on the walls. The bar is thatched, and a stream flows across the floor. He stands there and says this room has failed. The stream, look at the stream—it is not right, you should feel it, hear the water rushing against the hard, yet yielding stone. He glances over. Can I feel the water? No. See. It must be fixed.

"I want to feel the rain," he sighs. His eyes close, his fists curl tightly. "I must feel the rain." All the murals must be done over. It must be beautiful. When he stands here he must feel the rain.

He looks up. Do I understand? Each room will be different. He has had previous lives and the house will state what his many lives have been. His friends come over, people he knows in the life, and they find him late at night working on the rooms, and they laugh and say, Why are you doing this? They do not understand, they cannot see or feel beauty.

He hopes he has enough time before he is taken. People are trying to kill him. He does not know why. He is a good man. There are said to have been ten or twenty attempts on his life in the last three years. He hopes he has time.

Here, he will explain it. There will be furniture made of bamboo in the room with the stream where he will feel the rain. He motions to where he will be sitting.

He picks up a brass bell and rings it. A servant will enter and say, "What the fuck do you want?"

He pauses here and smiles. "And I will say, 'Bring me a cup of coffee.'"

It will be beautiful, he explains. He will be able to feel the rain.

There are three other things. At his wedding a photographer's lights caught a burst of light in his eye, *la estrella*, he repeats and repeats. He points out that at the entrance to the room he has carved a crown in the wall, a crown that gleams with jewels— *mas estrellas*. And there is the matter of his only letter, his first and last effort in a life of fifty years. He wrote it when his last wife left him. The note is framed and full of odd markings and squiggly lines that operate on a level that knows no alphabet. He holds it and reads out loud: "I love you." Then comes the pause, and he points to a light bulb he has drawn. Yet another *estrella,* a true star. Don't you see, he continues, the stars, all of them, are a sign. The star flaming from his eye in the photograph is a sign caught by the camera. He is marked. He is different.

He has these dreams which he must fulfill. There are things of beauty dancing in his head and he must make them real, actual things that can be then seen and touched and experienced. And he will, he will. He must.

If he is not taken too soon.

Even Al hiding in his adobe house in the barrio, surrounded by statues of saints and angels, sheltered by a huge Christ hanging from a huge wooden cross, even Al with his door bolted by a slab of wood, his curtains closed, his Bible open on the table. Even he has his bad moments. I'm over there sitting in his dungeon-like front room near the wood stove, and he starts talking about his dark feelings. He's been painting all day and the result hangs on the wall, *Death with Little Clay Man.* The canvas is sinister, Death hunches forward in his black robe, the scythe in his bony hand, the skull with the traditional grin. In a corner of the canvas is a small clay man, a prehistoric-looking figure. On Death's shoulder is a large blue oval, like an opal. Beneath the little clay man a red-and-orange circle swirls with energy and heat like the fires of hell and a black bird sails across this inferno. Al does not know what the painting means or where it came from. He is thinking of painting it out, blotting the whole thing out.

"I don't want to die and have people remember that I brought more ugliness to the world," he says.

And I agree with him because the beauty keeps breaking through. I remember walking through the *selva* with a Mexican man and his six-year-old boy, the child always scampering ahead of us. The man was well muscled, about thirty, his mustache trimmed, the face smooth. He had gotten hold of a spear gun and once a week he dove into the local river's deep pools and killed carp, catfish, and bass. These he sold in his barrio for a dollar a pound. He sometimes made ten or twenty dollars on a good day, excellent money in a place where the wage is four dollars a day and half the men cannot find anyone willing to pay them even that. Other days he looked for work. Yesterday, I watched him dive and fish, an old mask on his face, the gun in his hand, Levi cutoffs on his hips. His wife sat in the half shade of a Mexican bird-of-paradise bush along the river, a frayed rag over her head to protect her skin from the sun. Her lips were painted very red and her eyes glowed with pride as her man dove and dove and dove. That night we ate dinner at their hut, the whole dirt lot maybe a thousand square feet, the hut taking up a tiny corner of the place. They had four children. The next day, we went to fish with throw lines, and this was the time the man brought his son along. His small son wore new running shoes, the man stuck to his huaraches, sandals made from the tread of an old tire and tied to his feet with rawhide strands. We came to a small stream, the man jumped over easily, the boy hesitated. The father looked back at his son, and then turned, walked to a cliff, and picked up a small boulder. He pitched it midstream, the boy skipped across. The man never spoke to his son, the boy never complained, but his new shoes were saved. Love floated in the air with perfect silence.

*　　*　　*

At dusk, he comes off the hill, the figure big and broad, a mean yellow cur at his feet watching with fierce eyes. He wears an old shirt, the hair is gray and wild, in his hand a glass of whiskey. The dog growls and he says, "Easy, easy." The thorn forest of southern Sonora grabs the earth behind him, a tangle of low trees full of darkness and possibility. We are just off the desert, the southern-most outpost of saguaros guards a basalt-littered hillside a few miles away. I can see him squint to puzzle out my outline, the hot breath of flats of organ-pipes cacti laps against our necks.

"I did not expect company," he announces. "I have been drink-ing since noon."

I know the hunger.

I can sense our sameness: the whole world is sexual to us, down to the very last stone. Outside on the patio, sacks of cement are everywhere, stacks of tiles, mountains of firewood, crumbling adobe walls waiting for a savior to restore them or a merciful rain to finally end it.

He lives in one completed room like a monk in his cell. His old *mozo*, the seventy-four-year-old night watchman, relaxes, senses it will be all right. The old man has had six wives (none of whom he married—*muy caro*, very expensive, he explains), fourteen children, twenty grandchildren, and last night, he announces, he was drunk, *muy malo*, he offers happily, and got in a fight. A sharp knife is strapped to his ancient hip. He apologizes for his blade by saying he cannot afford a *pistola*.

We must go up the hill, the man who has been drinking says, up to a mud hut melting against the thorn forest, a *jacal* built by some peasant. The dirt path winds and skirts the dense trees reaching out to us with arms of thorns, up on the slopes the pink wash of blooming amapa trees floods the gray branches. The *jacal* is a thatched roof, dirt floor, and out front a small dirt platform framed by chopped limbs of hemotoxin trees, the wood corrugated with a weave of woody veins.

The lights of the town begin to appear below us, the quiet streets lined with colonial buildings mask what has happened here. For over two hundred years the spot flourished because of a silver deposit and the floor under this wealth, under the fine houses filled with gentry, their women wearing clothes from

Paris, drinking wine from European goblets, the bottom line under this gracious vision of grandees was Indian slavery, little brown men dying like flies in the mine as they hacked out the veins of silver from the earth. Eight thousand people lived in town. Five miles away, four thousand Indians lived like beasts in the pits. The population of the town was cut in half by the Revolution, the mine shut down in 1927 after a final labor revolt, and then rich Americans began coming, not many, maybe 150 families over the years, and one by one they are reclaiming the big houses of the grandees, restoring them, and spending their days sitting in perfect patios.

The hills around us are pockmarked with fields of marijuana and opium poppies. His project is simple, he says again: to build an ecological park in Mexico. To create a center to teach people to love the forest and the desert and the beaded lizards with their teeth dripping poison and the boa constrictors that slither across the neighboring hills. To love the jaguar that comes in the night and kills the stock, to love the birds, the screaming parrots that hurry past overhead.

We stoop, go under the thatched roof of the hut, the crow of roosters and the braying of donkeys floating up from the town. The stars are out now, brilliant stars with little competition from the feeble lights of the town.

He tells me a story. Once, years ago, he was in the desert and found a young badger crying out from the mouth of a den. The animal, barely the size of his hand, had been abandoned, so he took it home. Soon, the badger dug a little burrow under his house. Each morning and evening, he would sit on a log and watch the light change and the badger would emerge, sit by him, and watch also. The animal had been found when very young and therefore had imprinted totally on the man. The man had become the mother.

With time, the badger grew, became an adult, yet the

relationship continued. The man realized that the badger was the best friend he had ever had. He pauses in telling me this to give the point emphasis. Then, one night the man was lying in his bed in the house when he heard a scratching sound. He investigated, and chased the sound down to a tile on his bathroom floor. He got a tool, pried up the tile, and out popped the badger. The animal had tunneled forty feet to find his friend, dug for days and nights perhaps. Who can estimate the size of such a project for a badger? The animal's tunnel had sundered wiring, ruined plumbing, half destroyed the underbelly of the man's home. The next day the man went to a veterinary supply house and got a syringe and drugs. He returned home, tapped on the tile, moved it aside, and out popped the badger. He gave it a fatal injection. But the animal did not die. So he strangled it to death with his bare hands.

He pauses again in his telling, the night is sensual, there are the scents of wonderful flowers in the air. "How do you think it feels to kill your best friend?" he asks. "For a stinking house, for some pipes and wires?"

We leave the hut, slip and slide down the slope, and wander onto his patio. Here, over here, he beckons and I approach a crumbling adobe room, the roof and door gone and replaced by chicken wire. I swing my head up and stars explode into my eyes. At my feet I sense motion, and look down at desert tortoises. Then, in the corners, I sense shapes. Boys brought them in, he explains, after they'd been shot. The big redtail hawk perched in one corner has the end of one wing gone. It was rotting by the time the kids brought the bird in and so he whacked off the ruined flesh, cauterized the wound with a hot iron. The hawk stares but does not blink. The eyes are yellow. In the other corner is a Cooper's hawk, also rendered helpless by gunfire. The two birds sulk in the room under the stars, something strong and hot to the touch pouring out of their eyes. Their sharp talons clutch the limbs jammed into the mud corners, and they sit there and say nothing. The Mexicans feed them scraps of meat, give them cups of water. Each morning, children come up the dirt lane clutching dead snakes they wish to sell for the hawks.

* * *

I put trees in the ground, trees that will live for centuries and move softly in the night breezes when I am dead and dust. I dig a hole in the yard, and ease in a young boojum, a plant with the look of an upside-down carrot that can reach seventy or eighty feet given 800 years. This boojum is about seventy years old so I've got 730 years still in the bank.

In my pocket is a story that I cannot get rid of. It is about love and came to me over a cup of coffee with a friend. When he tells me the tale, I listen. Then I go home and write it down. Now I carry the scrap of paper in my pocket. I show it to a few people and say, here, look, a love story. And then they read it, and look at me strangely and say, no, this is not a love story. But I insist on this point. At the top, in big bold type, I have written the word LOVE.

This is a love story.
It is spring and he moves with cat-like grace from the car to the door. He is very thin, and wiry, a scant mustache rides above thin lips. His friend is with him, a pal since boyhood. He has come to be of help, he is eager to lend a hand to his pal. The thin, wiry man knocks real hard, and knocks again. He is the boss here, the hombre in charge. A hard knock. Many, many fear him. In the life, he kills for money. He says he does not enjoy this work but no one, not one living soul, believes him on this point. Both men are in their twenties and very alive at this moment. Perhaps they have done a few lines. They wait. She answers the

door. It is night, the very best time for such a visit. When she opens the door a crack, she is not really alarmed since she feels protected by major forces in the life. They enter. And then it begins.

She is not beautiful, not in the American way or even the typical Mexican way. Her face is strong, very Indian, and she is dark. The skin is dark, the hair long and heavy and black, the body thick and solid, the breasts round and firm but not unlifted. Her man is very powerful in the life and he could have anyone. And has. He has been to Los Angeles and fucked starlets, been to Las Vegas and had showgirls, enjoyed the very finest whores from coast-to-coast. But he wants her, he is obsessed with her. She strikes some deep chord within him and he has set her up in a house, steered little deals her way, made her his woman in every way he knows how. This is not a small thing. He is connected and the connections are hard bloody strands that stretch back to Sinaloa and Jalisco and Mexico City. And Colombia. His obsession with her is the very reason the two young hard men in their twenties have come this evening. Spring is barely a hint now, the nights are still cool in the desert but in the days the smells are back, the scent of early flowers, the flash of green as the trees leaf up. It is a good time to believe in new beginnings. And that is what the woman with the dark skin and heavy black hair has done. She has ripped the two young guys off of $80,000 in a deal, because she is protected, she is connected, she is sheltered by the love and power of the man who loves to fuck her dark Indian hide. So she lets them in.

The $80,000, that doesn't seem to be returnable. The power of her lover, that doesn't seem to be present. The two men enter grandly, they work well together, they are accustomed to each other's company, cousins in fact. One holds her down while the other slices off the clothing. They slash the face first, fine lines of blood that will leave an interesting thatch of scars. Then the hanging breasts are attended with quick incisions. There is really no rush, this is not some crime of passion. She has become a bulletin board and they are posting a message. The stomach, yes, the stomach also, the knife wipes from side to side. The blade, ah that blade, they go between her legs with that blade. And then they fuck her. Before they leave they almost beat her to death, but not quite, they are skilled, no, not quite. Why send a message and then at the last moment thoughtlessly kill the messenger? This visit will not make the newspapers.

After they leave the woman bleeding, beaten, and enlightened, the spring nights continue to come on. Some days there is a whisper in the breeze of the waiting summer fire, and then soothing cool waves wash again across the skin. He is getting a little nervous now, the coke use goes up, he can smell danger. In many ways things are good for him. He has a good supply of product, a captive dealer in Phoenix, another in Tucson. Money flows through his brown hands. Then, at that very instant when everything feels good—man, oh, so goddamn good, you know?—at that sweet moment the offer comes and it is a fine offer. The message comes, of course, through blood. His friend, his cousin, well, he has an aunt who raised him, and she brings the offer. She says this deal will be easy and the money, Jesus, lots of money. So he goes. He is nervous, just a little nervous, and packs a machine gun. His cousin is armed in the same manner. The woman, the blood, the aunt, she has supplied the guns. She drives the two men to the meeting. The parking lot in the shopping center is empty when she pulls in. The two men move to get out, and she stretches over across the seat and kisses her nephew. Earlier she had asked him not to go, softly dropped warnings like flower petals. He would have none of it. He sticks with his friend. Of course, she has had no real choice. She does not want to die, so she has made the delivery. The men waiting in the parking lot are not the ones expected. When the two men realize this, they do not really use their guns. The aunt has tinkered with the weapons and they cannot fire. Ah, there is a man moving in the shadows, and then he seeps into the light. He is the lover of the woman who now has a new face, new body, one inscribed with slashes, the one the two men beat up and raped. The two men are disarmed, their hands tied behind their backs. The bullets neatly enter their heads. They are tossed in the trunk, then the car stops and they are carefully placed on the dirt of the desert and the stars smile down at their blank eyes.

The woman? Yes, the woman. She is a waitress now and works tables. The man, the man who finally found the woman he could love, he is busy. For a while, the authorities come for him. They put him in a cage. Then he pays bond, over a half million. In cash. The case begins to erode. Some problem with witnesses. They seem to disappear or fall mute. Perhaps, he is weary of love now. It can cause so many problems. Certainly, it caused no end of problems for the dead. The contract killer, love killed him. That is how they got to him, through his friend, his cousin. He trusted him. And his cousin of course loved and trusted the aunt who raised him. Perhaps, when he died, he could still feel her kiss against his lips.

This is a love story.

Sometimes, late at night, I go to where the killing occurred. The parking lot is empty, the asphalt almost cool under the lights beaming down from their sturdy poles. Nearby, I can hear the roar of the Interstate traffic as people storm toward hopes and destinations. The woman with the scars still waits tables not far away. The best nights are those on which a light rain has fallen and I can hear the whirring of the tires as they hurry toward things worth doing. I always remind myself of all the things I should note if I am to be a good person, one sound and balanced. One night as I sat there, I reminded myself that twenty-two species of flowers were blooming in my backyard. And of course, that fact helped a great deal.

Years ago, Alfonso told me not to worry about the desert, that the desert always won. That night, I can still taste it, a night drowning in perfume—the desert gets that way during the bonfires of June when the cereus blooms like a wound in the heart. Of course, what he meant was that I should not concern myself with many things, that larger forces with deeper purposes were at work and things would turn out okay in the end. He can be very stern on this point.

Then the desert seemed to swallow him up, there was the drink, of course, and many other demons, and one day he reappeared after a decade or more with a new name and new eyes. He carves things from mesquite, cottonwood, and stone, he paints his dreams and the dreams are of a safe world where angels watch over us, and the animals stare with concern in their eyes. Of course there is the problem of Death with the little clay man. I am sitting in his dark house—he paints without natural light and when a canvas is finished, he has to take it out in the yard in the sun to see what in the hell he has created. On the wall is Death and the mud figure of a man and he looks at it with worried eyes. The eyes are often worried. The smile comes easily, so does laughter, but the eyes seldom let go of their concerns.

He's a solid guy, always battling his weight. He says, "I'd rather be dead than not wake up in the morning thinking of food." So we spend a lot of time sitting in cheap joints eating chiles rellenos, sopas, enchiladas, machaca, menudo, camerones, and endless bowls of chips and salsa. The house is immaculate, he seems to cook only about one meal a decade there. He confides that's the trick, clean the house up and then never do a damn thing in it. He jokes and then his eyes go black and he starts ticking off a litany of the people he'd like to kill. The Bible is always near his easel.

I look very very hard at his paintings. There is the drunkard who must dance with Death, there is the angel who loves the drunkard. Then there is the dead woman, a painting of muted colors with this corpse demanding attention. A woman lies in her grave, Al remembers the blue of the flowers the day she was put in the ground. A huge moon rises over the village, a small rancheria in Sonora where he often stays, his home away from home. The dead woman, that's the kind of painting Al creates and then frets over. Should he mention such things? Who in the hell will buy it? He makes a lot of paintings that people refuse to buy, all the ones that I like. There is this naked woman holding a rose just above the hair flowing from her crotch. There is a good-looking woman holding a clay pot and wearing a blue dress, her eyes a record of millennia of hurts. They all have the innocence of a person who has been totally corrupted and then partially cleansed. The colors are very bright also. There are sculptures too. A woman in stone nurses a lamb, an angel struggles to free itself from a slab of cottonwood.

*   *   *

The night is rich with scent from the many flowers. I am visiting again with the man who wishes to start an ecological park in Mexico. We stagger down the crumbling steps to the patio where mangoes and bananas spike up to the night sky, then walk out to the front veranda. The hawks stare at us from the silence of their room, the forms outlined, the eyes hidden in the darkness, but I can feel the heat coming off the trapped birds. A couple of Mexican guys are sitting on the crude wooden chairs and smoking as nighthawks bag some insects near the trees. Overhead hang tin lamps made by a local smith, the boojum is still in leaf, and the orchids bloom with yellow flowers.

Then Miguel arrives, a young guy in his twenties, slim waist, proud mustache, ready smile. He's wearing a white shirt, tight jeans, cowboy hat, and tucked into his waist is a .22 Colt Woodsman. The gun, no longer made, goes for about $300 a throw in the States. Miguel works for $4 a day. I do not ask how he got the gun, but simply if they are hard to get here. "Oh, no," he says with a smile. "They are easy to obtain."

He whips out the pistol, removes the chip, ejects the shell from the chamber, and hands it over to be admired. I can tell from the way he handles the small .22 cartridge that he is a man who still counts his bullets. In the sierra a man will hunt deer with a .22 rifle and one or two shells. The mountain over the town leans down into our conversation and I can imagine the bright fields under the stars, the orderly rows of marijuana and poppies. Today, the *federales* in a gun battle in nearby Navajoa have killed four men. *Las drogas.* A few days ago, in Chínipas, someone shot down a small government plane and killed four. The plane, it is believed, got too close to a field and so was taken out of the sky.

Near where we sit orchids cling to a chicken-wire screen and the gray-green stalks with delicate yellow flowers seem like tongues stroking the black air. Miguel asks, is it true that Americans have these glasses, and if a man has a pair of these glasses, he can look and see a woman without her clothes? He would like a pair of such glasses.

Miguel retrieves his gun, jams the clip back in, and stuffs it back in his pants. He is the hunter, the man of this pueblo who combs the sierra seeking game. He is the man who knows the animals. So I ask him about onzas, the lion of the sierra that is not quite a lion. The snout said to be more like a dog's, the color different, the pad of the feet on the forest floor more mysterious. For decades, Americans have sought the skin of an onza, the skull of an onza, the teeth of an onza. None ever turns up. This troubles no one in the sierra, since every campesino knows that onzas exist. Miguel as a matter of fact has killed one. But alas, at the time, he explains, he did not know anyone in the world cared about possessing the remains, so he left the beast to rot in the thorn forest. He says this matter-of-factly, as if the loss were a small detail in a busy life. There are a lot of details that seem to get easily lost down there. Miguel is from high up in the sierra but he has left his mountain town. He says someone there bumped off his brother. So he left.

No one believes in onzas except the people of the sierra and the thorn forest. I do not believe in the existence of onzas. But I can dream about them. The shoulders ripple with muscle, yet they still move with that cat-like grace, the big feet making not a sound as they course through the shadows. The breath is sweet, the mouth warm and cleansed from a drink that very morning in a shady mountain pool. The eyes never rest, the ears swallow whole the noise of the forest, and the cat never skips a beat when a flock of screaming parrots storms past overhead. The doglike snout drinks deeply of the warm air and the teeth gleam and wait, hungry for the warm gush of blood streaming out of a severed neck. In my dreams, the onza never makes a sound, not even a faint purring, and I can always feel the hot breath flowing from that mouth, a warm wave lapping against the tendons at the back of my neck.

Onzas, moving through the night. I like to think of onzas, then the body does not bob up in the well, the fingers are not lying about on the ground, the spines do not have these small precise dots as if someone had drilled them looking for ore.

The next day, I am walking up a dirt path, the narrow track wanders under arching trees and huts that huddle on the hillside. The sun falls from the blue sky and thuds on the ground amid the flowers, fences made of sticks race here and there defining little borders in a soft, green world. The yard is spotless, and an old woman sweeps the bare earth while chickens peck around her. The men sit under the overhang of the thatched roof, their backs resting against the adobe walls. The guy I've come for is squatting on the ground, his brown skin shining in the morning light. Most of his teeth are missing and he is slight and wiry, maybe a hundred and twenty pounds. The machete in his hand flashes against the block of wasima wood he is shaping. His thumbs are short, little stubs, and the fingers on both hands are gone. Behind him in a dirt-floored room stacks of tables and chairs look fresh and clean, the wood unvarnished and white. An empty light bulb suspended by a wire hangs against the mud wall and the green leaves of a philodendron trail out of it. Children crowd around me and stare but do not speak.

The man swinging the machete does not smile and continues sitting and whacking away. The body is very frail and looks sickly and I can almost smell some kind of terminal rot wafting off his skin. The green leaves of the trees shimmer in the tropical heat and stir faintly in the breeze like the tongues of hungry dogs. Flowers, orange, pink, red, and yellow, blaze around me. The man, maybe in his fifties, lights a cigarette, the end wet from the smacking lust of his lips. A few feet away a younger woman sits on a cot, one huge breast bared with a baby sucking on it. Her face is almost blank except for that faint aura of pleasure women get when they nurse. All I can hear is the hot breath of lust rolling off the hillsides, the arroyos overflowing with warm juices from a million ready loins.

I tell the man I am interested in a table and two chairs. He begins to explain how much work it is, how he must cut the trees, soak the branches, and then take his mutilated hands and slowly coil the branches so they will form a flat surface for the top. I can hear the old woman's broom whisking against the bare dirt. The children continue to stare at me with black eyes and suddenly break into giggles. The arroyo is roaring now with hot grease and oil, a musk rises off it and clouds of steam form. The scrawny man with the machete finishes his smoke as clucking chickens drift through the patio. He never smiles, not once. The baby pulls at the young woman's teat.

The hills around me are alive with marijuana. The child at the woman's breast is said to be doomed by monstrous statistics documenting overpopulation. The thorn forest the man goes to for his wood, it is shrinking. I have more money in my pocket than the man with no fingers will make in six months. I whip out an American twenty-dollar bill as a down payment. He rejects it. The bill this afternoon is worth tens of thousands of pesos. But not to him. He thinks I am giving him twenty pesos. He has never seen American money, he has never heard of an exchange rate. I see the man's machete flashing, the woman's full brown breast with the baby sucking.

Some paintings of Alfonso's have the woman's full breast and the love in her eyes. And then he will fall into a pit and the paintings will grow angry for a while. He has done this huge canvas. A skeleton sits at a table wearing a sombrero that says in Spanish, "Drugs Are the Death of the Mexican Revolution." A bandolier crosses the skeleton's chest, a bullet hole sprouts on the forehead, and a bloody tear seeps from one eye. In the bony arm, a syringe dangles and the fleshless hand clutches a small doll. Al has written on the painting. "Sellers of drugs are the assassins of women and children." He hates the painting and keeps it in the darkness of his bedroom.

"Nobody'll buy that one," he insists. But he is wrong. It is snapped up by a gallery in New York.

This does not seem to please him either.

"The whole world has become a dance of death," he says ruefully, "and I know I can't do much about that, except do my little dance of death too."

*   *   *

It is night and we have been gone for days. First thing, the man with the vision for a park must check his hawks and I can see him heading toward the room with chicken wire, his voice already beginning to cluck greetings. He's been gone a week or two and he must see how they are faring. The redtail is on the dirt floor dying of thirst and hunger. The old *monzo* has forgotten to feed the birds. The Cooper's is gone. The old man explains with deep laughter how the night before he heard this terrible screaming, this awful squawking in the room, and when he checked, the redtail was eating the Cooper's. I point the flashlight down and see a yellow leg with black talons curled on the end. That's what's left of the Cooper's. The redtail sits on the floor with its wings splayed back to support its weakened body and the bird slowly rocks. I hold it while we force meat and water down its throat. The eyes stare out yellow and the big tongue hangs there tired in the middle of the fierce-looking beak. The hawk barely resists, it is driven upon the kindness of strangers and submits. We leave it there in the room on the dirt floor still rocking back and forth on its splayed wings.

One day we are in a village out against the foothills of the sierra and see a military macaw fly over our heads. The bird is huge, more than two feet long, a giant parrot skimming the dry leafless roof of the thorn forest. The local people say the birds come each day and then go, that is all they know of the matter. One finally agrees to lead us up into the hills. The streambed has puddles of water here and there, the banks lined with big cypress, and after a few miles we come to a rocky barren hill with a small hut on top. We climb to the shack, the windows have no glass, an old woman comes out. She is barefoot, gray haired, and dark. Inside the small room I see a fruit crate hung with twine from the roof beams, the whole covered with cheesecloth and a small baby sleeping inside. Ah, the birds, the woman says, yes, the birds, and she goes through her tiny hut into the open ramada behind it, makes a slight movement with one hand, and three brilliant macaws explode into view.

The beak is dark, tail red and outlined with long turquoise plumes. The birds arc toward the trees and I sense they are gone, have fled. The woman watches us impassively. Suddenly the macaws swing back into view, tumble down toward us, land on a post set in the dirt of the yard. The old woman walks over, holds up a piece of tortilla, and the birds eat from her hand. She says they go out in the morning to feed in the campo, rest in her hut during midday, forage again toward dusk, then return for the night. How long have I had them? Oh, four years. They were very young when they came, my son, he brought them. Names? No, they have no names. As she speaks, the macaws watch, a few feet away, some chickens, a dog, a cat moving contentedly beneath the post.

These birds, Señora, these birds are worth one hundred dollars apiece, we say. Do you wish to sell them? Ah, no, she does not want money. If we bring her a weapon, a .22, then we can have the birds. She wants a gun.

Of course, it would be wrong to take the birds. They are living free, just roosting in her house and sharing its life. No cage could replace the wonder of their present days and nights. But they are so lovely. And we are filled with envy. Not for the old woman in the hut, dirt on her calloused feet, flies swirling around her life. Not for the macaws, all gaudy in their plumage. But for the moment when they sweep in from the sky, land on the pole, take food from a human hand and do not flinch.

So we leave and go into town. In the evening we go to a fine hotel where the patio spreads out as a sea of stout leather chairs, blooming bougainvilleas, cool tile floors, palms spiking the night sky, and waiters in white tunics scurrying about with trays of food and drink. Enrique, one of the owners, comes over to the table and sits down. He is forty something, the skin smooth and brown, the hair beginning to thin, and his mouth is always tight and rides uneasily under his anxious eyes.

For twenty-three years he's toiled in the hotel cleaning up the messes that drunken Americans love to create in Mexico. Against one of the patio's palms a wild orchid clings—the campesinos rip them out of the thorn forest and peddle them in town—and for twenty years Enrique has tended the plant like a favorite mistress. He has bathed it just so, the water trickling down into the web of its fine hungry roots that cling to the skin of the palm, and snipped its flower stems off at the end of the blooming cycle, and given it the dash of food at the exact right time. He has watched the orchid flourish and grow strong while he has added fat to his middle and begun to grow old.

"Ah," Enrique says, "when I was younger I could really drink. I would drink with friends for two or three weeks. We would have women of course, and spend days just drinking and fucking." He utters this recital without a smile and I can see the room, the smell of sweat in the air, Enrique unshaven, the woman in a slip, a little thick through the hips but the breasts round and large and slipping out the front of her sheer nylon slip, the small feet in high heels, the lipstick red, and the eyes bubbling amid a black corona of makeup. Her lips are full, of course, and every orifice swollen from the work. The room is noisy from the tinny scream of the small radio, the air heavy with cigarette smoke, and the whiskey glass is dirty, Enrique bellowing for more ice, and her moving with a swing of the hips to fetch the bucket, the hair between her legs moist, his eyes hooded with fatigue and the retinas cinders from the drive and wear and tear of lust. The afternoons were surely the best, the drapes pulled, her legs spread, and the pounding away while other men had to work for their money and hold grimly to ugly tasks that paid. The days would pile up like used Kleenex tossed carelessly on the floor and then it would end, as it always does, not like a meal when everyone has stuffed themselves and can eat no more. No, it would end when everyone was finally empty, absolutely empty of the anger that brought them to the room. The first few minutes outside are always the worst, the sun driving into the eyes, those fourpenny nails puncturing the skull.

What Enrique never talks about is the son-in-law. He is a past tense since he dipped into the life, ah that wonderful money and the excitement, and then showed up a corpse with his ears sliced off.

We get up at five in the morning. The redtail has regained no strength and continues to huddle on the floor, a pile of light bones and dulled feathers that has run out of the drive to live. I hear the words *"matar,"* to kill, and *"cuchillo,"* the knife. We go north, the thorn forest melting away, the desert slapping against our faces. I can hear the soft whish of the knife, the muffled choke, the blood dribbling down the breast of the hawk.

3

The dead whale looms as just a room of ribs, the vertebrae like ship's propellers, the discs the size of large Frisbees. The summer sun eats my skin as I walk the beach, big flies find my sweat and bite deeply.

Months ago, I'd gone with a friend to the whales, we'd traveled like pilgrims, flown out on a point jutting out of Baja into the Pacific. She landed the plane on a chunk of dirt where there was no airfield and the fishermen came over from their camp of shacks. They looked to see if we were truly not dead and the children stared at the ground and stirred the dirt with their small bare feet. Then they offered us lobsters. She wore this smile. She was the pilot in her bomber jacket with many pockets. The sun fell without a splash into the ocean as we ate a can of stew. At night we laid out under the wing and the January winds blew cold from Asia. The moon rose over the wing and we downed cups of mezcal. Her body is white above me in the pale light, the hair black and thick and curly over my head, the breasts swinging freely, and I reach up. I run my hand up her leg, her face is a cream mask, the wind whips against our flesh. Past the crash of the surf, the gray whales are coming back to Baja to breed and bulls patrol the coast guarding the cows calving in the lagoon. We slip off the ground cloth and the sand is cold and tears our flesh. I feel her teeth scrape against mine. At dawn we climb the dunes and the bones of cattle, skulls with full horns, catch the early light. The coffee still tastes bitter on our tongues. Smoke curls up from the shacks of the fishing camp, and the women stand outside brushing their long black hair. Out at sea, we see the small *launchas* of the lobstermen bobbing in the big Pacific boomers and the bulls steam through them like ships, columns of water shooting up as they blow. I want her in my mouth as the salt air rakes across the point. When we take off, fishermen and their children come out to watch and see if we make it. Our made-up airstrip ends in three hundred feet and the ocean waits. Her smile burns past the graves and as the plane pivots on its wing I see the bulls blowing.

Now summer has come, the heat is on as I run my hand along the curve of the bones, trying to remember the bulls sounding. Small waves lap at the shore behind me. Huts stretch along the beach at Punta Sargento, the walls formed by bent wands of ocotillo, a blanket draped on top for shade, the floors hot sand. No one is home now, the small no-see-ums that plague this stretch of coast on the Sea of Cortez have driven the Seris away. Just behind the row of small *jacales* are a couple of tarpaper shacks thrown up by Mexicans who have joined this Indian encampment to have a go at the fish in the channel flowing by Tiburón Island. The channel is called the Infiernillo, the Little Hell. I poke around in the hundred-degree heat.

The drugs seem far away in the sierras or along those arroyos that spill off the slopes and knife into the desert. Kilos, bales, machine pistols, gold chains, thin white lines against the false veneer of the tops of televisions, all distant and silent. A friend came over to my house one day and I told her I was going to Culiacán and she said, "Why? Nobody wants to know that." But I do. Caborca, a center for the life, is maybe 120 air miles away, and small planes, like bullets, are often the measure of time and distance here. In Caborca the bars have new trucks parked in front, the roll bars chrome, the paint often black. Men will sit

and drink, .45 automatics stuffed in their pockets. The names of
the saloons are wonderful—one is called The Mentally Retarded
Wolf. A priest, Father Kino, founded the town, an old church
still stands. Some think he should be made a saint. The town is a
mecca for campesinos in the north of Sonora. I seldom go there.
The village of the blue flowers, Alfonso's stomping ground, is an
outrider to Caborca. Alfonso has this pitch: we must go there, he
says, I want you to see the desert there, to hike through it. You
must write it all down, he says.

Crabs clutter the shallow waters, their chests an orange smear
as they come in close to deposit their eggs and then depart again
into deeper waters. David is out there now balanced like a stork
on one leg, a hand-carved ocotillo spear clutched and ready.
His arm cocks, the spear flies down, and he has another crab to
drop in his sack. For twenty years he's been drifting down here
to buy baskets, necklaces, and ironwood carvings from the Seris,
about the last Indian tribe in North America to come in from the
cold and belly up to the table of modern life. Back in the fifties,
some Seris could still wield a bow, start a fire with a wooden drill.
They're big, often hitting six-foot, and they filtered into Spanish
records as a breed of giants hugging the godforsaken coast of
Sonora.

When the Americans bumped into them much later, they
thought them cannibals. This is not so, but once an old man told
me a story that he thought suggested where such a belief came
from. Back in 1934, or 1935, the Seris were starving and down
to maybe 100 or 150 surviving members and a group of them
headed up the coast to Puerto Libertad, a bleak fishing camp of
Mexicans where for a time the son of the governor had stashed
his Russian mistress. As this party of Seris paddled along the
shore, they saw a bee colony high on a cliff, and Ramón Blanco,
the brother of a famous shaman, Santo Blanco, pulled the boat
over and scrambled up for the honey. He fell from the cliff and

died. The other Seris cut him open and ate his liver—to absorb his power. My friend who tells me this story late one night, well, he thinks maybe this is how those stories of cannibalism got going.

The Seris finally make it to Libertad and my friend has a pal living there. This man gives the Seris what's left of a sack of flour, and they rip it apart with their hands, stuff their mouths, and eat like the starving people they are. One of them has a beautiful fifteen-year-old daughter. He offers to swap her for a small dory. There are other details that flutter out: when smallpox hit Hermosillo in the early thirties, my friend explains, Mexicans sent blankets contaminated by the disease to the Seris in the hope it would wipe them out. And, he laughs, Mexican soldiers on holiday would come to the coast and hunt them like rabbits.

"Has this ever been written down?" I ask.

"No," he says sourly, "nobody wants to know about these things."

By the late 1950s, the tribe was almost extinct. Books and articles appeared about The Last of the Seris. But modern medicine foiled that scenario and now they're seven hundred strong, breeding right along, and they've fled this place to get away from the bugs and left all the crabs to us.

All around us the desert has been gutted of ironwood by the tribe for carvings they began selling to tourists back in the sixties; out in the channel the turtles they love to hunt with a spear totter on the edge of extinction, in the currents the fishing has spun downward for decades until the catch is mainly dog sharks. The encampment itself is a Seri statement forged by a hunting and gathering society that has slipped effortlessly into the era of modern litter: fish bones, Kellogg's Choco-Krispie's, Bimbo bread, Agua Mineral bottles, flat tires, crab shells, orange juice cans, potato chip sacks, fish heads, shark teeth, nylon rope, club soda, instant coffee jars, oil cans, tequila bottles, discarded tins of *frijoles,* tomato sauce, baking soda, salsa, worn rubber gloves. Empty cartons of corn flakes. Nearby are heaps of shells, the middens, that hungry Seris have been creating here for maybe two thousand years.

We left Tucson one morning, the freeway slick beneath our tires, the border a demand for official papers. Magdalena rises up along the river, we pull off at a taco stand. Cabeza meat, strips ripped from the steer's skull, the soft tortilla a sopping mess in my hand. Flies crawl along my fingers. A radio blares and down the road Kino snores in his wonderful open grave, Father Eusebio Kino, the man credited with finally opening this country up to my kind in the late seventeenth century, pointing the way for the hordes of Europe. Now he's a skeleton looking up with empty sockets at people looking down through a glass top. I sometimes imagine Kino hobbling about the desert in his glory days when over every hill he met some new human beings who had never heard so much as a whisper about Jesus Christ. Father Kino is getting old. He has worked for the faith in Baja. He has pushed the frontier north in Sonora and visited with his cross the Gila River people. He has proven California is not an island. He eats slop, wears crummy clothes, and prays a lot. At times he likes to be whipped. He makes many journeys, travels thousands of miles in this desert. He forces other people to think the way he thinks—he says that is his mission.

He is the question. A friend once told me, "In Mexico there are no answers. There aren't any questions either." He is right of course, but I cannot actually think that way.

A clear gallon jar of sliced red onion rests on the worn wooden counter a few inches from my hand. The thin whine of a radio cuts through the morning light. The cook is fat, his face three days' unshaven, his wrist thick. The cleaver chops thin strips of grilled beef into tiny squares, mesquite smoke eats into my eyes. In colonial times, three thousand Jesuits wandered Mexico in the course of a century and a half. Each stayed twenty to twenty-five years. They were educated men with big feet and crude sandals, crazed dharma bums who would have dazzled Kerouac, and they bopped into every village, disarming the wise old men, snatching up the children, making quick crosses in the air, looking for the stone axe, the wooden club that would translate them swiftly to Paradise, their brains oozing out into the dry, desert dust. The Indians on the eastern slope of the Sierra Madres grabbed one, crucified him, cut his head off with a machete, and as his face tumbled forward toward the ground, his soul slipped loose from his lips in the form of an innocent child and ascended to heaven in the company of angels. This is recorded in a slow hand by a quill pen dipped excitedly into an inkwell. It is recorded as an answer. Three thousand men, twenty to twenty-five years, let's say sixty thousand years of knowing, of watching, of hearing the chants in the night, whooshing the flies off the plate of food. The long nights without women, the tight focus of their eyes as the brown breasts sway into view, and the infant sucks the swollen tit, hot rush of milk, the priest rides uneasily over his dead loins.

We rumble south and hit the long stream of desert and white light that leads to Hermosillo, a city of about half a million Mexicans in the middle of a furnace. We plow into the center, park on a narrow side street. We cross the plaza fronting the government offices, wander down a side street, and then enter a huge gravel yard where men sit under a ramada, just men, not one woman, and everyone drains glass after glass of beer. The cantina. We move toward a run-down stucco building off to the side, enter, glide past the small bar where a skinny Mexican in his fifties pumps a keg with four light-blue glasses riding in one hand, and make our way through a wilderness of small metal tables. The room smells of beer, men, and piss. On the wall is a big photograph of an enormous fat woman and an enormous fat man. She is lying naked in bed, her breasts resting like watermelons on her torso, her face contorted with laughter. The fat man is showing her his dick.

* * *

I know dealers. They are out there hunting the deer, but when the woman weeps, they never flinch. I have watched, they never flinch. In the bar, the wood very fine and polished, they buy me drinks. Deals stagger around in the blue air, and they are always hopping onto aircraft. The desert becomes maps, plats, parcels, pieces of paper, kilos, bales, non-recourse notes. We drink a lot, and there are always women about smelling the money in the night. One name keeps popping up, the center of a black star. One day a woman in Tucson shows me a coffee mug with the company logo as if it were an icon ready for a private chapel. "Everything he does," she says with joy, "is first class." I think, has Father Kino come back from the dead?

He is lanky, the air around him always mechanically cooled. The skin is very pale, the mouth a thin line, the money very big. I ask him how does it feel to get out bed every morning with a couple of billion dollars in your britches. He gives a half sheepish smile and says it is not that simple, the money is not a pile of gold coins, it's in play, there's a lot of work. His secretary whisks in and out with small notes, he nods and gives brisk instructions. The notes are handwritten on little yellow squares of paper, just like a kid uses in school to slide a message to that girl. I can reach out and touch him, he's sitting right there in a chair. Under the rules of my culture this one slab of flesh controls thousands of acres, legions of people, hacks up land, crushes people. This is sanctioned—he is on a mission. I can make a living writing about people like him, just as they will pay me to write about drugs, a thing called the environment, problems in something called growth. He is a subject.

It is early in the morning when my call gets through—this is not easy, he is always in a meeting, there is so much to do—and the voice comes on the line. I can see where he is sitting, the perfect furniture with good wood, calm colors, cool setting, the windows staring out at Phoenix, the view blocked here and there by palm trees stuck like props in the trim, green lawn. His name is Charles Keating, Jr., but everyone calls him Charlie. He insists on this point. He has billions at his command, thousands of people acting out his wishes, square miles of land, junk bonds, commodity exchanges, gold, silver, currencies. He is the twentieth century's answer to the captains of the past, captains both industrial and divine. He is a riverboat gambler, but then the captains always are. But the office is not spectacular, it is safe, careful, exact. The office is like a beautiful woman—perfectly groomed, the teeth polished and capped, the dress snug but not revealing, and yet when I get close and smell the scent coming off the nape of her neck I realize under no circumstances could she ever perspire, and then something dies, something like desire. This is the feel of the office.

We chat and then I ask the question about a man I know named Ernie Garcia, the question he has no doubt been expecting, the one flooring the conversation. And he says, "Him? Yeah, he just left here. He looked awful." Two days later, I flip open a newspaper and understand why he felt awful. His marker has been called and Keating has gutted him like a fish and left him flopping on the deep padded carpeting of his office.

Charlie hates certain stains on his country. Once he showed up at a congressional hearing with half a ton of pornography. Once he traveled 200,000 miles in a single year denouncing images of men and women rutting. Charlie has been up for hours now, grinding out his day in his own bureaucracy of money. He is sitting there in Phoenix, he is hard eyed, and in a trance of greed. I remember watching him once, watching him play. He acted at first as if I'd invaded his home. For months we'd been at war, fat letters arriving from his lawyers in New York threatening ruin if I slandered their noble client in print. The issue was kind of simple: I had a couple hundred pages of stolen documents, the official federal audit and other niceties, and they showed Charlie's empire as buck naked with a stripped savings and loan as its centerpiece. He crushed me with the power of his lawyers—he had seventy-seven firms on retainer—and I backed off, could not get my material into print, and surrendered the point. Because he beat me, I hated him.

I also felt an anger in my belly over his world, a place that was creating the new desert of air-conditioned rooms, instant cities, new cars, the calculated edge in the woman's eyes as we snort coke and wait for a flash of mechanical passion. I am a dwindling minority, someone who sees my appetites as fed by rock and cactus and dry winds. And I am losing to a world of pavement, deals, fine saloons, and new clothes, losing on both sides of the line. Those huge hard plates we call cultures are grinding me up into a very fine dust. I wince from the pain and then look into the mirror and see my real shame—I love both of the cultures that are slaughtering my dreams. It is not that I am clean, but I am pure. That is something I can never be. But I know others who wish to be clean, wish to be pure. This I cannot do. I eat like a beast and then see my image and feel shame over the gore dripping from my lips. But my blood quickens and lust rises and I can never stop feeding. I can feel anger over Keating, I can have understanding about Keating, I can think of destroying Keating with some magic stroke of my pen. But I cannot feel superior to Keating. Most people I know, they can feel superior to Keating. I lack that facility. So I go to Charlie.

The room where Charlie sits is clean and still and has that air of death and sterility that overwhelms one in an empty church. The eyes—they are so lined and tired and obsessed—bore into the computer screens where the globe's oceans of money flow. Deutschemarks, Swiss francs, pounds sterling, yen. Second by second, the currencies mutate like microbes. Another screen displays Eurodollars, the Dow Jones, gold, silver, Standard and Poor's 500. Clocks on the wall march in step with Zurich, London, New York, Chicago, and the Phoenix war room. Men move quickly around the glass-walled room, placing orders over the phone, monitoring the play of markets. It is 107 degrees outside the building and the desert breathes dust across the city.

Charles Keating, Jr., sits in a chair and stares ahead at the bank of monitors. The sixty-five-year-old face is absolutely still with concentration, the body all but motionless. It is morning in Phoenix, but the time that counts is that of money. The blue eyes are clear and alive and seemingly oblivious of every other single thing on earth except the movement of the numbers on the screen as financial ventures of the nations ebb and flow like the tides. He lays off an overnight order in pounds sterling, a hedge against his position. I do not know exactly what this means—he tries to explain it to me—I just keep seeing hedgerows in England skirting fine meadows full of Guernseys.

Now he gets up, and his lanky, athletic, six-foot-five-inch frame begins to move. The face regroups easily into a smile, the lines diminish. He walks past a room full of well-dressed secretaries, all selected for positive attitudes and wholesome appearances, and most personally interviewed by him, as are a lot of people on the 1,200-person staff. Candidates, he explains, are sized up for attitude, and if hired they will be constantly in the ladies' room primping.

I am sitting in one office listening to a puffy-faced subordinate explain the company's fantasies about a real estate development that is actually dead in the water. Then the executive buzzes a secretary, Christ they all love to do that, to buzz the underling. She coolly floats into the room. Her feet are encased in high heels, her clothes have quiet tones. And nipples poke through the fine cloth of her blouse. Until that instant it never occurred to me that Keating's squads of females had nipples, or went to the bathroom, or sweated like pigs as they flopped on a bed. Charlie is the biggest single contributor in the United States to campaigns against pornography—and for him that runs the spectrum from *Playboy* to kids in the sack with five guys. I pester him about this obsession, and he can never explain it. He looks at me and says, no, it's not some kind of buried thing, not some cover for a personal lust for children. It is just a thing with him, he says. When I see the nipples poking against the woman's safe, careful blouse, I realize that everything Charlie touches is staffed with good-looking people and that all the people have a well-scrubbed sexuality.

I am trapped inside a corporation without a drop of juice. It is a machine. The walls are tastefully decorated with Southwestern art, desks substantial chunks of wood. There are no hours for the staff except long, no set vacations. One of Charlie's secretaries keeps a packed suitcase with her always and if the call comes to meet Keating at the airport at 3 A.M., she is ready to go off for days trailing him and taking notes around the boardrooms of America. Charlie himself has been at the office since three or four and will not get home until seven or eight tonight. He works seven days a week.

His office has an open door. The desk is a fine old table with a computer plugged into the money markets and across the way are two more monitors. The furnishings are standard—the glass-topped conference table, the soft couch and chairs surrounding a coffee table, shelves, quiet carpet—and almost invisible. There are no plaques or awards on the wall, just a large color photo-graph of himself with his wife, the six kids, and all the grandkids in his grassy-walled $5 million private compound. In a distant corner, a big, glowing globe slowly rotates. Outside the window,

a Tongan, one of 125 islanders he pays as groundskeepers, zeal-
ously tracks down a stray leaf on the lawn. A glass Madonna
shares a corner of his desk.

He buys things. The city council? Toss them $80,000. Need
five U.S. senators to straighten out a problem? Give them
$1,300,000. A new pro-football team has moved into town? Get
me $800,000 worth of tickets. That last magazine article said
things hostile to the company? Get me my lawyers. "We have a
legal department," Keating says with a smile, "and they special-
ize in libel actions." The girls down in the legal department have
been doing well? Here, take them across the street to the Bilt-
more, give each of them $500, and tell them to spend it in twenty
minutes on something nice to wear or the money is going to be
taken back. Three jets serve him and his staff, plus a helicopter.
Going to Europe? Hey, reserve both full-body company jets for
me and the family, one reserved for those who want to sleep during the flight. He has given $1 million to Mother Teresa. He once
gave $600,000 to his old high school so they could build a decent
swimming pool. His paycheck one year was $3.2 million.

He does not want me to see the planes. He does not want me
to go inside the hangar. The planes are legend. Once, a businessman I am interviewing hesitates, shuts the door, sits on the edge
of his desk overlooking a desert city, and says, "You've got to see
the planes to understand him. That's where he goes crazy." The
rumors purr from people's lips: gold faucets, electronic equipment, rare woods, fine leather couches with telephones hidden
in the arms. The planes. The crew is standing by. Always.

Charlie controls things. Once, I am in another city and I
sink into a soft leather chair. The man is on the phone, barking
demands. He must talk to Charlie, he absolutely must. He has
to get the half million by lunch or the paper will go from good
to bad. He puts down the phone and looks down at the hard
wooden top of his desk. He says, "I gotta get the money and they
just tell me that in a half hour Charlie's flying to fucking Paris."

Keating settles into a chair in his office and begins to talk. A secretary brings in a glass of orange juice—the refrigerator down the hall also has a couple of bottles of Dom Pérignon, Charlie's favorite. His voice is very clear and almost soft, a slight lilt of Irish mixed with a large dose of the nasal speech of Ohio. The body is relaxed, and laughter comes easily. Secretaries come in and out with messages but these hardly break his calm. He still has most of his reddish hair and he has the carriage of a man who tries to swim a mile a day.

He is relaxed. It all sounds so simple. He owns more than a billion dollars' worth of the desert. His corporation feeds off a savings and loan and says it has $6 billion in assets. He tells me that Arizona will be the new coast of the Pacific Rim, that the Japanese are coming, the economy is now global, the future is now—the past? Well, who cares about the past, it is over.

A man who has done business with him catches this simplicity. "What you gotta remember with Charlie," the man offers, "is that his family comes first, his company second, and fuck everybody else."

Charlie surrounds himself with paintings and statues of Indians in benign and submissive postures. He tells me his wife picks them all out.

*   *   *

Two more cold Tecates, the engine sputters and lurches west. Glued to the cracked dish is a Seri santo, a piece of wood carved and painted with a sun and a cross. The wood is red elephant, a *torote* that looks half dead when it is all alive, the leaves absent most of the time, the bark a kind of wax paper that flaps in the breeze. I keep just such a santo hanging over my front door to bar evil from the house. The Seris have had a ragged reputation; some scholars once thought they were Jonathan Swift's inspiration for his giant Brobdingnagians since at first contact in the sixteenth century the six-foot men towered over the Spaniards. After that it was centuries of crabbed references to a filthy band of savages who lived along the coast and on a big island, a people who worshipped the moon, had no houses, stole cattle and horses, refused to farm, murdered at every opportunity, and would not come in and sit at the table of Western Civilization. The women were handsome and had large breasts they did not cover. They wore robes made from pelican skins and stank. Newspapers argued they were cannibals. In the 1890s, some West Coast reporters landed on their island, Tiburón. They were looking for a good feature about Stone Age folks and they were promptly slaughtered. In 1904, a band of Yaquis took refuge among the Seris from their constant wars with the Mexicans. The Mexican army threatened to wreak havoc on the tribe if they did not turn the rebels over. So the Seris complied, showing up at the Mexican military camp with the hands of men, women, and children dangling from a pole. There is an old photograph of Seris, the hands, and the surprised Mexicans, all grouped around the pole on a fine desert day. The Seri language is very guttural and soft, and when they speak the lips do not move and the faces seem like masks.

But then I find masks everywhere, and there are also the walls, huge walls keeping everything in its proper place. Charlie! Charlie, you son-of-a-bitch, you stay here in Phoenix watching fifty clocks track the chrono-madness of the planet as you worship money, power, and the darkness of your star, but for Christ's sake, stay out of Seriland, and ethnographic musings, and sea turtles blundering north up the coast on their way toward the nets, the harpoon, death, and the meat pot. The rules demand this, the world is linear—just look at this sentence. But as the truck bumps and grinds like a stripper, Charlie, he's riding in my mind, and so is Ernie, and the drug dealers in Culiacán, and the deer that changes into a woman and weeps, and Kino fucking over an entire region because he read the Good Book as a boy in Italy. The Tongan is bending over in the bright sun on the perfect lawn to pick up the one errant leaf and . . .

We turn off down a dirt road into the desert. Red elephant trees pop up here and there, organ-pipe cactus waggle their candelabra arms, and the soil is brown and hot, the white light of day flashing down. Vultures ride the thermals, and outside of the road, there is not a sign of our kind for miles. The ocean beats against the shore and it's enough to make a developer's heart sigh. There are no signs. The Seris are farther up the coast fishing off their boats with nets a couple of football fields long. They used to toss dynamite but now there's only a couple of one-handed guys hanging around the villages to memorialize those days. They also used to sing, and a few visiting scholars bagged some of their lyrics.

> I am alone.
> If we were married
> We would go out early.
> We would kill a deer.

*   *   *

An evening electrical storm plays across the Catalina Mountains at sunset. It is August and the terrace of the Tucson Racquet Club is filled with tables of hackers, swimmers, and survivors of aerobics classes. They are all savoring that cold beer or glass of wine as the day dies in flashes of lightning and the blood-red glow of the sun. Ernie Garcia, dressed in his tennis whites, moves from table to table, laughing, talking, the body relaxed, the manner assured, the smile quick and frequent. He is twenty-nine years old and he is The Man.

He announced right at the start that he was going to make a

million by the time he was thirty and he is well ahead of schedule. E. C. Garcia & Company is hot. A big utility has weighed in with its bankroll (for a share of the company) and now Ernie Garcia and his band of young partners are playing with big chips in a red-hot Sunbelt market. And they have a reputation for winning, always winning, and winning big. They got the numbers. In 1983, the outfit takes in $698,828 in total revenues, in '84 the take hits $4,498,923. Then in 1985 gross revenues zoom to $27,797,498. And that's just a beginning. Downtown the four-year-old firm has taken the top two floors of the new United Bank building. Ernie is about to move to Phoenix and open up a northern front on the empire. He has a round face with heavy jaws and the quiet manner of a guy who keeps winning. And there is an endless source of new chips coming into view on his horizon, Charlie Keating's chips.

He is the boy wonder, the hero of a certain world. Later, when the indictments come down, the federal government will explain its notion of how boy wonders operate. It will be a world, the federal regulators claim, where Charlie Keating loans people with little or no collateral money from his federally insured savings and loan, and then through a blitz of paper deals quickly fired back and forth between the parties creates a profit, on paper. From that paper profit, Charlie will take about half to put in escrow for federal taxes. This money will leave the vault of his savings and loan and never be seen again. Players in this game, guys like Ernie, will walk in tennis whites across the terrace of the racquet club and radiate power and success. There will be no end to the envy and ambition in the faces of others.

The town's hot, the ground's flaming from bonfires of money, and deals can be done—slam dunk!—just like that. People seem to be getting off airplanes with suitcases full of money—national homebuilders, big savings and loan operators, rich Mexicans stashing some cash in El Norte, drug-dealing Mexicans stashing cash in El Norte. Ernie buys an office building and parking lot, flips it in a day, and makes a cool million. Just like that, they say. It's a whole new world—not construction, not real estate development, not homebuilding or any of that old-fashioned stuff. No, no, no. It's called Real Estate Processing. Boom. A done deal.

The terrace of the club has got a feel that summer that anything is possible, anybody can do a deal, anyone can jump in and jump out of the market and suddenly have big bucks in their fists. As Garcia floats from one knot of people to another, he is the embodiment of a primary American dream: when he speaks, everyone listens.

He is the Hispanic who knows no Spanish and has never visited Mexico—except the border. He is the man who in his early twenties made $100,000 in commissions a year as a stockbroker, even though he had never owned a share of stock. He is the man who at the very beginning made big killings putting together real estate deals even though about the only piece of earth he had ever owned before was his own townhouse. He is the man who forked over money to buy a big chunk of a bank even though he had never saved money himself but rather spent dough as he made it on living the good life.

He is The Man with the Golden Touch. The twenty-nine-year-old man.

When I leave the racquet club, a woman I know comes over from her car. She has just finished her workout and hands me her thermos. It is half protein drink, half Irish whiskey.

*   *   *

David has spun off the road and is following some ruts into the village of Punta Chueca. The houses are small cement huts with red roofs, a project built by the Mexican government in the early seventies to get the Seris out of their tiny *jacales* of ocotillo wands with a blanket for a roof and make them live like human beings, like proper citizens of the Republic of Mexico. Children swarm around us, and then squads of matrons arrive in long skirts, their hair black and hanging. The white trader has arrived.

David is pinned against the truck by a swirl of women each thrusting forward a fistful of shell necklaces or ironwood carvings wrapped in soft rags. Their faces are serious, the tongues clucking. The ground is sand, dogs hang back, and the word *dinero,* "money," snaps through the sea air. One woman keeps pushing forward with two bad carvings, the forms unfinished, the shapes dead and static. Her eyes are bright and tightly focused, and David keeps pushing her carvings aside, telling her he cannot sell them, they are not good enough. She snaps, "Why do you come, if you don't have money to buy my things?" We begin to edge toward the house, make it through the ocotillo-wand fence. The yard is a ruin of cast-off bottles, cans, wrappers, broken tires, spent tires, rusting pieces of metal. We enter the house, the women sweep ahead of us. They wear long dresses that reach the ground, and blouses trimmed with colored piping that they sew. The breasts are full, the cheekbones strong, the faces handsome. They are good-looking women. They do not wash.

The kitchen is filthy, the cement floor deeply stained with grime. On a shelf a few choice objects—a coffee cup and saucer, a plastic doll, and a small color ad for Disneyland in English cut out of some magazine—lined up as trophies. The furniture is scarce, a woman sits on the floor with her basket and strips of *torote* for the weaving. The plumb doors war with their curved bodies. The women tug at our sleeves, produce baskets and yet more carvings from mounds of rags they carry. The words are almost inaudible yet insistent, a constant pecking at our ears. They eye me, realize I am not a buyer, and dismiss me from their universe. A man comes out from the back room, he is tall, in his thirties, the mustache thin, the eyes hidden behind round sunglasses. He surveys the mayhem, says something very softly, returns to his room. On the kitchen table are dirty dishes, flies crawling across the congealing juices. The stove has a pot of rice and tomatoes without a lid, the whole dish sinking into a new crusty form. The room is hot and the voices of the women never relent.

* * *

We are eating dinner, thick slabs of prime rib in the dining room named after him, in the hotel he owns, in the city he spooks. His father was an invalid every day of his life, a pensioner. His father would sit out in the yard and a squirrel would scamper down a tree and the old man would feed the squirrel. That was his day, day after day. The son is different. Charles Keating, Jr., is rich, very rich. Those jets await his instructions. That helicopter whirls him around to view real estate deals. There are rumors of violent temper explosions, sudden firings. He will be sitting in a meeting and someone will walk by the door and Charlie will turn to someone in the meeting and say, "Go out there now and fire that person." And it will be done, and people in the meeting will feel good, feel that they are on the inside, they are near the power, that their hand holds the knife, while others ignorantly present the soft flesh of their dumb backs. Senators answer his calls, cash his checks. There are hundreds of people working for him. Some leave, they say they cannot take it even with the money. I am talking to a young woman, she is blond, and when she was just out of college she worked for Charlie as a secretary and made forty or fifty thousand a year. She left, it was not good, the money was not good, she says. He is a religion, a cult, she says, the whole thing is sick, she decides.

The hotel that surrounds us is his creation, a dull heap of marble and fine woods. He decorates his places with millions of dollars' worth of statues of Indians. They stand there in bronze very quiet and dignified, and they do not speak or smell. But when the city arrives to tax his collection of hotel art, the works are suddenly worth a mere pittance according to Charlie's attorneys. He is alive with energy. It is eight o'clock at night, he has been up since 3 A.M. and he cuts his meat with dedication. The Dom Pérignon magically appears, the thin glasses constantly refilled. Keating waves a fork around the room—his place, the restaurant is called "Charlie's"—and complains of the many hostesses he had to go through before he got the right one, of how he had to cull the staff repeatedly to rid himself of graduates of hotel management schools, self-proclaimed experts that could not be taught his methods. There was some hotel figure from Germany who would not bend. He is gone now. Ah, he tells me in a moment of reflection: "My biggest regret is that I have not fired people sooner."

Every morning a few miles west of here, eight hundred people walk up the winding road past the old Jokacke Lodge, past the small stucco building where movie stars like Clark Gable once tasted little dibs and dabs of desert off Camelback Road in Phoenix. This army of workers marches on a $300 million palace carved into the base of Camelback Mountain, the Phoenician. The hotel will have six hundred rooms, more than an acre of swimming pools, millions of dollars of public sculpture (Indians, of course), the requisite golf course and tennis courts, and will target as a market the rich people of the planet. The tile in one pool will look like mother-of-pearl. It will cost $200 to $300 a night to stay here and the prices will rise as the trade becomes established. According to normal industry projections, the rooms must go for $500 or $600 a night for Charlie to break even. But he will have none of such talk. He will make it work. But then, it's not his money, the funds are from his captive savings and loan, other people's money, and somehow, about half of the dough comes from the Kuwaitis. Charlie can put together deals like that. There will be wet bars everywhere, no one will ever stand in line for a drink. Keating is obsessed with the hotel.

He is an old man now, oceans of money have flowed through his fingers. He knows what it is like to own and what it is like to spend and what it is like to dominate armies of people. But he has yet to build, to sink that stake into the heart of the desert that will proclaim his victory over it. He will drown the desert with lakes, bury it with lawns, deny it with cement. His eyes have the look of a man who has just found a new woman.

Back at his corporate headquarters, there are paintings on the walls of deserts, men on horseback, blue sky arcing over the big empty. Inside the air is cool, the carpet soft, the light just right. Green lawns surround the building and the desert is locked up within the frames of the paintings. Charlie Keating's employees have no staff manual with rules to follow. Either they work out or they are fired. I know a woman he hired for an executive position. He asked her one question: how much do you weigh? After all, he likes to hire people with an upbeat attitude, women with scrubbed, wholesome looks, because they create a nice environment. The company has a one-chair barbershop in its headquarters so employees will not waste precious hours getting a trim; lunch is catered—people don't have to lose work time. He once gave a Corvette to a woman in his mail room for some job well done. He demands and rewards loyalty, they say.

Once, the story goes, a new secretary was typing a legal document when Keating and his lawyers came out of a meeting. The attorneys bombarded her with changes that must be made. Charlie leaned over and said, "Don't change a single thing," and then walked off. The lawyers tore into the woman again, make the changes, we're his legal brains, do as we say, he doesn't know what he's talking about. She made the changes. Later she was called in and reprimanded. The incident was staged as a test. She flunked. Loyalty. But she was lucky, she got another chance.

I tell this story to people and some find it horrifying. Some think it is the right way to do things. That is Charlie's edge, the one I envy him. He has figured something out, that life is really about nothing, that beliefs, rules, civility, all that stuff is for fools, and he refuses to be a fool. The doctors, they come up with names like sociopath or psychopath for guys like Charlie. The nineteenth-century writers, they would say, ah, a nihilist. I see an American, a free-wheeling force rooted in nothing but the vortex of the deal. A man who believes in nothing and can do what he wants because others have a fearful need to believe in something. So he gives them Charlie Keating to believe in.

I notice a quality in the air when he speaks. The voice is always alone, the rooms waits to be told what to do. That is why the walls are so very important, and why the air conditioning must be set just right, and why the maps and sketches and models must be made just so. For the voice to function, for the silence to surround it, for the fear to float through the building, no one must be allowed to see the desert and sense out there a real yardstick for fear.

His son, Charles Keating III, dines with us. I ask Charlie about a real estate deal, another instant city plan he is bankrolling, and I say I cannot understand why he is in the deal, how he can make money. He jerks his thumb toward his son and says, "The jerk got me into that one." His son flinches and says nothing. Charlie is six-foot-five and everyone around him, regardless of their height, is very, very short.

"I'm stupid," Keating explains about his expensive new hotel, "but I'm not so stupid that I don't know that that's generally where everybody breaks their lance. The biggest number of failures is the guy who builds the imperial palace and then it gets resold twice, and it finally gets down to the guy who pays the right price to make it work."

His venture is considered insane by many others in the hotel business—the Phoenix market has the highest concentration of five-star resorts in the country. The word on the street is that he is strapped by this leviathan hotel whose only market is his ego. He denies this with crisp sentences, cold strings of words that stand alone in the air with the sterile clarity of Irish linen. He has already off-loaded forty-five percent of the cost to investors in Kuwait, he says, and contrary to rumors, he has plenty of cash to finish the job with—"I'm not bragging, I'm just saying we don't owe." I mumble something, his eyes snap alert. The lounge piano is clinking away behind us, but Keating's ears grow large. He looks at me coolly, and says nothing. He knows I am stuffed with those stolen federal documents that flay his hotel as a farce, that sketch his empire as functionally bankrupt. It is all buried there in financial jargon, the jumbo accounts, the fire-fights about what is equity, what is debt, what is an inflated appraisal. The hostess sweeps past with two more diners, her body bright with fabrics, her body as barren as an old woman's. She has perfect teeth, blue eyes. Her hips lie dead below her waist.

I start rattling off numbers from the forbidden documents.

Keating says, "You read too much."

He taps the arm of his chair, a cane piece of furniture. A McGuire. He wants to take control and so he does. Here, his hard blue eyes say, I'll just show you what real business is. He sits in his McGuire chair and explains how to do a deal. Most hotels buy chairs that look like McGuires by going through purchasing agents who tack on twenty-three percent for installation ("all that means is they put it on the floor"). Often as not they stiff the customer with cheap Hong Kong copies of the real McGuire. The real McGuire costs $720 a chair retail, but anybody can haggle the price down to $360, or if you're real tough down to $325. Keating went straight to McGuire, told them he didn't want crummy copies, but that he would fill every nook and cranny of his hotels with their furniture. It was the biggest order the company had ever received. Charlie smiles. "We got the chairs for two hundred forty bucks."

He is happy now, back on safe ground, the deal, the numbers, the abstract of life. The golf course at his new hotel, the Phoenician, cost $4 million. But it played too slow. So he scrapped it, poured in millions more to speed up play. Numbers. Rage. Prime rib. Champagne. And find the right hostess.

The dessert cart wheels over, the pastry chef supervises. Keating's eyes gleam with anticipation.

* * *

We slowly edge out of the small room full of haggling women, and walk back to the truck. Now the buying begins: that carving, yes, that one, no, the basket is too expensive, those necklaces, yes, all of them. The pesos flow from David's hands, the objects pile up in the truck. The village is largely empty at the moment, everyone has gone off into the desert to pick jojoba beans from the small shrubs. Mexicans buy the beans for about $1.40 a pound and the village has managed to harvest about six hundred pounds in a few days. The beans are made into a fine oil, one that substitutes for sperm whale oil, and helps slake the thirst of military buyers. There is the fishing also, many of the men are off in the channel, El Infiernillo, Little Hell, with their nets. Just yesterday they caught two green turtles, a species protected by Mexican law. They killed them. The beasts are worth about $4 a kilo in Hermosillo. Once green turtles were a mainstay here, but now they are about exterminated. When David asks fishermen how they feel about that fact, about the turtles disappearing from the sea, they shrug.

So we go fishing. Ricardo Estrella stands with a long harpoon on the prow of the *launcha* as we plow into the waters of the Infiernillo, the Strait of Little Hell. There are five Seris in the boat, one running the motor, another to bail, an old man named Antonio Robles who inspects the huge drift nets that run like a maze across the channel, a boy who helps the harpooner, and, of course, Ricardo, the man whose aim must be true. It is not yet dawn, and in the gray light Isla Tiburón, Shark Island, looms across the dull water. The men are very alert. The turtles they are hunting this morning have been running in the seas since the Cretaceous period. The turtles created the world. Long ago when there was only sky and water, long ago when Ancient Pelican slowly flapped its huge wings across the emptiness, there was a terrible struggle and violence under the waves and a huge hulk emerged, Ancient Sea Turtle, probably a leatherback, and he created Tiburón in his own image, in the shape of the *cahuama*, the turtle of the sea. For a long time the Seris and the animals lived together, spoke the same language, and each evening would talk and laugh and gamble. Then one night, the Sea Horse cheated, a fight broke out, and when this dust-up ended the world as we find it this morning, a world with a gray sea clogged with nets and boats and men, a world of killing and many languages, this world was all that remained.

It is a very different world. The green turtle we are hunting is an endangered species and not an ounce of it can be brought back into the United States. The slaughter begins at the nesting sites 1,500 kilometers south on the beaches of Michoacán. Each year when the *cahuamas* return to these waters they are fewer and smaller. In Sonora, it is illegal to kill the sea turtle but the Seris, as an indigenous people, are allowed to take them for their own food only. This rule is ignored. A Mexican buyer waits on the shore with his woman and child and his old pickup truck. By evening the turtles will be in the state capital Hermosillo, slaughtered, cut up, and distributed to the numerous restaurants that advertise *cahuamas*. Two days ago I ate turtle in a place called El Coruco, the Chicken Louse. I asked a federal biologist in charge of the plants and animals of Sonora why I could eat turtles if they were protected. He looked at me with kindly eyes and said there are two reasons. One, the lack of money for patrols. And then he paused and continued: two, there is no honesty.

The boat slows, Antonio motions silently toward a dip in the net, he grabs hold, nods toward Ricardo, the harpoon slams down, the big barbed tip drives through the carapace, and a green turtle is pulled to the surface, boated, and lies at my feet thrashing frantically with its flippers. The black eye, about the size of a Ping Pong ball, stares out, the long flippers keep searching for the ocean as they scrape against the fiberglass hull. I cannot bear the sound of that scraping. In a half hour, we land one more and then roar back to the shore.

Ricardo and his crewmates start a fire for coffee and breakfast. The two turtles are tied to the trunk of a tamarisk tree and instantly thrash with their flippers and pivot toward the sea. A couple of Seris use the beasts as stools. I want to get up, take the sharp knife from my pocket, cut the ropes, and let the turtles crawl back to the bosom of the sea. Crawl with the dark hole in their backs where the harpoon drove home into their flesh. Ah, David says, I know how you feel, but they will just be caught again, caught in the nets, harpooned again, tied to a tree again, loaded into a truck, slaughtered in Hermosillo, and float in a bowl of soup at the Chicken Louse.

Ricardo comes over to our camp. He has been to Tijuana and Hermosillo and seen the greater world. And returned. Almost no Seri ever leaves, many not even for a visit, and the language is still spoken by all. Some have married Mexicans but the children are raised Seri. Ricardo wears a baseball cap that says "Gypsum Corporation" and he wants water, the water of the United States. What must it taste like? But our water is from Hermosillo. Fine, he says, let me taste it. Other Seris gather round, swallow deeply, smile, and say it is *dulce*, sweet. The water here is rock hard, the Seris all have discolored and rotten teeth. Those of the women are worn down to nubs from stripping limberbush for baskets. And then there are the missing hands, some of the old men have mere stubs from the days when Seris tried dynamiting fish for a while. Ricardo admires my thongs—the Seris have feet like planks and seldom wear shoes—and he wonders what they cost. One hundred forty dollars! *Muy caro!*

Yes, they are very expensive.

I must be very *rico,* rich, no?

I certainly must be.

The desert lies flat in the midday light as we head north again, the road runs offensively straight, the sides scraped bare of cactus and trees by the elegant decree of some government planner. Hot wind pours through the open windows. We arrive in Desemboque at dusk, the same white concrete government huts lining the grid of streets. David drives north of town a ways, parks by the beach amid the litter of the village. Ospreys nest on neighboring cardón, one stands against the dusk picking at a fish. I can catch the outline of a fledgling peeking up above the big nest made of sticks. We have a beer while cottontail rabbits move nervously through the small bushes.

In town, the store is open. White cheese, eggs, coffee, tough beef. A Mexican guy tends to the customers. He is heavy and seems to sweat while he is standing still. The Seris line the window asking for potato chips, pop, a couple of eggs, candy, fruit juice, crackers. The man behind the counter moves in fast bursts. He's just coming off it now, he's been gone to Hermosillo for a few days and is still cranked up on cocaine. The stuff's a bargain for him. His brother-in-law is a *federale* so the supply is endless and free. Down the dirt road a hundred yards a big graffito has been spray-painted on a wall: WE'RE A LITTLE CRAZY AND POOR.

An old man walks up to the store window, his one hand a stub covered by a sock, another victim of those early Seri experiments in dynamite fishing. A faint purr of outboard motors rides in the air, gulls sit on the sand as the tide rolls in, warring with frigate birds that dive and wheel to steal their fish. The beach is white against the blue. The Seri women stand around, tall and firm. David tells me they are convinced that white men have larger sexual organs. Not that it matters much. For more than fifty years observers have noticed the reluctance of Seri women to marry—marry Seris, Mexicans, marry anyone. For some reason, many do not marry. The village is full of women who are twenty and thirty. They do not live with men. Early visitors noted the reluctance of the women to go off with whites, the absence of the cheap squaw bought with a bottle for a night's pleasure. For that matter, Seris do not seem to drink much. The village has a few drunks, like anywhere else, and that is about it. What the women do is stand very tall, their hair wrapped in scarves, and when they speak they bring their fingers to their lips, or hold a corner of the scarf in front of their mouth. It is a soft and graceful gesture and it always seems to happen. I can sense they are talking about me, the fingers are up to lips, the faint sounds. When they walk they move with a grace and certain carriage as if they had a very heavy burden balanced on their heads.

Next door to the *tienda,* suspended from a tamarisk tree, a Gila monster hangs by the neck from a limb. No one knows why the lizard was killed or by whom or why it is hanging there. Men poke at the orange-and-black body with sticks and laugh. Small boys throw stones. The black tongue hangs out of the dead mouth, the fat tail is limp and the body slack.

* * *

The sky is blue in the morning light outside the windows of E. C. Garcia & Company atop the United Bank tower in Tucson and it is summer. The two-story lobby swallows up the couches of emerald green, the coffee tables of polished mahogany, the white marble floor accented here and there with darts of black. Music plays softly, the sound floating across the empty furniture. The place is perfectly appointed, like a pharaoh's tomb. A receptionist sits behind a wall of wood, the phone silent. One guy kills time reading a pulp novel, the attache case resting by his side on the floor. He is security from the building's management firm, shipped in that day six weeks before when E. C. Garcia & Company announced that it was short of cash and closing down the offices. He sits there every day from eight to five and is instructed "to watch."

It has been two years since I saw Ernie on the terrace of the racquet club where he moved regally from table to table, the hint of sudden wealth dripping from his fingers like a blessing. Ernie says he is at ease with himself. The deals come, the deals go, but he is at ease with himself. The company is under pressure now, he allows, the market has gone south, the investments sit like cement, the payments fall due. His face remains full, the smile ready. There was that recent evening in his fine house with the pool and tennis courts, the lanes lined with palms. The desert does not exist there, there is green everywhere, but what the eye sees—the rooms, the furniture, the rugs, the graphite racket in the hand, all of these things—the desert pays for. Everything.

E. C. Garcia & Company is on the ropes, the word is on the street, the talk is denied in the fine-paneled corporate board-room. The whispers are in motion. So on that recent night Ernie and his friends drink beer, lots of cold beer, and then they run out of it. Suddenly, he remembers that case that came as a gift, yes, that case from Charlie. He goes in and finds the Dom Pérignon and they sit outside under the stars with the desert air washing against them sipping warm champagne at a hundred a bottle. Life is a lark if you are a player.

Now Ernie descends the open staircase from the second floor of his tower complex. He glides down easily, his hand ignoring the polished brass rail that rides atop green metalwork. The tie is red, the shirt blue, the black-framed glasses large. He glances ever so slightly at the empty chairs and couches. And then he is gone without a word. Ernie Garcia is in town for a few hours to help shut down E. C. Garcia & Company's current Tucson office.

The complex is a ghost town with only eighteen employees left. The security guy engrossed in his pulp novel never even looks up. Two glass-walled conference rooms hug the lobby on either side, each stocked with the long table, the soft green leather chairs, the television with the VCR perched on top that is there to unroll tape showing the wonders of the deal. Now there is a stillness. The deals have stopped.

His corporation is being dismembered by that major creditor, Charlie Keating. The party is over. The fine quarters on top of the United Bank building are a kind of curio of the days when the money flowed and you only had to dip in your bucket for a refreshing hit of wealth.

The two-story warren of E. C. Garcia & Company is shaped like a shortened crucifix, a kind of Maltese cross. The bottom floor is land development, bookkeeping, the grunt labor of deal making. Blue prints lie piled up in empty offices, maps of once possible developments are tacked to walls like old pinups. Now banks of computers stare with blank screens at abandoned work stations. A handmade sign taped over one door reads: DIREC-TOR—INVESTOR RELATIONS. I have a picture taken of this sign, but later the photographer panics. What if Ernie is mad about the picture? Then he will give the photographer no more work, no more assignments to capture the beauty of a chunk of land that will become a slab of buildings. After all, who can tell when someone is truly dead?

Another room contains a model of the plans for E. C. Garcia & Company's once-big holdings south of town, the deal that mainlined lots of money into the fledgling company and became its first major killing. Tiny pecan groves and miniature buildings suggest a perfect future. The model is dusty.

An aerial photo gives the scale of those heady days—large white squares designating pieces on the Monopoly board that held the attention of Garcia. A freeway knifes through the largely empty ground and from the perspective of the aerial shot everything looks delicious—land crying out for the scratch of a pen on a document, for the showers of dollars, the blade of a bulldozer. The slap of a firm handshake cementing a done deal.

The color green recurs, in the rugs, soft chairs, hints of it running through the marble on the walls. Ernie Garcia likes the color green. His office is on the east point of the cross. His desk is a fine table—the serious operator in America needs no drawers, does not succumb to the undertow of paper in the quest for the deal. A brass telescope points south—leased, Garcia explains, from some interior decorator. He has nothing to do really with his whole office, he says, it is all done by an expert. Except for the color green. He does like that color. In the center of the top floor is the conference room, a windowless chamber filled with the heavy, long wooden table lined with soft green leather chairs. This is the heart of the tomb.

There is a quality to the lobby, a special loneliness like that of an empty theater after the play has closed. The hard marble floors echo each footstep. When Garcia crosses it, he, like everyone else, seems to pause for a split second, the body seems almost to hang in the air as the big space swallows the person up.

He is determined to come back. Just a little reorganization first. Out the window of the skyscraper, Indian ruins a thousand years old bake in the sun.

* * *

I think the marble makes him feel safe. Keating puts it everywhere, the stone cold, almost colorless and smooth. All his buildings have the feeling of potential tombs. The Phoenician may have gutted Italy's quarries. A marble staircase leading up from one restaurant is encased in slabs weighing between 150 and 400 pounds—the workmen beam and explain that they have spent all day laying in one eight-by-eight section. Near an elevator the walls gleam with book-match pieces—marble fashioned by taking a twelve-foot block and cutting it like a radish so the streaks in one slab match the next. If one piece is broken, the men must go to an entirely new block. All the units have yet more marble in the bathrooms. Everything in the Phoenician is big and expensive—the tubs and showers are big too; after all, the owner is six feet five inches. The grand ballroom covers 22,000 square feet with a twenty-two-foot ceiling, the pre-reception area gobbles another 17,000 square feet so that no one ever must wait for a cocktail. There are twenty-two business meeting rooms also, and everything everywhere seems wired for state-of-the-art audiovisual equipment with satellite linkups.

"Another mistake," Keating sighs when the a/v system is mentioned. "It got away from us in the beginning, before we took over. We made a mistake—using professional managers, outside consultants, and so forth. When we got into it, we were so far along that the difference between going back to sanity and staying with Star Wars was I think about a half million bucks. But the damage had been done, installation, equipment ordered—so we stayed with Star Wars."

But what's money? It all comes from a savings and loan Charlie bought in Southern California during the early high-five days of deregulation when suddenly all those deposits could be plopped anywhere a guy wanted. He bought it with junk bonds peddled by Mike Milken, the wizard of junk. Every time you kind of run out of deposits, you just buy more from brokers and promise a check in the mail in ten or fifteen years. And what the hell, the federal government insures the money. This is the new ecology where the rain does not matter on the desert flats. Money flows in new channels, spills out onto the soil, gouges mountains, bulldozes straight lines on bajadas, creates lakes, fleets of jet planes, bottles of Dom Pérignon at tableside. The patterns of this new world race through the circuit boards of computers as gold rises and falls, silver quivers, junk bonds are snapped up, stocks are bought and sold, land changes hands sight unseen. The computer room is windowless to the outside, the carpet sedate, the attendants like mortuary workers in their soft-spokenness, the quick fingers flying over the keyboards, a satellite above soaking up their messages. "My house is in Phoenix," Charlie explains sternly, "but I don't live here." He sits in a chair, stares at the screens lining the walls, the attendant bends over, catches a command, the money pours down a new channel in this global terrain.

Of course, at times when he talks, the whole hotel business is a mistake in Charlie's eyes. He blasted 165,000 cubic yards out of Camelback Mountain preparing a pad for the inn and then poured back into the hole 80,000 square yards of concrete for a firm base (enough for that four-foot sidewalk 600 miles long, a foreman tells me).

"We have to be responsible ourselves," he argues, the American captain of money lecturing me about the burdens of his power, "or it ain't going to work. I don't mind if it fails, facing failure. But it isn't going to fail because some professional German manager took over for me and blew it. They're going to know exactly where to point the finger if that baby goes down. And that's fine, I think that's the way you should live."

He canned the interior decorators and hired his wife, Mary Eileen. What the hell, he's lived with her taste most of his life and likes it. Now the 3,600-square-foot entertainment bar will have a big Japanese carp pond with a baobab tree growing up and spreading all over the room.

The Phoenician is a physical model of Keating's style gone public. Each of the squads of restaurants (one's on an island in the acre of pools and can be entered by bridges or by swimming through waterfalls) has its own kitchen so the food is always hot. One restaurant is built like a wine cellar, one room for drinking

reds, another for whites. There is parking for 1,500 cars underground. The outdoor hot tub holds thirty-two people, the health
spa takes in 13,000 square feet, the golf clubhouse 47,000 square
feet. Six-inch copper pipes lace through the terraces for dining
in the chill of fall and spring, and if they don't do the trick there
are fire pits scattered like mushrooms. Down by a lower pool
(the one covered with mother-of-pearl tile) there are cabanas
for businessmen so they can watch the wife and kids splash
around and still plug their computers into lines, link up with the
information networks of the planet, and have phones ringing in
their ears on their vacation. All over the hotel are ceilings hand-
painted by a guy from Cincinnati whom Charlie brought west
to gussy up his properties. "We're using a lot of gold leaf," the
painter allows. When a guest enters the main lobby, his feet will
click on the marble floor and above his head a dish sculpted into
the ceiling will boom his arrival.

The numbers never end, they're not supposed to. They are
a substitute for actually creating a place. The sidewalks must
stretch 600 miles, it is a necessity. The lakes facing the golf
course must hold millions of gallons, the lobby art must cost
exquisite fortunes. And the 8,500-square-foot theater must sport
a satellite linkup and hand-held electronic devices that permit
meetings to taste instant balloting. Say there is a new car model
and you are the corporate CEO showing off a film of it to major
dealers and then after you've saturated them with chrome and
smooth lines and drenched their bodies with a sound track of
calculated music, after the show has run long enough so that
they've forgotten the $500 whore who called room service at
2 A.M., then at that instant they can vote with the control box
in their hands and their approval of the new wave of metal and
machine will flash up on the screen.

Outside, roaming bands of Tongans plug 1,500 adult palms
into the grounds. The islanders are a hobby of Charlie's. He was

at a barbecue in Utah, and the guy holding the affair had a couple of Tongans running the spit. Keating bought a whole tribe, chief and all. He says you can't get good gardeners in Phoenix. They are huge brown men and move about his properties like squads of refrigerators.

The hotel leaves a chill on my flesh. I cannot conceive of wanting to stay in it. It is a mannequin, not a woman. But Charlie, he is wiser than I am. He knows my country. When he opens, his occupancy rate is ninety-five percent. A television crew comes out to do a documentary on the New West. They take Charlie up to his hotel and film him as he walks the grounds and talks of the dreams his fellow citizens dream.

*　*　*

Jose Astorga is old now, and wears a government official's cap, one without any badge or rank. His face is dark brown, the eyes hidden behind sunglasses, the hair white, the feet, like most Seris, huge and splayed from a lifetime without shoes. He is thrusting forward a small wooden santo of the moon. The thing is carved from *xoop incl,* red elephant tree, and he has not worked hard. The finish is rough and the features are sketched in with markings from a black felt-tipped pen. The years are catching up with Jose. Once, the Seris essentially abandoned their old, the tribe moving on in their constant pursuit of a good waterhole and a meal, the ancients left behind to become mummies in the desert sun. In his earlier years, Jose was a head man of sorts, a leader in a culture without structure. Back in 1960 an American asked him to make a paperweight of ironwood and Jose did and the entire ironwood carving industry blossomed for the Seri from that act. The carvings joined a stream of the new tasks that became the economy, the new ecology of the desert, a stream fed by casting big nets for a catch of sharks bringing in some pesos, the ironwood carvings, then the baskets. As a safety net, the desert and the sea provide basic calories when there is no money to spend at the store. David in a few days will drop perhaps a thousand dollars buying hundreds of necklaces, dozens of carvings, a basket for a collector who likes to stare at the patterns in his fine home back in the States.

But now, Jose is adamant. He thumps David's chest as they stand in the sun with the sand burning beneath their feet and he insists on the beauty of the santo. There is no real market for the objects, David is almost the only human being on earth who ever buys them. They are dreams carved into wood and must be made from red elephant, the first living thing God made. They are hidden things that creep out from the mind. In 1826, Lieutenant Hardy steps from his ship *Bruja* onto the fierce landscape of Tiburón Island. The people are handsome and big, the women wear the skins of birds around their hips, the breasts hang bare. They show Hardy a pole with feathers, a stone ball suspended from the tip, all to stop the wind. He sees a brushy pile, peers into it, and eyes a small carved figure with a big hat. There are others, different sizes and shapes, as well as a bunch of leather bags. He reaches forward with his hand, but "I was not permitted to explore." Santos flicker briefly on the screen called history and fall back into the darkness.

The dreams. Jose says he is a kind of astronaut, that long before the gringos claimed to have visited the moon, he, Jose Astorga, was there. He smiles as he states this fact, daring me to believe him or disbelieve him. Of course, the gringos have it all wrong, the moon is a woman, a señorita. Do women not bleed, does the moon not move through its phases? For Seris, the moon is the harsh mistress, a force in their tales that explains the world and the universe, an image that recurs in their santos as they try to harness the energies of the world to their own ends. There are houses under the sea, they will state, and deer graze on the ocean floor, goddesses roam with flowers for mouths, antlers sprouting from their heads. The whales, they boss the sea; the boojums, big carrot-like plants growing up to seventy or eighty feet, they listen to Seris, so one must be careful around them and guard one's words. The turtles are flesh and blood smeared against the lips, but they are also power. When a big leatherback wanders into the hands of the Seris every few years, they hold a big fiesta with the half-ton beast corralled in an ocotilla ramada, the back decorated with face paintings. They are careful what they say around the leatherback since they also understand Seri. Then after the four-day blowout, the beast is released back into the sea. All this mash of explanation swirls around somewhere in Jose's head as he tries to peddle his little carving for a few pesos to the stupid gringo visitors. The gringo has probably never been born that impresses a Seri. For centuries, Spanish soldiers and priests came away in disbelief at Seri arrogance. The tribal members never planted a seed, no matter how arduous the training, or herded stock. They were unimpressed with buildings or clothes. For perhaps two millennia they have baked on the sands along the channel between the mainland and Tiburón (Shark) Island, dreamed of giants, of the woman who is the moon, of one-legged gods, two-legged gods, a spirit whale that courses the gulf riding about the waves in the night darkness. Almost no one ever leaves—one Seri woman married a Mexican and went to Hermosillo and she is the tribe's disgrace.

Jose's face spills over with contempt. What, you do not want this santo? You do not want the power of a man who has been to the moon? David shakes his head no. The old man glares, and walks off, the sand scrunching under his feet. He is old, the tribe has passed him by, he sits under a tamarisk tree by his hut all day and the flies crawl across his skin. The moon talks to him.

A *chubasco,* a violent summer storm, blows in the night and there is wind and dust but still no rain. It has not rained in seven months at Punta Chueca. The dogs howl all night, but the Seris do not chastise them. Dogs used to be people, as did coyotes and ravens, and packs of canines throng Seri camps. They are everywhere piled up in clumps, mangy, strange-looking dogs. Jésus Montaño is speaking. He is about sixty, a traditional Seri who has not gone Christian, and he is speaking of Big Cave on Tiburón where the walls and ceilings are cluttered with paintings. We are going over to the island in a few moments with Samuel Comito and while we wait Jésus talks. Men once went to Big Cave for visions. For four days and nights, he says, they could not eat or sleep. Ravens exploded from the walls and their cries filled the air. If a man slept, it would be fatal to his quest. The little people, who are white and about a foot high, come out at night and if you sleep, they carry you away into their tiny pueblo. They speak a language Seris do not understand. It is like our speech, he explains, like Americano. But if you last the four days and nights, a vision will come and no bullet or knife will ever penetrate your body. And you will be able to heal. You will take a piece of *torote*, chew it, blow on people, and they will be cured. Once he saw a woman with a big pain in her chest and a healer blew on her for half an hour. Then a yellow thing wriggled out of the healer's hand and he took it away and the woman was well. The yellow thing looked like a rattlesnake's tail. Jésus's mother knew two brothers who lasted the four days in the cave. But what of now, Jésus? Oh, there are no more healers in the villages now, he says. Things change. He was born by Snail Well on Tiburón, as were his brother and sister, but now he lives in a government-built house in Chueca. Once the green turtles ran heavy and weighed a hundred kilos, not the twenty or thirty they reach now. Why are they so small now and so few? "I don't know," he says. Things change. It is like the cave with the paintings. Why does no one go there any longer? He thinks a moment and says, "No one wants to be hungry anymore."

The earth is his playground. The desert? A void. He will fill it. Charlie is sixty-five years old and working eighty- to one-hundred-hour weeks, and he sees no rest in his future. There is so much to do. The desert, don't you see? The desert is a blank sheet and what he does is write on that sheet. Look at the site of the huge new hotel—nothing but squirrels and rattlesnakes there before he arrived with his money.

Do you ever worry about going broke?

"All the time, every day," Charles Keating, Jr., says, his voice rising. "It's part of the problem of what we're doing. It's something the press and public doesn't appreciate. I come into the office with this hollow feeling in my stomach lots of times. We're not clipping coupons, we're not living off our old man's wealth. It's not a friendly situation. It looks good and I'm sure a lot of guys think they'd enjoy it."

He is totally involved with the question. The room full of his employees, the docile piano player plinking away at his back, the soft lighting, all this disappears as he stares into his personal abyss, running out of money. His fork is still.

"A lot of times I wonder," he continues, "if I made a mistake when I left the Navy Air Corps. You get trapped almost. You get too many responsibilities. I look at some of these young girls and young guys in my office, they've got families that count on you. It takes a lot. Maybe a start-up company like ours survives and becomes big and viable and impregnable in twenty-five years or so but that sure isn't us yet."

He pauses, just a second. He senses he has given an answer, but not the answer.

There is more, and he knows it. Christ, when his pal John Connally went bust in Texas after decades of being The Man, the power broker, the rancher, the god in a big office, Charlie dropped over a hundred grand to buy one of his paintings at the bankruptcy auction. He's going to hang it in his new hotel.

"It's not only the money," he explains. "It's the disgrace: yourself, your manhood. I'm not sure I'd have a big problem with that; on the other hand, I'm not sure I wouldn't."

There are stories of his anger, the rages, the screams. Charlie tries to bury this part of himself from view and few will talk about these episodes. He hates to lose. You are not surprised. He hates to lose. There is a meeting in the conference room and the key management people sit around the table. I hear this story from several people. The room has glass walls. Ernie Garcia enters and Charles Keating asks him if he will take the offer, if he will join Charlie's operation. This seems reasonable since Ernie's schemes have skidded toward ruin and Charlie holds the paper. Ernie is dead unless Charlie decides he is alive. Ernie says, no, he does not want the deal. Keating gets up, walks around the room shutting the blinds on those glass walls one by one. And then his voice slams across the space. He is famous for these moments. The voice grows loud and no one says a word.

He hates to lose.

The auditors, they began to arrive soon after Charlie bought his savings and loan. They noticed that he had abandoned home loans (granting only eleven one year, and seven of those to his own employees) and started putting federally insured money into junk bonds, strange real estate ventures, off-shore banks. Charlie hires lawyers, famous economists, and, in a tactic I relish, bureaucrats from the ranks of the regulators themselves. Of course, he buys senators also, but then everyone does. Finally, one spring, he crushes the regulators, makes them back off. This moment is in all the newspapers, a singular instance of clout. Charlie smiles as he remembers this moment. He shouts to a secretary to get the book. A photo album appears, drunken employees spill champagne, knock over plants, dance on desktops.

Keating appears in one shot wearing a T-shirt with a skull-and-crossbones sketched on his chest with a felt-tipped pen. The sweet moment of victory. Then he tells his secretary to show me the cross Mother Teresa gave his family, the one with a piece of the true cross.

*   *   *

Victoria de Astorga Barnett, Jose's sister, made a head out of red elephant wood with a crescent moon riding on the forehead. She is in her seventies, perhaps even eighty, and she made the head because she had a dream which she does not speak of. I saw the head resting on the top of David's radio in Tucson and that is why I am here. The lips are red, the eyes blue, the moon rides in a sea of cobalt. Victoria leans against the wall of her government house, dogs flopped in the dirt around her. Her husband, Miguel, sits next to her as she strings shells for a necklace. Her face is lined, dark brown, the eyes quick and very alert.

Back in 1941 Gwnyth Harrington, an American anthropologist, met Victoria and Miguel on the beach to the south. They had come over from Tiburón and were camped on the sand with their children. Harrington gave them paper and colored pencils and asked them to draw their dreams. They marveled at the colored pencils and drew houses on the bottom of the sea, faces with flower mouths. In photos taken then the family sits on the ground, Miguel stands tall, his face an impassive blank. Harrington collected santos also, and then she went away, and no one seemed to think of her visit any more. Now the drawings, the photographs, Harrington's field notes all have been published in a scholarly journal and Victoria turns the pages and a slight smile crosses her face as she sees herself as a young woman surrounded by children, a baby in her arms, her breasts full of milk.

I begin to haggle with her for a santo she is carving. Victoria names her price, I offer half. She snaps that I am a bigger miser than even David. For the first time I feel a little acceptance of my presence. A yellow bitch walks over and flops, the puppies cause a melee as they topple forward to suck.

Dawn comes and nothing happens. David and I wait to go over to Tiburón Island with Samuel Comito. He arrives at 6 A.M. The village is up, the women trailing off in their long dresses into the dunes (the local toilet), men washing their hair, the dogs stirring. Samuel is about forty, Christian, and carries a pair of shoes in his hand. He is very lean. We cross the two- to five-mile-wide channel in fifteen minutes, the boat coursing through schools of dolphins. Gray whales also frequent the coast and their bones blaze on the beaches. Tiburón, forty miles long, twenty wide, looms ahead, the peaks stretching to over 2,500 feet. There are Mexican marines stationed on the north, south, and east sides, small groups of four to eight. The Seris say they never leave their posts to patrol. I asked one soldier, a boy about eighteen in a swimsuit and holding an automatic rifle, if he ever shot any of the mule deer, and he said no, they never came close enough to the hut. He has been there for a month, and there have been no visitors, except, of course, for parties of Seris who gather plants and game. Tiburón is over seven hundred square miles of desert with no one roaming around on it. You can walk all day and never see a footprint.

We land, shoulder our packs, and Samuel puts on blue-and-white running shoes labeled British Nights. Seriland is full of odd English messages. Last night I saw a boy on the beach with a T-shirt that said, "Save an Alligator, Kill a Yuppie." Samuel carries a *bolsa,* a small woven purse, off his shoulder. We move off at a fast pace. We are heading inland about six or seven miles to a puddle of water where carrizo grass grows, the tall cane that Seris until about 1930 used for their balsa boats. When Thor Heyerdahl researched for his Ra expedition, he visited the Seris.

The tidal flat soon gives way to classic Sonoran Desert—palo verde, ironwood, cholla, organ pipe, cardón. There are mule deer tracks everywhere and fresh droppings. Samuel glides across the ground, inspects some dung, and reaches into his bolsa. He pulls out a .22 revolver and a handful of hollow-point cartridges. "*Buro,* mule deer," he smiles.

Trees clutter the land, and we move through thickets alongside a wash. Huge jackrabbits bound away but we never catch sight of a deer. For Samuel, and other Seris, Tiburón is the mother lode, the homeland where they constantly return. As he moves, the landscape opens up like a pantry. Huge wild fig trees grow thirty feet high along the banks of the arroyo. Samuel plucks a fruit and eats it. His hand caresses a low shrub with a red skin, and he pronounces the roots good *comida.* The red elephant tree is fine for making santos, sacred fetishes; the limberbush provides the fiber for the baskets. It is always this way with Seris. You walk behind a woman with a twenty-pound bundle of cut limberbush branches on her head, and her hands touch each plant, break off a leaf, smell it, perhaps chew it. The desert is alive with potential cures for the many hungers and ailments of our flesh. We are now up against the hills, Samuel points out a dove nest with eggs, good to eat he says, and the ground grows rocky. Suddenly miles from the sea there are shells everywhere, a campsite of the ancient ones, he explains. Pieces of pottery lie on the ground, clumps of stone record old fire rings. Until this century there was not a roof on Tiburón or anywhere in Seriland.

We clamber up the draw, and come across a stone wall. A blind built for hunting, where the men would crouch with bows and arrows. Just ahead we see the blaze of carrizo, the wands ten or fifteen feet high. Samuel stops, his nose twitches, and he breathes deeply. He smells animals. The gun is in his hand, the body crouches, and then moves ahead with catlike grace. Suddenly, two ewes and a lamb stand about twenty feet ahead of us. The pistol cracks, they scramble up a rock face and stand again. More shots, they move off. Samuel drops his bolsa, bounds ahead. Two huge rams stand still, their horns more than a full curl. Desert bighorns were introduced to the island in the early seventies by the Mexican government. Samuel fires again, and then he and the sheep disappear. It has taken twenty, perhaps thirty seconds.

I sit down and hear him blasting away with his little .22 pistol. *Borregos,* sheep, are not so good as deer for eating, but worth the cost of a bullet. Tiburón is the Mexican equivalent of a national park and wilderness area. A few miles across the channel the land is being massacred—a recent study by scientists at Arizona State University, the Jet Propulsion Laboratory in Pasadena, California, and Mexican colleagues found that Sonora has a constant temperature about four degrees higher than neighboring Arizona. This is because of overgrazing, a land murder by cattle estimated to be at the scale of three hundred times carrying capacity for the past century. Tiburón has escaped this carnage.

Samuel returns after a half hour. He has failed to hit a sheep— with ammunition so expensive, Seris do not seem to become dead eyes. But he is buoyant. He has seen *borregos.* He describes how he recognized their rich smell as we had moved up the wash. He laughs at his failure—Seris never seem to run out of laughter. Then he carves his initials into a fig tree. On the way back to the beach, he knocks down a jackrabbit with two shots, then stones it to death. He carefully cleans and skins it. *Comida.* Food. When his small son sees the meat later, he brightens, and Samuel lets the ten-year-old boy carry his *pistola.*

*   *   *

It is April 9, 1987, and night has fallen on Capitol Hill as five senators and a squad of bank officials meet in the office of

Arizona's Dennis DeConcini. Senator John Glenn from Ohio, who has been to outer space, is there. Don Riegle of Michigan, the head of the Senate Banking Committee, is there, a man who years earlier as a simple member of the House of Representatives published a journal of one term's struggle in the life of an earnest liberal congressman. Alan Cranston of California, a former Olympian, a man who this very evening is spearheading a move to lock hundreds of squares of battered desert into a new national park, is there. John McCain from Arizona is there, a man who spent years in the Hanoi Hilton, the son and grandson of an admiral, the war hero come home to his place at the table. And of course DeConcini. I remember seeing DeConcini years before in a fine hotel. I am sitting in the bar and suddenly I catch him moving across the patio outside. His shoulders are hunched forward, the face bent down, the hair thinning, the body soft as dough and bulging at the gut. He looks like a man who sells aluminum siding and has not made a sale in days, a man whose wife no longer waits up for him, who knows that dogs always piss on his tires. And then out of the shrubbery come a half-dozen people, their white shirts rumpled, their neckties flapping, their pace at a trot as they trail him. They are speaking, moving their arms, but DeConcini never looks up. His lips barely move, the entourage nods its collective head, some make notes. He plows ahead. He is The Man, The Senator, and they are the dogs sniffing the wind for a whiff off the bitch of power.

The five senators represent a lot of money since together they have received around $1.3 million from Keating and his companies and staff—depending on who is counting. Riegle received more than $70,000 a few weeks before the meeting. He'd been out to Phoenix for a ride in Charlie's fine chopper. He will later return it. Two years later, DeConcini will return his share of the money. And there are odd details, like the $800,000 Charlie funneled into a voter registration drive in California that was essentially a Cranston operation. Later, a senate ethics inquiry will probe the behavior of the five. (Glenn and Riegle will eventually be dropped from the investigation.)

DeConcini will later explain it as typical Hill business: "just another example of elected representatives going to bat for a constituent who appeared to be getting pushed around by bureaucrats."

Keating has no problem with the money. He paid the senators so they would help him with government agency auditing of his savings and loan. When anyone asks him, he tells them just that. No, he didn't give the money for good government, or some conservative agenda, or out of some crazy generous impulse. He gave it to buy influence for his savings and loan. Period.

The meeting opens with Glenn and DeConcini taking the offensive against the squad of bureaucrats. "To put it blunt," Glenn says, "you should charge them or get off their backs. If things are bad there, get to them."

"Our 1984 examination," a federal official explains, "showed significant appraisal deficiencies. Mr. Keating promised to correct the problem. Our 1986 examination showed that the problems had not been corrected. . . . Merrill Lynch appraised the Phoenician. It shows a significant loss. Other loans had similar losses." Here the meeting pauses, as the senators troop out to the Senate floor for a vote.

When they return, the federal official picks up where he left off, and his words are not the mild vagaries of a bureaucrat. "Lincoln," he says, "had underwriting problems with all their investments. . . . It had no loan underwriting policy manual in effect when we began our 1986 exam. . . . The examiners looked at fifty-two real estate loans that Lincoln had made since the 1984 exam. There were no credit reports on the borrowers in all fifty-two of the loan files."

DeConcini won't buy this argument: "Are you saying their underwriting practices were illegal or just not the best practice?"

Another federal official jumps in, saying the practices "are unsafe and unsound." Michael Patriarca, a man with twenty-five years under his belt policing big commercial banks for the Treasury Department, says, "They're flying blind on all of their different loans and investments." Riegle has had enough now and asks, "Where's the smoking gun? Where are the losses?" James Cirona, head of the San Alfonso office, responds simply, "This is a ticking time bomb."

Look, Patriarca says, "there's file stuffing. They took undated documents purporting to show underwriting efforts and put them in the files sometimes more than a year after they made the investment."

"This is not a profitable institution," Patriarca insists. "They didn't earn $49 million. Let me give you one example. Lincoln sold a loan with recourse and booked a $12 million profit. The purchaser rescinded the sale, but Lincoln left the $12 million profit on its books. Now, I don't care how many accountants you get to say that's right, it's wrong.

"I think my colleague put it right," Patriarca allows, "when he said it's like these guys put it all on sixteen black in roulette. Maybe they'll win, but I can guarantee you that if an institution continues such behavior it will eventually go bankrupt."

"Well," Riegle says, "I guess that's pretty definitive."

It is 8:20 P.M. on Capitol Hill, the meeting has droned on for two hours. And so it ends. A year later, the federal regulators back off and Charlie has that champagne party for the staff. He shows me the pictures, the album of Polaroids, Charlie in his T-shirt with a huge grin, people wearing the drapes. It's the same day he shows me the crucifix with a piece of the true cross that Mother Teresa gave his family.

* * *

Jose Astorga is standing in front of the small *tienda* in the late afternoon. The Gila monster has been cut down from the tree and no one speaks of it. The women gather round and try to sell David things—so far he has bought 332 necklaces. In the States, people can't seem to get enough of the necklaces. No Seri woman wears one.

Jose is animated, good spirits fill his old body. He turns to one woman, a pretty woman who is pregnant and has the air of joy that women carrying a child often have. He tells her what she needs is a *macana de cardón,* a cock made from the arm of a giant cactus.

* * *

I look up on the wall of my house and what I see is a photograph a friend took decades ago of a skinned coyote hanging from a hackberry bush. My friend says the animal was left because of witches, something to do with witches. The body is lean as a whippet's, the teeth perfect, and the tail rigid like a cock ready for a hole. The feet do not quite touch the ground and the eyes are gone, perhaps plucked out idly with the tip of the knife. The animal is silent, I cannot hear a song escape its thin lips.

I opened the mail this morning and in it was a clip from a paper on the East Coast, the tumble of paragraphs recounting the five senators on their knees with Charlie Keating in the center. The account contains the transcript of the meeting that took place long ago, back in the vaporized past. The senators are in a room on Capitol Hill browbeating bank officials to leave Charlie's action alone, let the man be, for Christ's sake. The type is a fine serif and this makes the words look very serious. The last time I saw the transcript it was typewritten pages that had been boosted from the secret catacombs of the federal government. I sat in my office late at night and read and reread it. Then I went to a store and bought a bottle of wine, and came back and continued sitting under the cold fluorescent lights reading and rereading. The senators purred on through the pages, this one bagging a hundred thousand from Charlie and his friends, this one forty, that one fifty, this one seventy or eighty, another happy with something in the thirties. The wine cost two dollars and forty-nine cents and did not require a corkscrew. I drank it from a coffee cup. At first light, I finally gave up reading.

Then came the lawyer's office, seventeen stories up in a tower that stared out at the desert heat. I stood by the floor-to-ceiling window and looked down at the block. A tiny air space between the sludge of bricks sheltered a tree, maybe twenty feet high, a green prong marching upward into the sun. Does it have a name? It must. Such an act should be remembered, memorialized. I can hear the lawyer's voice on the phone talking to another lawyer in New York. The words are careful and clipped, a dance of sounds and meaning circling around the threat of a lawsuit. Something about you print that and you will be sued for millions of dollars. Stolen documents. Illegal. The New York voice is calm as it pours out the speaker phone. Perhaps the man at the other end of the telephone line is glancing over at his secretary whom he will fuck for lunch, and winks at her as he handles some problem in the provinces. In the office where I sit is the investor of the magazine I helped invent, the man behind the magazine I work for, the one with the money. Outside the office door, the covey of secretaries, their skin pale, the hair clean and limp, the skirts long, it is the fashion at this moment, and the cloth hides their hips from my eyes. Their bodies are barely scented, the eyes noncommittal, and always floating around them is the purr of the air condition-ing as the tower of glass and steel breathes in its asthmatic way. I wonder if the secretaries ever scream, if they howl astride, if the cool air can be conquered, if sweat still trickles down. The sun burns through the glass walls of the tower. Of course, I know that I am dead. The transcript will never see light of day except in a mutilated form. Nor will the pages and pages of Charlie's books, the dense pages of numbers going the wrong way. Tonight perhaps, in a restaurant, my lawyer will study the wine list, his eyes will look up and notice the top two buttons on her blouse carefully undone. There will be French bread with real butter, of course, molded into the shape of a fruit. The waiter will wear a starched shirt, never spill a drop, and go home to a cheap apartment. I know I am dead because there is no money in what I want to do, just big bills and fat lawsuits.

I turn around, the others in the office look content. The phone call has ended. We have made a deal. Things will be left out, other privileges will be granted. It is only fair. There are limits. And finally, the constant question, the one I am always asked when Charlie is the issue: just how do you know the documents are right and Charlie is wrong? I look down again at the tree knifing green upward. I am sure it will never quit trying.

*   *   *

Once David was in a fine store in Tucson that sells Indian arts and suddenly Imelda Marcos entered with her bodyguards. Her husband was still the boss of the Philippines then and she had the power. For one hour she bought. Her finger would point—this, that—and when she finished she had spent $35,000. Among the purchases were Seri baskets and carvings, including one ironwood piece of a turtle, flippers reaching out, swimming through the water.

The heat is on in midday and the two women sit, legs tucked to one side and the baskets before them. They work with an awl made from the bone of a mule deer and pause from time to time to sharpen it on a pumice stone. The mother is very old, and strips basket-weaving material with her teeth from a supply softening in a plastic bucket of water. The water may not be used for washing hands or for anything but basket making. That is the rule, lest the spirit of the basket be angered—an act which can result in miscarriages. There are three sisters in their twenties, and they will not marry. They sit under the ramada by the sea, the mother and the oldest daughter making baskets, the two others watching. A basket can take months, sometimes years. It is slow and tedious work—the gathering of materials in the desert, the dyeing of the fibers, the stripping, the endless and boring hours of weaving. The women wrap their baskets in old rags to keep them clean, and to shield them from the view of other weavers who might mock their work. The Seris make many kinds and sizes of baskets. They sell for small fortunes—enough sometimes to buy a truck with. No Seri uses a basket for anything these days. They prefer metal tubs, plastic buckets.

Dogs sleep in the sand, a cat curls atop a barrel, a small girl watches the women work, the awl punching in and then, sometimes, a small screaming sound as the fibers bind against each other. This is the spirit of the basket crying out, the thing that must be placated if Seris are to be safe. An old woman comes up and offers to sell her hairbrush, a fistful of fiber from a desert plant bound at the base with fish line. As she speaks her other hand picks nits from her rich black hair. The afternoon creeps along. Below, the tide rolls out, and gulls cluster on the new sand with dumps of pelicans. The village is very quiet, the women working talk but in a low tone that barely penetrates the lapping of the waves against the shore.

In a corner of the ramada, Armando sits, his legs beneath him, an ironwood carving of a turtle in his lap. His T-shirt says "Property of City Jail." He had polio at age three and has never walked. He scoots across the sand with his hands. He has no crutches or a wheelchair. He keeps stacks of old magazines beside him full of color photographs. David brings them down for him. Once David watched him flip through an old *National Geographic* and suddenly a picture of a man in a wheelchair came up. Armando looked at the image long and hard. But he said nothing. He smokes a lot of dope and David calls him El Chimney. He is about forty now, and he has never had a woman.

His carvings are very distinct. He always makes his creatures move, the pelican with wings extended in flight, the turtle with flippers thrusting ahead to grab the water. When Imelda Marcos had her one-hour shopping spree in the Indian arts shop she left with one of Armando's turtles. He flips through another *National Geographic* as the afternoon wanders on, then points to an image and asks me to explain. It is a photo of a man in China, his face a nest of long needles as he undergoes acupuncture. I smile.

Armando likes his dope a lot. He has his dreams.

A while back a couple of Mexicans took over a crumbling adobe building in Desemboque and opened a taco stand. The place has a few tables, lots of flies, some carne, salsas, and torti-llas. It is a place to go. Jose wanders in, his step deliberate, his air one of a man on an important errand. He sits down and shows his work, a crude head with an outline of blue dots. The santo, he explains, is good for stopping bullets, for getting a woman, for tapping the power of the moon, for calming El Infiernillo, Little Hell. The three crosses? For El Señor, Christo. He holds the small wooden head in his leathered hand. For dreams, he explains, for tasting the power of dreams.

I walk over to the *tienda* and find Miguel Barnett standing there. He's about seventy-four now, his big feet are bare, his skin almost black from the sun, and he is wearing a red Seri kilt over his trousers. I look at his big blue belt buckle, which has stamped in large type: LED ZEPPLIN. I buy him a 7-Up. He's got this weird faded tattoo on his forearm and I ask him about it. He says he got it when he was forty, when he went to Big Cave on Tiburón looking for power. I ask him about the four days and nights, the little people, about what he saw. He says he cannot explain it in Spanish, he lacks the words in Spanish.

*　*　*

The room is small, the shelves plain and lined with rows of records, the documents recording Charlie's deals. Federal auditors lived in this room for over a year, searching earnestly for proper forms, evidence of collateral, evidence that guidelines had been followed, that caution and prudence had been exercised. Charlie looks about the room with contempt, his lips very thin. It is a Friday, a fun day in Charlie's empire when the staff does not have to dress formally. This means that the women wear softer dresses and that the men do not wear neckties. Charlie is in slacks, white shirt, and, true to the spirit of the day, without a tie.

He is uncomfortable in the room. He is power and this is the place where enemies try and cast spells against his power. Don't they understand that deals happen too fast for forms, that power vanishes if subjected to analysis? Do they really think this life is rational? We move off and walk down the quiet, sterile hallways of headquarters. Keating moves at a kind of ambling lope, his long legs devouring the ground. Near the door on a fine pedestal is a bronze statue of a grizzly bear rearing up and trying to embrace an Indian in a death grip. The Indian's arm is moving forward with a huge knife. A small brass plate on the statue announces it is Keating in combat with the Federal Reserve.

Charlie will not comment on the small monument. He says the staff gave it to him. Everything around Charlie in the end is something given to him, not something that comes out of himself. It is all bric-a-brac surrounding the power. And you don't talk about the power if you wish to keep it. The firing, the firing is always done by someone else, by someone sent right out of the meeting to slaughter that person who just caught Charlie's eye. Charlie's favorite hatchet man is said to keep a picture of the Grim Reaper in a drawer of his desk.

*   *   *

Miguel Barnett stares at the scholarly journal with the photograph of him taken almost fifty years before. At first he held the magazine upside down but then he hit the page with the photo and realized his error. His unmarried daughter is beside him as his eyes burn into the image. He jabs a finger at his image and says softly, "*Fuerte, fuerte,*" I was strong, strong.

The santo is almost finished, Victoria sits in the dirt beside him and sands it. David begins to talk of ticks—do the dogs ever have ticks? But he cannot remember the word and struggles. Victoria and Miguel's unmarried daughter watches with amusement. She is all dressed up—a light blue mantilla on her head held by a barrette of pearls, the skirt is a rose print, the blouse blue and delicate with lace. A belt of golden grape leaves with purple fruit encircles her waist. A pink ribbon dances in her black hair. There is a revival tonight at the evangelical church in Desemboque and she is going. She will pray and sing until dawn. She has already changed her clothes three times today in anticipation.

David sputters on but cannot come up with the word and so begins to describe a tick: that thing that pinches. The daughter smiles and says, "*Panocha,*" a kind of sugar cake that in Sonora is slang for pussy. And all the women laugh with pleasure. One looks over at the daughter in her fine clothes and says, "Her pussy is ready." She says nothing but leans against the wall and smiles.

*   *   *

"It's a bellyful to carry," Charlie rolls on. "It's risky. Dangerous. There's the possibility of failure with it every day and every night. But in a way it's a challenge, it's invigorating. There isn't any point in not being a player—you're here."

There is the Continental property, and Rancho Vistoso, and the hotels of course. And then there is Estrella, the star, the city that will hold 200,000 people someday, harbor families who will not read smut, and the kids will play in the park and all the faces will be white, the hair blond. Just a matter of the financing, getting the blueprints blazed into the raw ground.

He is alone. He is always alone. His corporate headquarters is like the family rec room with daughters and grandchildren, wife and son popping in. But still he is alone. His staff is replete with lawyers, accountants, and vice-presidents. But this doesn't change his solitude. He operates in well-defined, crowded arenas—bonds, stocks, currencies, real estate, hotels—but he is not really part of any organization. He makes the decisions on the McGuire chairs, the pounds sterling, the shifts of francs, yens, and marks. American Continental exists in buildings, stock certificates, developments, brochures, but mainly it exists where Charlie Keating happens to be at the moment. He is sitting in the crowded glass room, the eyes are intense as numbers flash across the computer screen, his face a mask of concentration. Alone.

One day months later, he tracks me down in the city and so I get up from my chair, leave the meeting, and take his call. The voice is very excited and I can hear lots of noise in the background, people shouting, orders being barked, bodies moving about in their various missions. It is Keating, and his huge new hotel, his $300 million wonder carved out of a desert mountain, will open in one day. The newspapers have just buried it in two pages of type as a loser, a mistake, a boondoggle, a waste of money.

"What can I do?" he asks. "Why in the hell are they acting that way? I'm just trying to make a buck and give people jobs."

The hotel has artificial lakes and the first tee is on a mountain ledge looking down at the strands of green.

*   *   *

They have built a special shed, maybe fifteen by fifteen for the basket. The man opens the door, I walk in and the light is poor, the air hot and stale. An old boat motor leans against the wall, a yellowed bra dangling down. The basket is off to one side inside a corral. It is about six feet high, almost as wide. The old woman has been working two or three years already. Seris like big things. It is a *sapim*, a giant basket. Such a basket should be sung to.

> Rock it away, rock it away
> Rock it away, rock it away
> The *sapim* pulled out its soul
> Rock it away, rock it away.

It is infused with *coen*, a spirit, and if this spirit is violated, the basketmaker might die, or perhaps one of her family might die. When this basket is finished they dream of the sale, thousands of American dollars. It will, if sold, wind up in a museum and each night when the attendants go home it will be very lonely, on the weekends also. Once, when Seris made such a basket, two men would carry it on a pole to the beach and then a balsa canoe would ferry it over from Tiburón Island. Everyone would gather at a spring and for four days and nights there would be a fiesta. They would sing many songs. Then they would carry the giant basket out into the desert and for eight more days have a fiesta. Men would bring in deer, everyone would drink cactus wine and dance. And then, when all the proper acts had been done, the giant basket would be left out in the desert and it would slowly age and rot and become dust ground under the heel of the sun. Some of this still continues; David has been to a giant-basket fiesta that lasted four days out in the dry washes.

But now the baskets are not abandoned, they are sold to rich people or rich institutions. Three such baskets are under way in Desemboque right now. There are many stories of how baskets came to the people. The nighthawk, in one, gave a basket to his daughter-in-law so she could go out and gather cactus fruit. When she returned laden with a load, she threw dirt in the nighthawk's face.

* * *

The call comes just like that. It is Ernie and he is fine. The assets have vanished into Charlie's hands, that's true, and the nice offices are gone also. Some limited partners have filed suit. Yeah, there're always details in business, you know. All in all, the experiences have been a good thing. Getting back to basics. The voice sounds good. E. C. Garcia & Company is coming back, the voice says. Just wait—thirty to forty-five days max, the financing is falling into place. The voice is very alive, cheerful. There are notes of caution, things that hopefully will not be publicized, words that could make things harder or even make things go bad. Ernie wants a smooth ride. But the juice, he can feel the juice again. And that is life itself in his desert.

"There are a lot of opportunities out there," he says. A year later he refuses to talk to federal officials when the hearings begin.

* * *

The moon, she rides just above the sea, a three-quarters moon, *la señorita,* her loins full, the blood coming once a month, worlds I have never seen lie waiting in her womb for conception. Her breath is dank with richness. Her eyes have the assured daze of a woman arising from a bed after a long night with a man she has gutted and drained. In the village the brothers and sisters are singing at the revival, and for a brief moment coyotes in the surrounding desert bark at the welcome night. I have a santo by my head in the moonlight, a long crescent with a yellow band, then red stripe, then belt of blue, the face rising, lips pursed, nose strong into the white pale milk, into that glow dripping from the sky. The sea is calm, the sharks cruising restlessly, the whales sounding up and down the coast. This afternoon we were out with a Seri in his boat and set the net, one two football fields long, for small dog sharks. The sea was glass and as we trailed out the net a whale breached the water nearby, blew, and dove.

The santo does not move. I roll over and listen to the singing in the village. This afternoon we were walking down a village street when a man came up clutching a Xerox copy of pages from a book on Seris written in English fifty years ago. Women soon gathered around, their long skirts limp in the hot, flat air. They pointed at the photographs taken in 1930, and soon fingers would jab and names come out of dead tribal members. There was a song, "The Whale Song," and they wished to know what it said. So David stood out in the sun and read,

> The whale is swimming
> Back and forth in the water.
> He drinks very much water
> And goes here and there,
> And here and there.
> He comes to me
> At the edge of the land.

The people nodded and said nothing. The book explained: "the ballad gives a very impressive picture of the huge mammal which they look upon as the Chief of the Fishes, coming up to the edge of the water in answer to this song." An old woman thrust forth a fistful of necklaces and asked if David was going to buy them. The man with the Xeroxed pages from the book walked back down the hot sand street and disappeared into a government cement hut.

* * *

The end comes with the spring. It has been a hot spring, a very hot spring, and the saguaro are coming into bloom a month early. I have been getting calls for months, the end will come, the people are being moved into place. It is certain, it is over, all over. They move at 7 A.M. in the morning and take over the files, the offices, the records. The money. There is only twenty million left in the savings and loan. A few hours before, Charlie declares his empire Chapter 11 but this does not stop the agents of the federal government. The newspapers make a tally. It promises to be the largest bankruptcy in the history of the state, perhaps the fifth or sixth largest in the history of the nation. The exact size remains to be seen—there are many records to peruse. But it looks to be a billion or two short in the cash drawer.

It is not easy being technically dead and yet actually alive. I have a call placed to a man who has a credit line worth tens of millions of dollars with Keating. I wish to check up on a small little detail. But the man will have none of it. He is not interested in history. Life, I learn, goes on. He says fuck Charlie.

The press conference is held in a fine hotel, not one of Charlie's. I go first to his headquarters but plainclothes guards stop me before I can get out of my truck. No, not here, they say. The guards wear cheap white shirts and carry walkie-talkies. Their guts are slack. I can tell they are not Charlie's people.

The room is very prim, the frieze flutters with butterflies dancing against a band of blue, the tables in back lined with coffee cups, real china, and pastries. Outside a hundred people are held back. They are employees of Charlie's, reserves. All his grandchildren sit in a row, the little girls wearing Communion-like dresses, fresh ribbons in their hair. Charlie is pinned against a wall with his wife under the television lights as the cameras get their footage. He is no longer in absolute control, he must now talk to the media. A television cameraman pokes his video recorder into the faces of Charlie's grandchildren and slowly scans the rows. Suddenly, a large guy in a suit tears away from the wall where Charlie is being interviewed and comes over and stands right behind the cameraman who is intent upon his shot. The big guy has a thick neck and head of rock. He bends forward, right up to the cameraman's ear, says something sharply, the cameraman snaps backward, and *boom!* his head collides with the big guy's. He is stunned and almost reeling. The big guy walks away easily and there is no more footage taken of the grandchildren. It is hard not to like such moments.

At the last moment, Charlie's employees are let in. Almost all are women and very clean and white and well scrubbed. They stand in the back of the room and look earnest.

First, John Connally's son, one of Charlie's employees, addresses the present situation. He apologizes for the slide show that they are about to flash on the screen, but, he notes, this very morning when an aide went over to headquarters to get better imagery, he was stopped by a federal guard who told him, "If you take anything, I'll take your fucking head off." Connally's son looks to be in his thirties and has the serious air of an elder in the church at collection time. The slide show is brief, a cavalcade of lakes, streets, houses, hotels, swatches of fairways, pools, dining rooms, industrial parks. There is no desert in this presentation, it has gone away. I am standing in the back with Keating's employees surrounding me. They eye me warily in my Levis, their faces questioning my financial resources and suspecting I am a carrier of dreaded sexual diseases. And then, they crisply applaud.

Now Charlie rises to the podium. He reads a prepared statement denouncing the government for crushing a thriving concern with rules and regulations and constant harassment. His voice is firm—he leads with an anecdote he attributes to Abraham Lincoln. As he turns the pages his hands tremble.

Then he finishes, and is whisked out a side exit. The press is allowed to ask no questions. His employees applaud. They say the failure is billions of dollars but that is only a number.

In a few months, the government slaps him with charges of racketeering and asks for the return of, say, a billion dollars. Charlie is interested in having lunch. I drive up to Phoenix and curl up in a diner with the 160-page indictment. The deals spill across the pages: a piece of desert that the Feds figure Charlie flipped back and forth between subsidiaries and straw borrowers until its value on the books rose fifty-nine times in a few months. Ernie, the golden boy, shows up in the angry federal script as the man who borrows around $20 million with no collateral. All this weird wheeling and dealing tunnels back into a complicated scheme to get money out of the savings and loan's vaults and into a tax escrow fund, a place from which it seems to vanish forever. Names flutter across the pages, the nice solid names of chamber of commerce types I've bumped up against. Now they appear as people who can borrow millions without a worry, and then never pay the money back. As I read on, the jukebox in the diner keeps playing Elvis and Chuck Berry.

I look forward to lunch in the swank Phoenician hotel. But Charlie never is able to break away, something about talks with lawyers, his aide tells me. The guy does chat about the current difficulties, seems the company has shrunk now to fifty souls, all of whom are outnumbered by defense attorneys. The guy can hardly finish a sentence, and seems real uncomfortable in his nice suit. He says this country has changed, that it is hard now to do something to help people, to give them jobs, and a purpose in life. This country, he continues, would kill off a Henry Ford now. Just look, he says by way of example, what it is doing to Charlie.

* * *

We leave early in the morning. Victoria gives me a necklace made with a very long strand, then turns away. Her body is erect, her face dark brown and passive, her mind a country closed off to me and my kind. The desert is a green mash of ocotillo leafing out, organ pipe, cardón, saguaro, the tortured trunks of elephant tree. The light is still soft, the heat has not yet come on. Dust rises from the dirt road for hours.

Just before I left Miguel Barnett told me of his night in Big Cave on Tiburón. He used a translator because he said there was no way to express what he had learned in his limited Spanish. It was all long ago.

For three days and nights he did not eat, did not drink water, did not sleep. Then he walked to the mouth of Big Cave and over his head he twirled his bull roarer, two finely sanded pieces of ironwood held together by the sinews of a deer. The wood made a whooshing roar and this opens *la puerta,* the door to the cave's real soul. Now he enters, sits under the paintings in the darkness, and lets his mind float. The night is long and suddenly a shaft of light strikes him, the outpouring of *la puerta.* The little people appeared, they were very short, maybe a foot or eighteen inches, and they spoke Americano. Things began to change, and their blood mixed with his blood, their flesh with his flesh. They taught him songs in this language he did not understand, songs that would give him power and healing. A sign came to him—here, he will draw it, three forms, two that look like J's, and one with the aspect of the silhouette of a bullet. This became his sign—not his name, he insists—his mark, his brand. He tattooed this sign on his left forearm. All the old men who had gotten the power wore their signs there.

He rolls up his sleeve, the veins huge on his old arm, the skin almost black, but the tattoo has vanished. He says he is old now, he is not sure he has the power any longer. No matter. That part of Seri life is over, another Seri explains. The young will have none of it. They are Christians, and such things are forbidden to them by their new Protestant faith. This fact is simply that, a fact. It does not seem to disturb him. The Seris are a very practical people, they gave up the balsa for dugouts, dugouts for plank boats, took to motors in 1948, absorbed fiberglass boats in the '80s.

The tip of Tiburón peeks around Tepopa Point, the dogs laze in the sun, out in the bay dolphins feed, and in the channel of Little Hell, the *cahuamas* are running. Miguel rattles on, his voice a low singsong. He is a very erect, thin, tall man.

He tells me that if I go to the cave I must be careful not to sleep. These things, these things he describes, they could happen to me. The little people are there. The island is there. The *buro* are there, the ravens, the coyotes, the plants Seris believe have *icor*, souls or essences.

The man translating for me tells me a story. Once some Mexicans came and captured a Seri in Big Cave. They took him out in a boat, tied a heavy rock around his neck, and threw him overboard. When the Mexicans returned to the cave, the Seri was waiting for them.

That is what I want to believe. I keep having this daydream, this hope, that some things persist. Fortunately for me, various priests in the now disguised temples have fabricated an entire science around this fantasy, a science designed to shield the naked human need I am feeling. This fantasy is called Ecology. I enjoy it often, like taking a hit off a good pipe of hashish. With this science, plus other baggage assembled by scholars, I can humor myself with notions of cultural persistence, with metaphysical pipe dreams called business cycles, with Jungian voodoo about archetypes and the common floor under the mists of myth, with catechisms of plant succession and the foreordained inevitable climax. Like an evangelical, I am even provided with a way to distinguish the children of light from the children of darkness. The saved are called natural, the damned unnatural.

Charlie, he is a slave to Lucifer. Miguel Barnett, he is one with Our Lord. The Seris murdering turtles, they risk their immortal souls. It is a wonderful perspective because it requires no thought. But I am plagued with memories of the future. Actually, that was the name of a cheap saloon in southern Mexico in the days of Porfirio Díaz, the tyrant who created the fuel for the bonfire called the Revolution. In these memories of the future, there is no particular purpose to things, or a meaningful pattern that can justify words like *evolution* or *progress* or *climax* or *success*. There is life, an impulse, wet loins oozing across the faces of the clocks. And none of the children have faces that earn words like *light*. Or *darkness*. It is like the fiestas Mexicans are always holding to disrupt the quotas set by time-and-motion experts.

It is all in one moment for me. I am standing out in the hot sun by the Sea of Cortez and Jose Astorga is explaining a santo to me. I pulled out my notebook to catch the ethnographic lore I sense he will impart. He traces forms in the sand with his ancient finger. First, he draws the numeral 9. Then he traces the numeral 3. Then he draws a perfect set of tits.

Then he looks up and laughs.

Ah, I see. She is standing over there by the mud wall, the light blue mantilla caressing her long black hair, the pearls, the delicate lace of the blouse. Her pussy is ready. For what, no one asks.

4

Chalo has found love now, he sleeps under the stone in the grave-
yard with seventy rounds in his body. A Bible verse dances over his
head, a carved dove flies toward heaven, and two boys sit near his
grave and look up with respect and dark eyes.

Is this his plot? Truly?

A man busy cleaning the grave of his recently dead child glances
over and says, "The guy who took seventy? Ah, yes, there he is."

I am looking for the Virgin when Héctor hands me a cold can of
beer. He's pretty well smashed and his wife is good and drunk
too. He sways slowly forward and backward on the soft sand of
the arroyo just below the tongue of cobblestone leading up to the
village's tiny plaza. Pilgrims walk past, some of the women and
children wearing red shapeless cloaks like those of monks, each
garment with a small white cross hand-stitched on the shoulder, the waist cinched with a rough white cord. They have made
mandas and now it is time to pay back God. Up on the small rise,
hundreds gather in a day-and-night vigil in the old stone church,
and outside against the cold wet wall, dozens come together
under the magic cactus.

There is a song sung by mariachis that goes, *"Estoy enamo-*
rado de tu crueldad, I'm in love with your cruelty." The song
plays in my head. The night air is filled with sounds. Hawkers
peddling blankets bark at the crowds, young guys with a gift for

gab and microphones taped right under their noses. They chant
their pitch, their arms flailing as they slam down one blanket,
no! make that two! no make that three, no, no! six, seven, eight
blankets! plus a huge rug tossed up into the air, a rug crowded
with a hungry Bengal tiger. Peasants gather around to hear such
a wonderful torrent of words. There is no sign out on the paved
highway to announce this place, just a dirt road that trails off
into the thorn forest. Normally, the village harbors 200 or 300
people, but tonight there are perhaps 10,000. Mayo women
tend stewpots of goat under ramadas whacked together the day
before with machetes. Vaqueros and their *novias* flow past, the
men wearing tight jeans, shirts with snaps, straw cowboy hats,
their women poured into Levis, the hair teased into a heap, the
eyes gemstones in dark wells of mascara, the cheeks aflame with
rouge, their feet often as not in high heels. From the skin of these
women comes a scent that wanders out like a tongue offering the
promise of flowers and musk.

Down the wash, Gypsies have set up a theater with a bunch
of poles supporting blankets to form the walls. A projector on a
truck aims at a tattered screen, and from their PA system a voice
coaxes one and all to come and see movies about Caro Quintero!!
the bandit king of barrio Tierra Blanca, the giant from Sinaloa!!
the man now jailed in Mexico City for killing that American drug
agent, the hombre who sent wails through the government of the
gringos!! All this for a dollar and twenty-five cents.

I am lying under a huge tree on the edge of the wash finish-
ing off a big clay tumbler of tequila. A young goat is tied up just
behind me, its throat to be soon cut for the meat pots of the
fiesta. I hear that voice roaring out of the PA system, then suddenly a *corrido* comes from the speakers, one celebrating Lamberto Quintero, a cousin of Caro's. The song flows like honey
down the wash, licking the faces of the thousands of short brown
people:

On the 28th of January, a date we will always remember with
Don Lamberto Quintero,
He was followed that day by a pickup truck as he went toward
Salado just making his rounds,
They passed the carrizo thicket, just drinking a few beers.
One of his companions told him that they were being followed
by the pickup,
Lamberto smiled and told him, pass the machine gun.

The Gypsy woman sits on a bare bench while the song unfolds.
Her dress falls almost to the ground, a headdress of pink flows
down her back, and between her full ruby lips rests a *cigarro*.
She is maybe thirty, her small children seem to appear magically
from the folds of her dress, and before her black eyes an endless
stream of people passes. Many have walked forty or fifty miles
because of *mandas,* those promises. People move in loose squads
up the hillsides and the arroyo and they leave in their wake a
moving sludge of piss and shit. Clots of toilet paper flap in the
night breezes like newly opened flowers.

Under the tree, listening to the songs about the drug lords,
the American world of drug wars, drug problems, drug crises,
doesn't mean much to me. I see the roundness of the women's
hips, the sullen masks of the men, the bright eyes of the *niños,*
the air of sex and despair. I am in love with your cruelty. I get up
and go back to the beer stand up the wash. Héctor is still there,
and now his brother staggers up. The brother is dead drunk
and beckons a mariachi band over. They cut loose with a bass,
a guitar, trumpet, and drum. Suddenly the brother's legs start
ramming the ground like pile drivers, he holds one fist before
his bent head like an object of meditation, wheels, spins, and
then erupts with howls, yips, barks, and strange cries. He dances
alone, falls against the beer stand, rights himself, and is back at
his celebration. Héctor nods approvingly as his brother dances,

his wife curls against his side toasting the brother with her can of beer. She is fat and her face glows with happiness and lust.

Héctor wears a small plastic Buddha around his neck—his wife found it in the sierra one day. He is Catholic but this fact does not exclude Buddha in his eyes. He is about twenty-five and this is the fourth year that he and his wife have come the thirty-five miles to the fiesta. For three years they walked, but this time they took the bus. He must come, he made a vow. Up the hill, the Virgin stands serene in the stone church, outside on the wall an organ-pipe cactus pokes out from the sheer stone wall, the green thorny arms reaching upward about ten feet off the ground. The cactus never grows and is never dry. This is a miracle. Beneath it, the faces are very Indian, the people sprawled out on blankets on the wet ground. A yellow glow lights their faces from a thicket of burning candles under the cactus. Here and there an open tequila bottle sits on the stone pavement and all the conversations are soft.

Héctor is laughing now as the brother storms along with his dance. The Gypsies' shouts fill the night with the legend of Caro Quintero. Héctor leans forward, motions at his wife, and asks if I want to fuck her. She beams and her fat head nods.

Chalo lived at this particular time with his sister. One night he was cleaning his gun. This is what he later said. There was an accident. He shot his sister dead. He was cleared of any charges. They say he got off because he was a cop. People recount this event with quiet voices, not the soft voices that give confidences, but the low voices that state the obvious, the commonplace.

That is one story. The other story does not mention the sister, the gun cleaning, the shot that kills. In this tale, Chalo kills a cop and goes to prison. When he comes out, the authorities make him a federale. The man who tells me this shrugs as if to say, "Some crazy world, no?"

Indians are walking up the arroyo in the still morning air. All around them the thorn forest presses in, a green wall of small trees that is here and there punctured by giant cactus. The sky rattles with the cries of parrots. The Indians are in loincloths and mutter in the soft gutturals of the Mayo language. They are enjoying the last few moments before history begins. Suddenly, they stop. Before them a woman is sitting on the top of an organpipe cactus, just sitting there on this shaft of thorns as if the huge plant were a throne. Her face is serene, pain seems not to touch her.

They hustle about and pile up stones so that the woman can dismount. But when they get their heap of rocks almost finished, she flies off through the air. This is the appearance of the *Virgen de Balvanera*. The date in the calendars of the Spaniards is 1683. Soon silver is found where the Virgin appeared, an enormous strike that finances a town of grandees. The mines themselves foster the mining camp where the fiesta occurs each year. Families grow very rich, and one on a rainy wedding day orders silver ingots laid as a walkway to the church lest the bridal dress be soiled. The cathedral in the town of the grandees is said to have two five-hundred-pound silver balls buried under its floor. In the hills above the mining camp, someone is said to have buried forty burro-loads of silver during some time of troubles.

I can look up onto the hillside and see the seeping wounds of the mines. I can open my ears and hear hymns to drug dealers, and killers, lift a can of beer and smile with thousands of other drunks. Shout "Salud!" to Héctor and his wife, consider his offer of fucking her. No problem, he explains, she goes her way, he goes his. Women stream past my eyes, the dresses hand sewn, satiny, hips tightly fitted, then a flare below with layers of ruffles, high heels, the asses bouncing, hips jutting, the breasts barely revealed, scents rising off the scrubbed flesh, and the faces masks with layers of makeup, passive, almost sullen images of haughtiness.

The peasants have come for years, years beyond telling, walking ten, twenty, thirty, forty, or more miles, short brown people trudging through the night, some in those shapeless red cloaks, the twisted thorn forest arching over their heads, marching to the village because of that vow, that wish, everything slamming together here on November 20th since time began with a Virgin resting on top of an organ-pipe cactus. There are similar fiestas everywhere in Mexico for different Virgins, for various saints. They exist because people hurt, because work is hard, because women are desirable, because miracles are necessary, because few can stay sober without sometimes being drunk.

People sprawl everywhere in the village, smoke rises up from their cookfires, the community takes on the look of a place seized during some revolution. I walk into one building and the patio is cluttered with family groups, the women in long dresses huddled over little blazes, blue coffee pots resting on the coals. In the tiny plaza an old Indian woman with long black braids sells holy bread with prayers written across the loaves. I buy one that says, "For my fucking race."

Chalo loved to hunt. He would be out in the selva on his horse. He holds his rifle and his eyes search for the deer. The thorn forest is a tangle, branches grab at the flesh, the path is not obvious. To enter the trees is to be blinded by life. Orchids grow on the trunks, parrots call overhead, the boa constrictor slides silently along. A man tells me this over drinks in a fine hotel. He is a waiter and Chalo, he says, was his friend. They would hunt often, Chalo loved to bring down the deer. I sip tequila while the man talks reverently about his dead friend. He is wearing the white uniform of a waiter, his hair is carefully combed, his manner formal. I can hear the crack of a rifle, see the deer fall, feel the warm stickiness of the flesh as the animal is gutted with the sharp knife, smell the smoke off the fire as the meat slowly roasts. The man looks down at me and says Chalo was a very good shot.

It is night now and I leave a cantina on the alameda with my head spinning from hours of drinking. A man takes me to his small taco stand in the market. He grabs a six-pack of Modelo from the ice chest. Chalo? Ah, you want to know about Chalo. Certainly, I knew him, he would come to this very cafe and eat tacos. He was powerful, he was a cop, he killed his sister, he abused women, he was a narcotraficante. *It is like this: a matter of economics, a matter* economica. *The mota, well, people in the United States they will pay big money for the mota. In Mexico, people are poor. You see?* Economicas.

The son leans forward and smiles. The fiesta, he explains, will not be so grand this year because of the pressure on the *marijuaneros*. His father listens and then adds, "Marijuana is very expensive. Death is cheap." For months now, the Mexican government has focused on making Sonora and other places *limpio*, "clean." Road blocks of *federales* search vehicles, choppers spray the fields of *herba mala*. A man of the town tells me, yes, things are tight right now, many cars are suddenly for sale as the income of the drug world dwindles for a moment. "There is a lot of lead in the air," he cautions. A painted wall dominates the entrance with the message: *"Narcos . . .* Out of Sonora. Respect Yourself! . . . Say No to Drugs." A man tells me over coffee that thirty-five drug dealers have been run out of town.

Up on the hill in the *cárcel*, twenty-three men visit with their families. Women are permitted this day. Three of the men are in jail for murder, the other twenty for theft or drugs. The floors of the cells are dirt, the walls topped with jagged pieces of broken bottles, and here and there the roof has collapsed in what was a mansion of the rich before the Revolution. Little heaps of horsehair clump on the ground since the men must fashion belts and lariats if they are to eat. On a wall someone has sketched a fine marijuana plant. A two-year-old child squats and pisses through his jeans. A young woman comes to the door of a cell, her face flushed, her hands tugging her dress back down on her hips. Her eyes are glazed with pleasure. A man's face appears in the shadows behind her, the lips a straight line, the chest bare. A peasant of about thirty sits under a gaping hole in the roof, a heap of horsehair at his feet and in his hand a chicken wing. An old woman, his wife, glares up from his side, and his six-year-old son squats and gnaws a bone silently. The man knifed a fellow member of his village over use rights to a piece of land. Another man from the same village came home one day from his field and stabbed his wife to death. He suspected infidelity. His sentence has not yet been determined—it will depend on whether or not he can prove she was sleeping with another man. The dead woman was from Guanajuato where the traditional *corrido* is *"La Vida No Vale Nada,* Life Is Worth Nothing."

The cells are surrounded by a stout stockade and up there Pancho the guard strides with his twelve-gauge pump. He wears no uniform, none of the guards do. Pancho is feeling very good. Tonight he will go to the fiesta, and then in a few days his sister will be married—yet another glorious drunk, and, thank God, the end of his days supporting her. Today, the problem in the *cárcel* is simple: the prisoners cannot go to the fiesta. But they are trained up to suffering and dream their own dreams. One *corrido* of the narcotics world says, "I dreamed that I would die at the hands of a man who is valiant."

Chalo loved his work and his work inspired fear. The band leader leans against an old wall and explains that Chalo was a bad man and no one wept when he went down. The cops in the area, well, they were afraid of him when he came to town. He killed five people in town, the man says, five for sure. He had six women, and there were children also.

Up by the church Héctor and his woman lean against the stone wall. What is the story of the *Virgen de Balvanera?* He does not know, but he says she produces *milagros,* miracles. And he needs one badly, that is why he has been making a pilgrimage for four straight years. His wife, the woman swilling tequila beside him, she cannot conceive.

I walk down to the front of the church where an Indian woman stands with a girl of three who is dressed in the red habit of a penitent coming to the Virgin. The girl has been sick, the mother says, so the entire family has made a *manda,* a promise, and come to the village. As she speaks, the father, the uncles, the aunts, and the other children watch silently with black eyes. What is the story of this Virgin who grants *milagros?* Ah, yes, she explains, the story, Señor, goes this way: There was a cave at the village where the painting of the Virgin was kept but then the rich people of the neighboring town came and took it away. The next day the painting reappeared in the cave. That is the miracle. So the church was built, Señor. This she knows to be a fact because her grandfather lived on the hill above the church and he told her. What of the cactus? Is it part of this *milagro?* Oh, she says, this I do not know, Señor, but the cactus is very strange, is it not, growing there out of solid stone and never being dry.

Just below, a man sprawls on the wet ground drinking a beer. This is the fourth year he has walked forty miles. He burned his foot with a cigarette and the infection got very bad and then he made a vow to the Virgin and now he is well. His face is unshaven and he looks up at the young women strolling past in their best dresses and offers, "My heart aches because there are so many beautiful Mexican girls. My dick is throbbing."

"Who is the Virgin of Balvanera?" I ask as I walk through people huddled around small cookfires, babies squalling, women softly patting tortillas for the *comal.* Try Ramón Garcia, there, over there in the old white mud house just above the plaza. I open the gate, walk up the stone steps, and cross the porch which is clotted with pilgrims camping out. Ramón comes forward, his face warm and his manner gracious. Ramón's family has lived in the village for two hundred years in the same house, and he explains that the story of the Virgin is this: the cactus in the old stone wall never grows, never needs water. That, he says, is all he knows.

Except for one night. We are in the *sala* now, a huge room with a ribbed ceiling supported by big beams. Five years ago, Ramón confides, he was a terrible drunkard. He was sitting in this house in this very room when he looked up at a portrait of the Virgin on the wall and asked her to help him stop drinking. Suddenly, ten or twelve men with rifles appeared from corners of the room and they threatened to kill him. His family locked him in a room for three days and nights and the men with *armas* came at him constantly. For a year afterward, his body shook. He has not had a drink since. So every year at the fiesta, he renews his vow to the Virgin and lights a candle.

Chalo loved to go after criminals. He never brought them back alive. This was at the time he was a cop. He would go out and find them, and then something would happen. They would resist, perhaps, or try to escape. Who can say? No one knows how many times this happened. These killings are not entered into his tally. After all, this was when he was a cop. It is just that he never seemed to bring back prisoners. Many say he was very cruel.

The stalls around the plaza are wrapped in orange, blue, white, yellow, green, red, purple, and pink crepe paper, the knives chop up carne asada for tacos, fat sizzles around the doughy churros browning in washtubs of hot grease over the wood fires, ears of corn drip with butter, cheese, and chili, the barkers scream at the shooting gallery, hotcakes hiss on the grill, there is the constant murmur of old women wending their way through the crowd to the Virgin, the yips and howls of men drunk with love and the night, the slap of huaraches on the wet cobblestones, the bleating of goats, braying of burros, shrieking of toy whistles in the mouths of children, the loaves of holy bread saying For My Beloved Father, For My Beloved Child, For My Beloved Mother. Down in the arroyo, the Gypsies crank up their PA system again and boom out the *"Corrido de Lamberto Quintero,"*

> Now close to Salado the ambushers erupted
> And there the enemies of Lamberto left two dead men behind them.
> I wish this was only a story, but mister this is the truth.

The small stone church is packed now, people spread out on the floor sleeping, and the endless line of pilgrims approaches the image of the Virgin who reigns in her glass case. They kneel, make the sign of the cross, kiss the glass, and then quickly move on into the night and the beckoning cans of beer, the bottles of tequila. There are eighty to one hundred candles burning now beneath the cactus and three or four mariachi bands play at once before the church. A drunk stands by the altar swaying to the music. A second drunk stands before the church door directing another band with a can of Tecate. A cop strolls by, his jacket says in English: Park Staff. His hand holds a twelve-gauge pump.

Chalo was sent to Nogales, Sonora, on the U.S. line to buy guns for his police agency. His superior instructed him as to what weapons to purchase and to whom he should deliver them. But when he came back, he gave the guns to a different unit and did not follow his instructions. So his chief was very angry, and charged him with being a contrabandista, *a smuggler. It is said that this was the moment in which Chalo changed sides and became a gatillero, a triggerman, for Rafael Caro Quintero.*

I give the Gypsy woman some money and go into the theater. The seats are wooden benches, the walls blankets, and behind me an old projector pokes out from an opening in the big truck where the family lives. The moviegoers are all peasants. *"Policía de Narcótico"* flashes on the screen and the announcer says "to knock out the drug traffic in Mexico you need the most violent cops in the world." A blond woman with large breasts is suddenly coming at me, then a man appears in the foreground. She presses against him, holds him with her arms, then rams a long dagger into his neck. A naked woman with large breasts writhes on silken sheets, her face in ecstasy. The room is very large and filled with fine furniture. A man appears in the doorway, he is a shadow raising a weapon to his shoulder, and then he blows both her breasts off with a shotgun. Now a trim woman with a fine hard body enters. Her stomach is firm, her breasts also large. A man pumps the magazine from an Uzi into her bloody crotch. Above the stars shine in a black sky, and in front of me an old woman rests her hand on her cane and stares intently. This is the preview.

The movies, the movies do not bother me. They are kind of exciting and I catch the fervor of the crowd huddled under the stars in the arroyo while the ancient projector of the Gypsies cranks on. A movie about Caro Quintero comes on, there are many guns, the flash of Uzis, and everyone laughs and is hypnotized by the unfolding action. I am in love with your cruelty.

Chalo was out at his rancho in the selva, riding his horse with his dog trotting along beside him and worrying out the path ahead. That is how they got him. No one knows how many were awaiting him in the wall of green but from the number of rounds, the

educated guess suggests that four weapons were required for the
work. The killers cut down the horse and dog also. They say that
the man, the horse, and the dog fell as one, a single beautiful cas-
cade of flesh and blood and screams. Chalo, he took seventy to
eighty rounds, the mortician counted them out when he dressed
the body for holy ground.

Pilgrims continue to march up the wet cobbles to the church.
Up on the hill, sheets of metal ten feet high have enclosed the
basketball court for the *baile*, the dance. The band fires up and
couples line up to pay: $10 for a man (two days' wages), $2 for a
woman. People are streaming up the arroyo shoulder to shoulder.
The village is 10,000 strong, beer is everywhere, and desire flicks
its tongues against all the faces. Men piss in the corners against
the wall. Pancho, the prison guard, is here, he is fine with drink
and beer follows beer. The band plays the *"Corrido de Lamberto*
Quintero" and Pancho howls with pleasure.

> This man who was never serious, always happy and full of love,
> Who sang love songs for his sweetheart was caught off guard
> When the bullets snatched away his life.
> The clinic at Santa Maria has my testimony and now,
> Two days after his death the sounds of shooting are heard again,
> And now there are ten dead men left behind,
> They are there for obvious reasons.
> You who were there on the bridge over Tierra Blanca,
> Who remember when Lamberto passed by,
> You will never be able to forget him.
> For my part this is certain,
> He will be missed in Culiacán.

Couples wheel, the women dressed in their finest, the men
with polished boots and blank faces. Pancho raises his beer can,

"Salud!" A young guy comes off the floor with a good-looking woman on his arm. Pancho's face lights up. The guy just got out of the *cárcel* where he spent six months for stabbing another man in an incident over a woman. Pancho says when the young guy was in the *cárcel,* every week a beautiful woman came to see him, each week a different woman.

The dance will go on until 2:30 A.M. and then afterwards the arroyo will be lined with rutting couples sprawled out on the sand. Up on the hill, pilgrims will be making the sign of the cross before the Virgin and kissing her glass case. As for the cactus looming from the stone wall, it never grows. And it never goes dry. *Estoy enamorado de tu crueldad.*

Chalo is in the place of love now, in the burying ground on the edge of town which is very old, centuries old. They say he killed a man, and then the man's brothers, well, they sought revenge. But no one pursues this matter. He was a cruel man and it does not matter. He died three months before the fiesta for the Virgin of Balvanera. He missed the party, the good drinks, the blackness falling off the mountain into the arroyo as people drank and howled at the stars.

His grave marker offers this message: "We love you—your parents, wife and children." Now he belongs to the worms, and the Bible verse carved into the stone:

But I in justice shall behold your face; on waking, I shall be content in your presence.
—Psalms, 17:15

5

He is sitting on the wall smoking a cigarette and telling of the thorn forest and his village. The home place seems strange down there on the border of Sonora and Sinaloa. When he was a boy he would walk the almost forty miles into town, but now he has prospered and owns shoes. He has a good house, a pool, and does not go to the nearby fiesta for the Virgin of Balvanera—that is for Indios, for the dark-skinned people, the *borrachos*. Long ago, when the Americans had their First World War, two gringos from Texas fled the draft and came to the village and now their descendants flood the area. "Imagine," he says, "a pueblo of blue-eyed, fair-skinned Mexicans."

His brothers stayed in the village but in recent years it has gotten very bad there, many shootings and killings. *Las drogas.* He has had to bring his mother into town for her own safety. But that is not what he speaks of now. It is evening, we have been drinking, the Mexican sky bleeds stars. In a while, he will go to visit his girlfriend, then home to the wife, and a good night's sleep. He is explaining the uses of the forest, the various barks, herbs, fruits, roots, remedies, the lore of *brujas,* and *curenderas.* And, of course, the cats. There is the *leon,* the lion, and ocelot, and the onza, yes, yes, Señor, it truly exists. And the *tigre,* the jaguar.

I quicken. The cats always seduce us, the grace, the silence, the dreams of giant purrs rolling off their bloody mouths. We find their tracks, stumble on their scat, smell the strength of their urine, but as for the animals themselves, we seldom catch even a glimpse, a few brief flashes in an entire lifetime. We look down at the paw print in the soft, moist ground and imagine the claws. A few months back, a *tigre* swept through his ranch, slaughtered a calf, and the man and his vaqueros took up a kind of pursuit. Of course, they failed. Without dogs, a man has almost no chance of treeing such an animal.

But his brother, his brother had better luck recently. He is still living back in that crazy village of blue-eyed Mexicans, and he hired some Tarahumara Indians from the sierra to help out. The Tarahumara are famous in Mexico for their foot races of a hundred or two hundred miles, for their refusal to become Mexicans—some still live in caves—and for their keenness out on the land. When a jaguar started killing his brother's stock, the Tarahumaras took up the pursuit. And they were successful. This is the interesting part, the man says. Mexicans, he explains, will eat mountain lions. You see, he instructs me, the lion eats cattle and deer and so is sound meat. But the jaguar, the jaguar eats anything, including men, and therefore it is not clean. But these Indians, they cut up the jaguar and made jerky, and then they pounded that jerky into powder and mixed it with spices and made machaca. And then, they ate it.

He looks over at me with a smile and shakes his head at the imagined horror of such an act. I say nothing. I imagine the Indians eating the cat, putting the power of the beast inside their own bodies. I become hungry.

*   *   *

Storm clouds scud low off Tonto Rim and the air rushes raw with cold fingers across the desert. The men walk slowly into the Gila County courthouse, the Levis worn, the fingers scarred, hands big, guts hanging over their belts, their shirts all with metal snaps. The faces are well creased by memories of sun and wind, the hats, they are different here, deliberately out of fashion, crown high and barely dented, brim pulled down fiercely in front and back. They nod to each other and barely speak. There is little need, the blood goes back three, four, five generations. The men under the hats share these things: they hate lions, they kill lions. And they love lions. These matters will never be spoken, but in the Rim country most of what is, is never said. Or it will not be at all.

They have killed hundreds, lassoed them, shot them, tracked them with hounds up the rock and into the trees. Shot down the mothers, brought home the kittens and raised them in cages. Crossed their yards each morning, the cats standing up, the blank green eyes reaching through the bars.

"You wonder what they're about," one rancher says. "You watch your ten-year-old kid walk past the cage and then look into those eyes."

I am sitting in the back of the room and do not speak but watch. I have driven up here in order to listen to the lion world. To consider nature, that fine word we feel more than understand. Ignore drugs, ignore them absolutely. Forget development, Charlie, finance, wine in goblets with fine stems, the voices on the phone with whispers of deals, testimony, fissures of bankruptcy streaking across the country club faces. Of course, there is no Mexico in this part of the desert, it is safely kept out of sight and mind. There is also the matter of love. And I have come to meet Harley Shaw, the one man in the state paid to think about lions.

My interest goes back to a time I cannot remember, perhaps when as a boy I hunted all day in the desert for deer and then as light began to fail turned back toward camp and followed my tracks. For more than a mile, I saw the dusty print of a lion in the outlined tread of my boots. Probably it started at that moment, realizing something I had never seen had followed me and watched me for hours. It may have been the Yaqui barrio that clung near the freeway in the city. I would go down there as a boy and stay all night to watch the dances. The Yaquis have songs, songs I did not understand until decades later, but songs that I heard and that seeped somehow into my imagination.

The Yaquis have a lot of songs and there is one about a female mountain lion. No one sings this song much up on Tonto Rim.

> Flower lion, flower lion,
>   walking in the wilderness, flower lion.
> Flower lion, flower lion,
>   walking in the wilderness, flower lion.

There are also songs about deaf mountain lions. And mad lions. But that is the flower world.

When I was a kid I sat in the Yaqui village late one night in the house of a man who talked in Spanish or Yaqui, neither of which I understood. His face was pleasant and blank to my eyes. The house was bare and simple, naked light bulbs hanging from the ceiling, a white porcelain sink standing free and gleaming like a treasure in the corner. The hours crawled by. After a while the man, he was the village headman with a secure job on a highway crew, offered me a jar of chiltipins, small red balls of explosive pepper. I did not know what they were and threw a fistful into my mouth. The man laughed silently as I bolted for the faucet.

Later, I sat under the ramada of an old man in his eighties. He swept out the church for the priest. When he smoked a cigarette, the end was soaked from his hungry lips. As a young man he had been a warrior in the Yaqui wars that raked Sonora until the '30s. Now he made flutes from cane. I still have one.

There is a place that is the desert—except that it is the desert made perfect. The deer are there, as they are here, and the flowers. This place is called *sea ania,* there the people are called *Surem.* The Yaqui learned of this place when a man who herded sheep and goats began to envy the hunters he saw decked out in the hides of many animals. He made a bow, fashioned an arrow, and went into the forest. He saw two large antlered deer rasping their horns together and a third, a smaller deer, moving around them. Then he understood: the large deer were making the music and singing, the small deer was dancing. He learned the songs and from that moment on the wall fell between this world and the flower world, the *sea ania.*

They say, for those who know the way, it lies to the east beneath the dawn.

One night at the dances I see this man. He is crawling across the dirt plaza toward the big wooden cross. It is black, mesquite smoke drifts on the March winds, the ground shakes with the stomping of the dance. The Yaquis huddle in a village of shacks less than a mile from the freeway. They are surrounded by the night moans of the city, a pudding of cement and tract houses that has flowed across the desert floor and trapped a half-million Americans in its grid of streets. The dancers do not hear the city, the man crawling does not hear the dance. He is drunk, he is a disgrace, he has, I suppose, violated the sacred rituals of the tribe's Easter. The dancers are in the flower world, the other reality where deer explain the nature of life to Yaquis.

They can do this but I cannot. The village has these problems, the heroin dealers, the lack of money, and of course the drunks. These matters cannot enter the flower world. The drunk has crawled on another ten years, he is covered with dust and strange grunts and cries pour out of his foamy mouth. No one says anything to him. No one tries to stop him. He does not exist in the flower world. So he does not exist.

Men who are not dancing sit on benches and smoke cigarettes. They wear deer heads. The drunk is struggling to his feet now, he is at the big cross that dominates the plaza. He cannot keep his head erect, he weaves and staggers forward. I am the only human being in the village who will look at him, but then he and I are not in the flower world. He lunges forward, drapes his outstretched arms on the cross. There, the silhouette against the fire: crucifixion.

Before the Spaniards arrived, all the people divided into two groups—the *Surem* and the *Yoemem*. A young *Surem* girl listened to a talking tree and when her people heard the tree's prophecies they decided to hold a dance. When it ended the *Surem* went into the earth. They are enchanted. Some argue that they became ants or dolphins, others say they still look human—they are just magical. To this day, a *Yoemem* will stumble on a *Surem*, a visitor from the enchanted world, the flower world. Such a meeting may kill the *Yoemem*.

This is the way Felipe Molina reports the matter in a book. He is a Yaqui living near Tucson. He also notes, "for that reason, my grandfather and especially my grandmother disapproved of me going into the desert alone."

Perhaps, that is where the interest in lions began. For years, decades, I find their tracks, their dung, their lairs. But I never see one. I look for almost twenty-five years before I so much as catch a glimpse, the green eyes burning in the night.

Harley Shaw stands up in the Gila County courthouse and explains some new rules on killing lions and reporting the killing of lions and the how and the why of it. He is the bridge in this room between the men out on the land and the people who never see the land but make the rules for it. The walls of the room are decorator-selected soft tones and there is no clue within this chamber that this is the ground that spawned fables of the West. Zane Grey, a dentist, sought out this place to hunt and fish and pump the memories of local people for tales, odd yarns that he could stretch into short books for insurance salesmen bored with their jobs and their women back in Pittsburgh. The Pleasant Valley War left blood just to the north, the grizzly staged a last stand here. Just on top of the Rim in the town of Young with Moon's Saloon on the main dirt drag, the village hugging the edge of Pleasant Valley. In the '50s a woman tells me the boys were lounging out in front knocking back some cool ones when the first motorcycle to ever beat its way out of Tonto Basin came rolling down the street. They shot its tires out so as to have a better look.

The lions have never left, never given ground.

When Harley Shaw went to college, he wrote a paper in his freshman English class on Ben Lilly, a legendary hunter who died in 1936. Lilly started in Alabama and worked his way west slaughtering bears, coyotes, wolves, and lions. Once he guided for Theodore Roosevelt. He married twice, but these ventures did not work out. His first wife went insane, his second wife he abandoned. He was a solitary man, a religious man, who followed his hounds on foot six days a week subsisting on a little parched corn. At sundown on Saturday, he tied his dogs—Ben Lilly would not hunt on the Sabbath. If a dog failed to perform up to his standards, he beat it to death. He ended up in Arizona's Blue River country exterminating the last holdouts among the grizzlies and wolves. His name still conjures up tales in that region. For hunters, Ben Lilly is truly a legend—Texas folklorist J. Frank Dobie once wrote a book stating just that in the title, *The Ben Lilly Legend.* Shaw as a boy was fascinated by wildlife and so Lilly, the premier killer, was a link to the natural world for a boy growing up in the valley east of Phoenix.

Now Shaw is older and he is Arizona's expert on mountain lions. He remembers his fascination with Lilly and a soft grin graces his face. Harley Shaw has spent eighteen years following the lions on foot, on horseback, behind dogs, from airplanes.

He has never killed one.

*   *   *

Like us, lions kill. In the Southwest, their house occupies about 150 square miles on the average, and they move patiently through its many rooms. They are 5.5 to 7.5 feet long, the weight ranging from 75 to 190 pounds. We seldom see them: perhaps if lucky, once in a lifetime. But they always see us. They like to watch, they will follow us at that slow walk for hours. They almost never attack—in Arizona perhaps once a decade according to our records. They seem not to regard us as a suitable source of food. But the kill is the thing and what they like is something around a hundred pounds and alive. Studies in Arizona find about one out of every five kills is a calf. They eat what they kill, not what others have killed. We have studied this matter and we have numbers to comfort us. Every ten and a half days, an adult will kill. Or, if a mother, every 6.8 days. In certain regions, at certain times, under certain conditions. Because we really know very little about them, very, very little. Our major contact with them has always been on bloody ground, the kill.

I am standing in a patch of chaparral on the edge of Salt River north of Globe and the rancher is angry in that slow, hard way that ranchers vent their emotions. The voice is flat, almost monotone, the face placid. In one month he has lost thirty-four calves to them with calves worth hundreds of dollars apiece. But it is more than the money. It is the kill, the neck punctured by those large teeth, the small animal ripped open like an envelope. It is logical to argue that he was merely going to raise the calves to a certain weight and then ship them off to eventual slaughter. But this fact does not abate a rancher's anger. The calves were under his care, *his care,* and he has been violated by a force he never sees but whose presence he constantly suspects. He calls in the expert hunters and has seven of them taken off his land. That was months ago, but still he is not at peace. The fury of finding those dead calves in the morning light will not leave his eyes. He reaches the conclusion that many others have who stumble into their country: they like the killing.

And perhaps they do.

We will never find out.

We do not know how to ask.

It is just before Christmas. A mountain lion workshop clogs the lobby of a fine old hotel with 150 biologists, guides, animal control folk (trackers, trappers, poisoners, and hunters), plus a handful of conservationists, all tossing down drinks during the get-acquainted cocktail hour. A rumor floats through the room, one brought here by a government hunter from California. A woman, about fifty-one, has been found. The skull said to be punctured by a large tooth mark. The other whispered signs offer unmistakable evidence of a kill. The autopsy, well, that's the kicker, the autopsy, according to the rumor, suggests that the woman was alive while being eaten.

The kill.

I have come here with my simple question: What is it like to kill with your mouth? The biologists turn away when I ask. There are things about the wilds, we are not supposed to say.

And this brings us down to perhaps the fundamental fault line between us and lions. Our basic contact with mountain lions is the kill and yet what little we know suggests this is not the major portion of a mountain lion's life. Harley Shaw has studied lions in Arizona for eighteen years and he is the host of this big workshop. He is fifty-one now, the hair and trimmed beard silver, a bearlike man who is not tall, the eyes and voice very alert and deliberate. At times, he can be a bundle of statistics and graphs and scat samples and radio-collared plottings of lions. But now he is sitting down and just talking.

"Lions," he says, "more than other animals, have time for contemplation. They lay up, seek high places and vistas. So you wonder what goes through their minds."

You certainly do.

As soon as we knew they were around, we tried to kill them. When the Jesuit priests hit Baja at the end of the seventeenth century, they ran into a culture, one now vanished which we recall as the Pericue, that refused to slay lions. Imagine it is three hundred years ago and Father Ugarte, a large man and a strong man, wants the lion dead. The cat comes in the night, slaughters the mission stock at his outpost in southern Baja, then vanishes. The Indians will not kill the beast—if they do, they say they too will die. The priest is riding his mule on a narrow path, he sees a lion, throws the stone, the animal dies. He places the warm body across his mule, rides back to the mission, and shows off his trophy. The Indians watch, the priest does not die. See, he says, now you are free, now you can kill the lions.

We have not stopped since that moment. As a people, we've had a hard time abiding lions because they want what we want: meat, especially venison, lamb, and beef. Take Arizona. Between 1918 and 1947, 2,400 lions were killed in Arizona. Mainly, they were taken out for killing stock. Legendary men emerged like Uncle Jim Owens of the Grand Canyon country who is said to have bagged 1,100 cats in his lifetime. A man named Jack Butler is reported around 1929 to have killed fifty-eight in eighteen months in the Sowats and Kanab Wash area around the Canyon. Government animal control people tried poison, traps, dogs, bullets—everything in their arsenal. In 1947, the state legislature took a look at the situation and decided to offer a bounty, one that floated between $50 and $100 for the next twenty-two years. They were moved to add this incentive because decades of lion killing had not seemed to dent the lion population. When the bounty finally became dormant in 1969 (it is still technically on the books ready to come to life if desired) another 5,400 lions had been knocked down.

All over the West (with the exception of Texas) attitudes about lions began to change in the sixties, and first one state and then another shifted them from varmints to game animals, started issuing hunting tags, and generally tried to manage them just like deer, bighorn sheep, elk, and antelope. Arizona made this shift in 1970 when it allowed one lion per hunter per year, stopped funding the bounty system, and gave control of the beast to the Game and Fish Department. Stock-killing lions could still be taken out by ranchers if they contacted the government.

What is the net result? No one's really sure. There are somewhere between two thousand and three thousand lions in Arizona—nobody has any good way to count them. The hunt has now been limited to six months a year, and Game and Fish is busily studying their new charges. Each twelve months between two hundred and four hundred of the cats are killed (the state figures run around two hundred, but some critics figuring in estimates of unreported rancher kills tend toward the high end). And after a century or more of slaughter they are still out there. In the American West there is no place where lions are endangered. They have survived without our help, they have survived in the face of our hatred.

*   *   *

Whenever I drive to southern Sonora, I pass through a corridor of Yaqui land and Yaqui villages. The women wear long dresses and scarves, the men Levis and straw hats. Both look very dark. On the southern edge of their land, I hit Ciudad Obregón. Once the town was not called Obregón, but after a different man. To the *Yori* he was Jose María Leyva, but to the *Yoemem* he was Cajeme, He-who-does-not-drink. When the Mexicans came to take the land in the 1880s and to plant Mexican colonists there, Cajeme raised four thousand men, built a fort, won battles, drew blood. The Mexicans, of course, did not surprise the Yaquis with their behavior, the tribesmen believed that the Mexicans originated in piles of garbage and came writhing forth reeking of their birth. Of course, they kept coming and finally Cajeme's forces gathered in the foothills of the Bacatetes and lost. He fled, fought on with a few followers, and was captured. The Mexicans took photographs.

And then he went before a firing squad.

It all began almost as soon as they met. The Yaquis lived on the bottomlands of the river and that was the land the new people wanted. The war began whenever you wish to begin it, but for a century, from the 1820s to the 1920s, it periodically flamed up and licked the fabric of Sonora just as a buried inferno slowly eats out the veins of a coal mine. The Yaqui leaders appeared at the appropriate moments—Juan Banderas, a man who had nightly visions and rode by day with two thousand armed Indians in the 1820s; Cajeme in the 1880s; and finally, in the 1890s, Tetabiate, "Rolling Stone." At the Peace of Ortiz in 1897 the Mexicans had promised, according to the Yaquis, to leave their country and let them alone. It is May 17, 1897, and a large platform has been built by the railroad tracks at Ortiz. General Luis E. Torres waits, and out of the dust Tetabiate rides in with four hundred men each carrying the white flag of peace. But the Mexicans deceive, their promises are lies. According to Yaqui accounts of that day, General Torres looks up and sees the Archangel Michael watching and then the General promptly shits his pants.

The war, of course, continues. During the first decade of the twentieth century, Yaquis are rounded up like beasts and marched to the hemp plantations of Yucatán, where most die. The diaspora reaches out from the jungles of the Maya to the barrios of Los Angeles. Tetabiate is hunted down and killed. For decades his grave is visited by those seeking fire so they can face the future.

At times, the tribe that sought the flower world and understood the songs of mountain lions presented a different face to the world. But then so do lions, when the kill becomes the matter at hand.

I have a friend who has spent a long life in the desert and he loves to tell stories of his life on the line. He is very good at the telling. There is the old Mexican he knew who lived through the Yaqui wars that terrorized Sonora for decades. The man was on a train south of Hermosillo when the Yaquis stopped it. They lined up all the Mexicans and said, *"¡Culo o mato!* Ass or die!"

My friend asked the old Mexican, "What did you do?"

The man answered, "I am alive, am I not?"

* * *

Almost no one has ever seen a lion kill. There are millions of people living in the desert, they are crawling up every canyon, the families are picnicking under the willows by every mountain stream, the bulldozers claw at every roll of the bajadas, the satellites spin by day and night with giant glass eyes watching everything that moves. But still almost no one has ever seen a lion kill.

But we can guess some things from the kills we find. Harley Shaw has seen many kills, made his notes, puzzled out the action that is now dry blood, broken bones, empty eyes with flies buzzing in the air. He has written a book, *Soul Among Lions,* and then rewritten the book and then rewritten the rewritten book. He has drifted into an obsession. The thing floats around as a manuscript, the publishers look, consider, hesitate. It is not a normal book by a normal biologist. The facts are all there, the slender scraps of fact we have sifted from the world of the lion. But there is a feeling gnawing at Harley as he studies his field notes and tries to understand how the cats eat. He has gotten too close, and he knows it. "I have begun," he writes, "to dislike the ways humans view themselves." He has begun to see the world through a lion's eyes—he cannot see that world, he has learned too much, sensed too much to ever think he can see that world, but he has a feel for its presence and that has changed how the things now look through his eyes. Now he is there, he is so close, it is all in his notes, in his mind, in his senses as he thinks about lions, and it is not nearly enough, barely a beginning. He has about studied himself out of a profession, biologist. As he notes dryly of his work, "You will be forced to reexamine your beliefs."

They are out there right now, looking down at us from the sierras, cruising silently across the desert floor, lying up on a cliff and watching, waiting for the glimpse of the right thing. They cannot run, cannot really run at all, and everything must be a brief sprint. The lion drops down, creeps, slides, it must get within fifty feet or less if it is to succeed. The lion is alone, in this act almost always alone, a single force that must always do its work alone.

This colors the act.

The object of desire should be around a hundred pounds or less. The lion weighs seventy, eighty, ninety, perhaps a hundred pounds—sometimes a lot more, but not usually. The animal is not as large as the feeling the name *lion* conjures up in our minds and hearts. The lion does not seek a fight, a combat. This would be a dangerous choice. The broken rib, the torn muscle, and that half step is lost, the micro-second of speed and grace vanishes, and then the hunger comes and weakness follows that and the thing spirals into death. So the fight must be avoided.

The object is close now, a deer, browsing, alert, but as yet unaware. The skin of the deer is a fur almost gray in this light. It drifts among the chaparral, a ghost that is alive. The sun is up and warm on the gray fur but still it eats, feeling safe in the cover of the brush. It begins to happen, the lion is close, belly to the ground, and now it surges, slithers forward, and nears. The cat rises up on its hind feet and those big front paws with sharp claws sink into the deer's back and the animal goes to ground instantly. The mouth opens—feel the warm breath?—and the jaws settle around the back of the neck and the teeth penetrate the muscles near the base of the skull.

There are nerve endings at the base of the big teeth, very sensitive endings, and as the fangs plunge and tear through the warm flesh these endings pick up that gap between the vertebrae and the teeth slide in, the lion swings its jaws, the neck snaps. Death washes across the deer's face. Harley has seen many kills and if the lion is an adult, an experienced killer, it is over very fast, it seems—the sites show little if any signs of struggle. With younger cats—and it takes a lioness almost two years to train up her kittens to a good and proper kill—it may be messier. Attacks on humans usually involve cats under two years, those who have not mastered the feel of the kill and the risks of the kill. Sometimes when a doe is killed, the fawn lingers around and is killed later. There is speculation that such objects provide training for kittens.

What happens next the biologists can only guess, but this is the guess: the lion leaves the kill, goes off a short ways, and lies down for perhaps an hour. The stalk, the leap, the teeth probing for that gap between the vertebrae, the rush of hot blood against the tongue, all these things have stimulated the lion and it is not a proper time to eat until calm returns to the well-muscled body.

Now it is ready and rises and walks slowly back to the deer. The lion drags it across the ground to some place that suggests safety, perhaps under a tree or a rock. It is time to feed. First, the cat clears the hair with its teeth from the deer where it will be entered—typically just behind the ribs, Harley notes. The procedure here is thorough, much the way humans prep for surgery. The claws flash, the deer is opened up. First the heart, liver, and lungs are devoured, then, it seems, the back legs with the meat on the interior of the legs taken first. The stomach and intestines are pulled out and ignored. Eight to ten pounds of flesh may be swallowed at this first feeding.

Then the animal is covered. The cat will toss up grass, brush, soil, rocks, something, to cover the kill. Why, we can only spec-ulate—to hide it from other animals? to keep the meat cool to delay spoiling? Harley once found a mule-deer kill on solid rock. The cat had placed a single twig on the animal.

The lion retreats, perhaps a couple of hundred yards, and beds down. It will lay up where it can see and come back often to check the kill. What does it do while lying up there, the desert a vista before it, or the oaks of the canyon a carpet unrolling in front of it? This is not a small matter. The kills come every three to ten days in the desert. It depends, in part, on how long the meat lasts before going bad. Or so we suspect. We really have no clear ideas why lions abandon kills. There are just little glimpses. One cat in Idaho stayed and fed off an elk kill for nineteen days. What goes through the brain for nineteen days as the meat is engorged and then come the quiet hours sprawled up high, the eyes staring out at the big empty?

Normally, the lions will not eat carrion. If they do not kill it, they do not eat it. This has made them hard to poison. The wolves, they are gone from the Arizona desert. The grizzlies are gone. The lion is not.

Of course, kills vary. If the animal is large, the lion cannot reach up and sink those claws in deeply. Then the teeth go to the throat—Harley has a photograph in color, everything very red and bloody, of an elk's windpipe with a big puncture in it, the hole a memory of the cat's tooth. Then the lion kills by suffoca-tion. But this is to be avoided. Those who follow the cats, whether to study them or kill them, agree on one thing: a lion is not likely to leap from a ledge or drop down out of a tree onto the back of a large animal. Such a ride is dangerous and for lions danger is not the drug it seems to be for human beings. They will kill anything: steers, horses, sheep, elk, desert sheep, deer, javelina, people. They must eat. But all things being equal, the object of desire will not be too large, it will not struggle, the claws will grip the shoulders, the mouth will open, the teeth, those wonderful teeth with sensitive nerves at the base, will probe and find that gap between the vertebrae and the neck will snap. Death descends like a summer shower, the lion walks off and rests. Then an area will be cleaned of hair for the incision. . . .

* * *

The *Yoemem* have this mad-mountain-lion song where the beast jumps on the deer and drags the head around and when a coyote ambles by, why the lion punches him out.

> Over there, I, at the edge
>   of the flower-covered enchanted water,
>   on one wood branch,
>   I am brown,
>   dangling, hanging,
>   mad mountain lion.
> Mountain lion is mad,
>   there in the wilderness,
>   is mad.

* * *

The lobby is fine soft couches, lamps casting warm yellow light, good wood in the tables, a fireplace that swallows large logs. On the ceiling beams, delicate floral abstractions open and spin across the painted surface. The floor is tile and cool to the eye. A woman plays the grand piano and sings the songs that you hum in elevators but can never name. One hundred and fifty lion people mill about this lobby. They drink, form small knots of conversation, eye each other's name tags. They have come from all over the United States and Canada, wherever the lion still hunts. Harley Shaw is the host. He wears a dark sportcoat with leather patches and looks like a professor of Elizabethan poetry with his silver hair, trimmed silver beard. This is the world of the *per diem* people, those who work in state agencies, federal agencies, who plunder government for grants so that they can continue their researches in universities. These are the lions' official modern keepers. Everyone standing here with a glass of wine or bottle of beer in hand cashes checks signed in blood by the big carnivore that courses the mountains and flats leaving carcasses in its wake. This is not part of the rumble of conversations.

The lobby is filled with people who focus on the killing, men dressed in tight Levis, wearing cowboy boots, the faces weathered, the hair trimmed, that careful mustache, the deliberate hat with the brim exactly bent. These men speak little if at all, they are ranch people, sometimes descended from lion-killing families. Now, as the West shrinks and business takes the land for esoteric tax purposes, they hang on as federal and state killers of the wild things that make up the West that has always held them in its thrall.

They traffic in stories, anecdotes, glimpses of the trail and the hunt. Harley moves easily with them: they know what he wants to know. Science here searches folklore like a hungry scavenger seeking a clue that will destroy the mysteries. There was this cat in the Big Bend area of Texas that took to attacking people in the park, so it was captured and shipped to Florida where a big state project seeks to salvage the last few panthers huddled in the Everglades under the glow of the hot, cocaine night skies. Now the problem lion lives in a cage in a research center. Captive lions not subjected to mobs in zoos tend to be very shy and try to crawl under things when they see people. This one stares the biologists straight in the eye, gets up and presses against the wire. So they do an X-ray, find a dark mass in the brain, and speculate it may be a tumor or a viral blob. They consider killing the lion, cutting open its head and looking at the brain. There has to be some reason why it does not cower in our presence.

There are many things to be explained. Recently, a lion was killed on the road near Fresno, California, and others are seen often on the local golf course even though it is fifteen miles across the big agri-business fields to the sierra.

Death, that is the only place in which we can get near. Why do we want to get near? Why do we crave to get so very, very near? That is not a question to be asked, it is forbidden. We have our excuses. I will tell them to you. There is this thing called depredation—that means the lion eats things we want to eat, kills things we wish to kill. The calf stares blankly up at the hot sky, neck broken, underbelly ripped open, body gnawed, bones crushed like small sticks. The sheep scattered willy-nilly, twenty, thirty sheep dead, so dead, and only one or two even eaten. The rest, just killed, wantonly we say, killed for sport we say. Killed for reasons we cannot comprehend. And if we do not act, act right now, the lion will be back at nightfall and kill again and again and again. Depredation, we say.

Besides depredation, we say science. We want to answer the mysteries of life, curious questions of gestation, digestion, population densities, nurture, movement, prey selection, social organization. Diet. We want to put radio collars on them, we want to dart them with drugs and take their vital signs, spend many hours sorting out the remains in their scat. Weigh them, measure them, consider blood type, disease vectors. Learn how to determine their age by putting calipers to their teeth. Science, an excellent screen for our desires.

Besides science, there is envy. That is the one we will not speak of. Not at all, seldom if ever. Envy. We go where they are. We take a truckload of dogs, pull the horses in a trailer behind us. The hounds are released, we saddle up and ride. We carry guns. We carry our food, cover our body with fabrics in order to endure the weather. Sometimes we have radios so that the hunters can communicate constantly. It has taken us years to train the dogs, hundreds and hundreds of hours on the trail. And if we are lucky, we may tree a lion. The cats, they are out there alone, they carry their culture inside their bodies, they move anywhere, set up a universe wherever they decide to lie up. When hungry, they kill and dine day after day after day. They breed—meeting by some miracle of scent like two lonely ships in an endless sea—train up their young, push on.

I am having a drink and I tell a woman of the kill, the special nerves at the base of the teeth feeling the gap between the vertebrae. She says, "I want to feel that."

"Be a lion?" I ask.

"It doesn't matter," she says. "I'm willing to be either."

That envy. And from that envy comes our love. It is not a normal love, or perhaps it is, but at any rate it is not the love we normally admit to. It is not a desire to share or nurture or protect. It is much stronger than that, more powerful in its effects. It is a desire to join them.

So of course, we must kill them, kill every damn one of them.

* * *

The Greek restaurant is near the University and this is a quick break for a faculty member. A big new road may knife through some barrios, here are the plans, here are the arguments—stop the road. His hair is blond, his eyes alert behind the glasses, the issues crisp. Development versus neighborhoods, cars versus whatever, the present versus the past. And of course, his house, which sits in a barrio about to be amputated by the new road.

Before the road, there was Don Jesús, a Yaqui who had taught the man I'm having lunch with some deer songs for a book. A curious thing happened when he was doing the book with a Yaqui who lived in Arizona. They'd been down there in Sonora and Don Jesús took sick. The professor and his Yaqui friend could not stay with the old man because they had to get back to the States. They drove north to Arizona and their homes and that night they both had dreams. The faculty member woke up his wife to tell her that he had dreamed of Don Jesús. The Yaqui also dreamed. In his dream, he is watching a woman making tortillas and sees the image of the Virgin of Guadalupe on one, an angry cloud appears on the horizon and the rain comes down. The drops are on fire. The man's uncle tells him such a rain comes once every few centuries and he begins to sing a deer song. The stanzas tumble out and the uncle becomes Don Jesús.

Down on the Rio Yaqui, people say that during Don Jesús's last hours his heart was over Arizona and from that fact the dreaming came. The rain of fire is another matter.

The songs do not seem to end. The voices speak a strange language, one that sounds hard to the ears. The flower world beckons, but who can believe in it? The *Yoemem* sing.

> Where the enchanted spotted mountain lion ate,
>   a fawn's head was found.
> An enchanted, enchanted buzzard
>   was not hovering there.
> An enchanted, enchanted big coyote
>   was sounding there.

*   *   *

They see a thin line between us and them. And they guard this line with guns, poison, and words. We are standing, beers in hand, and the talk flows with missionary ease. Darrel C. Juve works for the Department of Agriculture in Arizona but he does not farm. He kills. The term is Animal Damage Control and what he does is patrol that thin line between us and them.

He's in his late forties now and his world is plain. "A lion," he says briskly, "is nothing but a big housecat. Curious."

It's not just the lions, no, no, there are coyotes out there, bears, and if you look up, my God, the birds. Juve speaks without a smile, his eyes scanning people to see if they understand, if they can handle his message. Ravens? They kill. They kill calves, they kill steers. Drop down from the sky and peck their eyes out, blind them, and then comes the hard death with these black birds pecking, pecking, pecking.

We've made some progress. Take the wolf, he's gone. "There's a good reason," he almost snaps, "why they were wiped out in the West." And then he pauses to make sure his next words truly sink in: "They destroyed millions of dollars of livestock." His face has that tension in it, the tension flooding a man who knows, who really knows, and yet has learned that others will shun his knowing.

He's got eleven people under him, the calls come in each day, there is no way to keep up, no way at all. The lion complaints alone would bury his force if they dealt with all of them. People, he continues, have lost touch with reality. Only four percent of the population produces the food for the other ninety-six percent, and now you see people going into supermarkets and tossing a nice plastic-wrapped chunk of meat in their baskets and they have no idea where or how that piece of flesh got there.

"People don't understand," he says with cold anger, "that for them to eat, something has to die. We try to attach sentimentality to animals without ever thinking about what is really going on out there. *Humane* is not a word spoken by Mother Nature. The mass media depict wild animals in unrealistic terms."

He is struggling now, trying to rein in his feelings, to make the words seem like a reasonable position, one arrived at after much research, the product of cool detachment by a scholar sitting in his study before the fire and musing over a glass of fine sherry. But he cannot maintain the tone.

"They," he flames up again, "they think there is a 'balance of nature'—that's bullshit. There is no balance out there."

Out there. The heart of darkness. The ground where we are not in control. Wait, twist the lens, see it zoom into focus? Yes, that ground, the world seen through a lion's eyes, the warm blood-soaked breath flowing out the cat's open mouth. We deny it, we abolish it with fine shots in calendars, with musings about the intricate relationships between all living things. We avert our eyes so that we can always see Eden. Juve, ah, he insists on the teeth at the throat, on those long beaks tearing at the eye of a terrified calf. He wears glasses, Levis, an oval belt buckle inlaid with a coyote (made by a convict, he explains). His brown hair is trimmed, the face seldom smiles, the voice is almost always urgent, the words clipped. He is the man with the mission. He has been Out There. An image rises up from the snap of his sentences: Nature is this teeming, unruly bitch at the gates of our lives, ready at an instant to violate our humanity. She waits out there by the picket fence so white against the green lawn. You stroll out, open the gate, and suddenly she walks out of the desert, dressed smartly, the lips full and inviting, the eyes dangerous with desires. Her hair is black, the teeth very even, the cheekbones strong, the voice, well, you can hear no voice, you merely sense a kind of purring coming off her body. She moves toward you, seems almost to glide, you turn, smile, tip your head silently forward as to say hello. Her dress rustles, a soft silky kind of sound, the hair is long and stirs with the breeze. She is at your throat, the teeth tear and warm blood cascades down your body. Out there.

That is one mountain lion. Harley Shaw thinks the lion exists through human eyes, and the different eyes see different lions:

stock killer, hunter's trophy, curious biological machine for studies by scientists, noble beast of the sierra and bajada. It all depends on who you are. For Harley, the lion exists in a very strange place: he says he cannot conceive of them except in front of hounds. Dogs have shaped his lion world, they are the door or window or what-have-you that permits him to go to the lion world.

He does not think this view has any particular merit. It just is that way for him. Out there, that black place full of sun, is very hard to reach, in the case of the lion almost impossible, and we can only stay a very short while—idle moments standing under a tree while the dogs bay, the wait for the dart to drug the cat, the quick measurements and sampling, your hands running over the warm fur, then retreat, the groggy animal staggering off and vanishing. Flies are buzzing around a kill, you measure scratch marks, you are being watched, you can sense this fact, feel it, but you cannot see. The lion?—the lion is that excited sound in the dogs' throats, the lion is that long slash on the deer's shoulder. The lion is something you make up to fill a big empty spot inside you.

She is standing before an auditorium of lion people, the hair blond, the dress blue, the face smooth and open. The room is dark and the light at the lectern splashes up on her and she seems like a spirit, a clean-smelling angelic form, reading thoughts to the soiled and the human. Slides flash on the screen as row after row of biologists and lion hunters slump in their seats. She is from New England, from some institute or foundation, and the slides express her feelings about the wilds. Big color images of the desert in a real estate ad, huge close-ups of lions with their big tawny faces seeming dignified and noble and innocent. The mouth on the cats in these slides is always closed, the teeth a secret kept from the camera. Of course, there are two kittens sitting on the snow. She reads a poem by D. H. Lawrence, "Elegy to a Mountain Lion." Out There vanishes.

Can we call this love? Juve, like many men who kill animals, has ready explanations for the killing. There is a need. The coyotes, they'll take your dog. The bear, he will eat your calf. The lion, he murders everything he meets. The ravens, they are at the eyes. They must be stopped.

But there is another level in their words. The talk will drift, the drinks will take hold, the pretense of positions will become too great a weight to carry day and night, and then the talk will change. For a century we have been cleaning up the desert, setting this house in order. We have the records, incredible records where everything is columns of bounties paid, wages paid, damages reported, poisons bought and spread, traps set and accounted for, skins piled up and assessed, skulls sent to natural history collections. We have a record. The wolf? Ah, the wolf was easy to take out, he was not that smart. He could not adapt, not at all. The wolf lost, and because he lost to us, he lost our respect. You can hear this behind the words, you can. He lost our respect. The grizzly, he was easy too. Big, stupid, and now gone, and never ever coming back to the desert. We will not permit it. He does not deserve it. We took him out. The coyote, my God, the coyotes, they cannot be beaten, we kill them with guns, traps, poisons. Still they keep coming, and coming. The coyote is our enemy, we must fight him if it takes forever. And then you can hear a kind of love come into the words. The coyote is worthy of our respect. And the lion, nothing seems to touch the lion. They are out there, walking slowly in their kingdoms, and we kill them, kill hundreds of them a year in the desert and still they keep walking slowly across their kingdoms. The men slumped in their seats in the auditorium, the Levis skintight, the black cowboy hats hugging their heads, brims bent low in the front and the back, the large oval belt buckles recording that good day at the rodeo, these men who kill lions worship them. You can hear it in their words, in the horror which they describe of the sheepbeds after a bloody night, the rich language that flows from their mouths when they recount the long, deep rips in a calf's small soft body. The feeling is also there when they speak of the hunt. The cat is so hard to find—if it is hot and dry, the hounds can find no scent; if they find scent the ground is so broken and difficult, the cat sees so well, senses everything, moves so silently, broods without whimpering, slaughters without being seen, lives without our knowing. Except for the blood.

You can hear a kind of love in their words. Without the cats they would not know who they are, would not have a clue. For the lion is something that exceeds their grasp, they have tried everything and still he exceeds their grasp and from this fact, the love comes. The lion has kept the world from getting too small. The men who kill lions are ever vigilant to maintain this reality. Some men hunt lions with trucks, the dogs riding on the hoods until a track is struck, the lead dog wearing a radio collar with a beeper and when a cat is treed and the lead dog bays, the collar lets off a special beep and then the hunters zero in thanks to the radio. This, the men who love to kill lions, this they want outlawed, this they want stopped. They also oppose the winter hunt in the crisp snow because it makes things too easy—"Murder," one snaps with contempt. There are other abominations they oppose. Will-call hunts, where a guide trees a lion, leaves his hounds and a friend under the cat, and then calls that doctor or dentist in the next state who will pay $2,000 or $3,000 for the trophy, and the client then hops a jet and within a day is under the tree, fires once, the cat falls dead, and the hunt is successful. There are also men who trap lions, then cage them, and when a rich man wants to hunt, release this captive just ahead of the hounds. All these things the men who love to kill lions hate. They will admit this fact, they will say it in their low monotones, their lips barely moving, the sentences very short, often merely fragments of sentences.

Love, that word cannot be said. You can feel it, but no one will say it. Who will admit to loving something that will not love you back? There is that rumor floating around the room as we stand and drink, a whispered thing where the men huddle and clutch the beer bottles in their hands. In another state, the whispers go, a woman has been found. She is dead, middle-aged, there are the marks, the right marks on her body. She has been killed by a cat. The autopsy, people almost whisper, suggests that while she was yet alive, the lion fed on her. This can be determined, the murmurs continue, determined from the hemorrhaging. Alive. The rumor floats around the room, an electric current reviving the tired air. Months later, the story will become a vapor, a thing that never happened, that does not check out. But of course, that does not really matter. For there will be new rumors, new tales. They are necessary, the menace is essential to us for reasons we can barely state. The mountains would have a new frightening emptiness if we could not imagine the soft padding of those clawed feet, the unflinching eyes scanning our every move, the muscles rippling under the tawny fur. He is out there. Out There. Love.

But no one will say that word.

Harley Shaw sips his coffee in the saloon. He is very calm, very careful. There are things he thinks about but finds difficult to say, almost dangerous to say. Much of this is in the book that he toiled over. He seems small now as he sits and sips his coffee out of a clear glass cup. The book (and he has finally found a publisher) contains his odyssey—the break that spun him out of turkey studies into lion studies, the early years training the hounds, learning from the lion men, collaring the cats, charting their wanderings. The bad time when he caught a mother and her kittens and a lion kitten died. The sinking—that is what it feels like when he talks or when he writes—the sinking into the idea of lions and then the country of lions and then into some place we do not have a word for. He tries to find the word. He uses that German concept, *umwelt,* the idea that any species is the product of the entire universe and encapsulates the entire universe in its being. Yes, the *umwelt.*

He has worked himself out of what was going to make him Mr. Somebody. That is the problem. The hounds are gone now. He no longer follows them in the saddle, listening for the bay, riding hard over the ridges to see a treed cat. The darts are no longer fired, the chemicals slowly dribbling into the blood, the lion's eyes getting glazed. The radio collars are still. Harley no longer clamps them around the cats' necks. Here he becomes hesitant, careful in what he says. He utters circumspect sentences like "I am not opposed to darting lions if we're gaining some new knowledge." He cannot turn his back on knowledge, that is his business, his job. Gaining that little kernel of fact, writing that journal article—"deep down you know you're doing it to gather knowledge and if there is any immortality it is that you are leaving something that may change things."

But this time he is the thing changed. He has run out of reasons to bother lions. He has run out of the arrogance to think he can penetrate their world. He hates the bureaucracy he works for, he has turned against his own species. He thinks lions should be left alone. To kill.

"You follow them step by step," he explains softly, "and then you relate to them."

The saloon is richly oiled walnut, the barmaids wear fine black slacks, white ruffled shirts, black ties at their delicate throats. They stand by the back bar slowly polishing fine glasses. Their skin is very white, the hair perfect, the movements silent as a cat's. The word *lion* seems as alien as the word *love* in this room. We sit in a cell designed to seal out the air, the scent, the scat, the tracks, the warm blood coursing across the tongue, the tooth seeking ever so surely the gap, the twist. The neck breaks.

How many are there? We don't know. How are they organized?

We can guess. How many types, how many subspecies? We still argue. How do they decide what to kill? We speculate. How long do they live? There is no counting. What do they matter? We have no idea.

Harley backs away from the questions. "We should go camping," he says. Maybe in the dark hours, the fire crackling, our tongues loosened by liquor, the blackness protecting our faces, maybe then our minds will be freed from our roles, maybe then we can talk.

You can love something that is not beautiful, that is not useful, that is not easy. That is not safe. But you cannot know it.

Harley is talking again, even more softly. He admires things that can be solitary, he says. There have been some bad marriages, hard nights, solitary is not a thing to be despised if it can be endured. He sees the lion clearly now in his mind, the beast floods the room with its scent, the big pads move silently across the saloon floor.

"Out there," he says suddenly, "out there alone without tools, without shelter, without food. Down deep I have an image of myself as being totally wild. And I know I never will."

Out there.

Love waits. With long teeth.

6

He is always drunk. Drunk in the morning, drunk at noon, drunk at night. The anger burns within him and the booze rises off his skin as a hateful steam in the dry air. It is summer in the desert, his baby daughter sleeps in the cheap house with a small fan blowing air over the crib. He needs a drink, my God, he needs one, oh, so bad. He unplugs the fan and leaves to sell it for a bottle.

We sit under the trees and drink too much and talk about the desert. We argue and he never gives in. He insists that my concerns are foolish, that the desert always wins, always endures, always, always, always. This is years ago, of course. It gets so I can no longer take it, the drinking, the air of imminent catastrophe. I go dry for a spell and he disappears from my life. Now I am standing in line at that fast-food joint and this man looms up and says, Do you remember me? He is forty-one, the body thickened with age, but he is the same person. Except for one thing, the eyes. The eyes are no longer as angry, no longer cloudy, no longer feral. He has not had a drink in twelve years.

I say, "What are you doing now?"

He says, "I make beautiful things."

I think that is a brave thing to say.

He says, "You must come to León with me."

Where is that?

So we go.

The moon is over León, a crescent moon waxing between a quarter and a third. The village strung along the arroyo glows in the white light, the cottonwoods stand guard along the channel. Coyotes cry and their messages ride the night wind. Dogs answer without conviction or heart. I can hear a faint rustling of the creosote, catch the outlines of saguaros to the west against the sierra. I look at the mountain hoping for the warm glow, the burning fire of gold beckoning to be freed from the earth. This happens here, anyone will tell you that. But there is no golden flame this night.

I can smell mesquite smoke coiling off the fires. The small mud house sits contentedly on the lip of the bajada right where the fields begin. The fence is cut ocotillo, the gate a yellow car door, both framing the yard. The wands of ocotillo look black and bristly. From the open windows of nearby houses my eye catches the warm breath of kerosene lamps shedding yellow against the cool stucco walls. Perhaps three hundred people sleep here tonight. On the horizon I see the night lights of a nearby town where the drug people run the streets, of Magdalena where Padre Kino's exposed bones sit in a shrine before the church. They have been baking in the hot earth for more than two and a half centuries. That small button rests on the Padre's sternum, a thing unexplained. The skull is very smooth and the grin is the usual one from the gates of hell.

Far to the north, I can make out the glow of Nogales across the sierra, the city squatting like an angry beast on the border. But mostly, there is Sonora, Sonora is everywhere here and Sonora pulls you down to its dirt and ways and dreams.

Al is in the hut sleeping. That is what he comes here for, he says, to dream. Painters have these habits and odd needs. The hut's three windows have no glass, the small fireplace in the corner is newly made from raw adobe and leaks smoke like a sieve. My bed is six forked ironwood posts buried in the dirt floor, the mattress saguaro ribs. No one in León sleeps on such a bed anymore. Don Pedro, the eighty-year-old man in the neighboring house, about fifty yards and two small gullies away, he made this bed because Al requested it. This is the kind of bed that at one time everyone in León slept on. But that was long ago, before even the *problema* came to the desert valley. Before the world beckoned with solid rewards. Al wants to go back, he has to go back because for him the dreams are better if he goes back.

When he was a boy, he lived on a farm outside Caborca, another Indian village Father Kino impaled with a cathedral. It is farther down the drainage from León, just at the point where the stream surrenders, sinks into the sands, and lets the desert begin to hold absolute sway. Sonora is just dirt in those days, dirt roads, dirt houses, everything dirt. When his family wishes to get out and travel, say to Mexicali, to go and see a paved street, they travel five miles away to the train line. It is night, they build a fire by the tracks, a big bonfire, the engineer sees this orange glow in the desert night, slows, and they hop on. The Mexicans who work the farm get time off every four months and then go to town for that woman and that bottle. Now the farm is devoured by Mexico, nothing left of the houses and huts but one palm tree and a woman's shoe. Al went back, always a mistake, and that is all he found. The rest is straight furrows tracking across endless irrigated fields. Caborca, it too is changed. That is Caro Quintero country, a center of the *problema.*

The hut has no electricity, no water, a bird nests in the chimney and the smoke backflushes into the room. The floor is dirt. The toilet is the desert that rolls for miles behind the house unto the sierra. Beneath the creosote lie the bones of steers, gleaming white under the hungry moon. They are relics of the droughts that rake the valley from time to time. Everything here takes Al back to the dreams.

He has tried to capture this very moment. In his painting, the moon is huge, a monstrous yellow crescent rising like a beast behind the sierra. The village is ever so orderly, the white *capilla* with its small cross looms slightly larger than the small perfect white houses. The ground is brown and if you put your hand to it, you will feel the warm blood of the campesinos. That is Al's painting of the moon over León. Like all his work, he signs it Alfonso. And then a date. The signature is very large, very insistent. This art thing has not come easily to him. For five years he painted without realizing that by mixing white with a color he could make it lighter, paler. He really cannot be taught but must learn everything his own way. His eyes see things that others do not. His village lives inside his head somewhere.

Tonight, for example, the moon is white, not yellow, it does not rise from the sierra behind the *capilla,* but hangs like a milky torch in the center of the sky. And the buildings, while white, are not nearly so clean and pure or so ordered. The ground under my feet is rough with broken stones and pale in the white light. I cannot see the brown earth now or feel the warm blood of *la gente* of León. I stand in the yard and listen to nothing. Alfonso does not awaken. He comes here to dream as the moon drifts over León.

The place? From whence sprang this place? Don Pedro says, as the old men say in thousands of Mexican villages, that when he was a young boy the oldest man then alive did not know the beginnings of León. Doña Flora, his wife, sits by the kerosene lamp, her face corrugated with deep wrinkles, a glowing Fiesta cigarette in her hand, and listens. She says finally, "Only God knows the beginning of León."

They are amused by the question. It does not matter to them. León is now an *ejido*—a Mexican land collective recognized by law—but it has been a communal village for a long, long time. Somewhere in the dust under my feet lies an Indian hearth, the outlines of crude buildings, stone tools carelessly left, metates worn out from the ceaseless grinding of corn. I have a stone axe head perfectly formed that a farmer found in the spring when he plowed his field here. For thousands of years people have huddled on this ground and worked out ways to suck life from the desert. No one knows the beginning of León. It is the present that matters, the endless present that unfolds by minute, hour, day, season, and year. That is what Alfonso comes for, that is where the dreams live. In the brutal warm tasks of daily life.

On a rise a few miles east of the village is a small shrine by the road. A man was driving back from Magdalena, he was driving very fast because there was another car packed with men chasing him. The shrine marks where they caught up with him and killed him. No one remembers the reasons for his murder. That was years and years ago and the shrine now looks naked in the desert and wants paint and the visit of a fistful of paper flowers. There is no love, it seems, still bathing this memory. Someday, perhaps someday soon, no one in the village will remember the man's panic-stricken ride on the dirt of the Magdalena road, the car cutting him off, that shot in the night. His frightened eyes as death descended and his retinas went glassy and then blank. Perhaps then the shrine will crumble back to the earth, the man's family will lose sight of the fact that he is their ancestor, the scab on this old wound will close over, and only the desert will know. No one will care.

I am standing outside under the moon sipping mezcal from a tin cup, the brand "Bacatete," named after the range that the Yaquis always retreated into, the rock pile that was their ultimate sanctuary in their endless wars for their land and their customs. A Yaqui deer dancer prances on the label but none of the Spanish words make note of the flower world. Al, Alfonso, does not mind the drink. He says, "All of my friends are drunks, or ex-drunks." I can see the sense in his remark. That happens on this ground. It is hard to hold to a mean here, a harmony, a point of balance.

I have come here to rest and hide and sink into something. Technically, this is narcotics country. If there is a heart to the beast, a center to the squalor of the life, it is here, exactly here.

The business is said to be everywhere. You wish to take a walk and so, of course, you check with Don Pedro.

The east is fine?

Sí.

The south?

Sí.

The west toward the sierra?

No problema.

The north?

Oh, I would not walk north today.

The problem, the hydra-headed creature that stimulates the wives of presidents to scold, that fires up American politicians to babble about a drug war. Ah, that blistering television montage of crack houses, bodies flopping in rubber bags as they are trundled out of cheap tenements. Of slow-burning joints whispering up from ashtrays in public-service announcements that warn one drag will destroy your precious mind. The crazed eyes of lawyers as they pummel my legal tangles but first must make a quick trip to the bathroom and hop a little ride on the train called cocaine. The bodies found in the arroyos, left packaged like Christmas presents. Those young men with gold chains, tight Levis, new pickups with chrome roll bars, young men crowding the cheap cafes on the south side of Tucson, there they sit cradling pistols between their legs as they discuss The Deal. The brightly dressed women with eyes widened by mascara who follow these warriors much as *soldaderas,* the camp followers of the men, did in the *revolucion.* The man dreaming in his room with gold gilt on everything, frescoes over his head, his shoulders squared as he sits on his throne and enjoys the fruits of his passage through the life. The man who has had fifteen or twenty attempts on his life in the last few and oh so swift years.

I remember standing in the moonlight by a fine house built on stilts, a big house far away from León, one that overlooks the lights of my city raging below. My hips are sweltering in the hot tub and I look up at the blond woman dressed in high heels, the rest of her skin white and naked. She bends over to hand me a joint, sweet smoke clogging my nostrils. She cannot seem to make it through very many days without a joint. Her breasts swing before my face, her smile is wide and warm and purrs, yes, yes.

Or the line of white powder on the smooth wood top of the saloon bar, the woman carefully measuring it out. I look into her face and see the covers pulled back, soft, half-dark bedrooms dance in her enlarged eyes. The rush of desert air across my face at night as the truck races, the headlights of oncoming traffic seem huge and yet so soft—I want to reach out and stick my hand in those headlights and feel the warmth—the tape player rippling with currents of sound and everyone and everything and every place on the surface of the earth good and proper and in tune with me, in tune with me at this very instant. Until it begins to wear off and we will need more.

My eyes scan the sleeping valley where León nestles, drink deeply of the light dripping from the moon, and what I see is Doña Flora's face, deep canyons worn in it by decades of life, and what she is saying is *"mal dar,"* bad give. Yes, I think, *mal dar,* bad give.

But that quickly passes and only her face remains, the smell of fried coffee on the stove, the taste of warm tortillas in my mouth, the yellow light of the kerosene lantern washing lovingly across the spare walls. Daylight comes and Don Pedro is carrying a ladder across the desert, leans it against the whitewashed wall of the hut, clambers up the crude handmade rungs, and sticks his arm in the chimney to search out *"el nido del pajaro,"* the nest of the bird that is backing all that smoke into the room.

It is night again and a bat flies through an open window and flutters crazily in the half light cast off by the lamp and Doña Flora advises that its urine will burn the flesh like fire.

Or it is afternoon and Panchita, the eleven-year-old girl, asks Doña Flora if the woman Alfonso was seen with walking down the street of the town, if that woman is Alfonso's wife. Doña Flora beams and says, "Oh, my dear little Panchita, that was another slice of the pie."

It is noon in the village and we sip bitter coffee on the man's porch. The women retreat, one wearing a sweatshirt that says "California the Golden State," the other a young girl sporting a T-shirt with a desert landscape in color that announces "Magic Land." The head of the *ejido* laughs and talks. Each year he buys a brand-new pickup and no one asks how. An old man waits for the bus to wind its way down the dirt lane. His head is gray but it looks like he has never lost a single hair, his face sports the local field of stubble, his teeth perfect and white and offering a grin a foot wide. One of the old shoes on his feet has a huge round hole. That is why he is waiting for the bus. He has been up against the sierra and when he swung the pickaxe it went right through his foot. He laughs about his clumsiness. I stare down at the hole the size of a silver half-dollar. When the women come out of the house again to retrieve the coffee cups, the old man says, *"Me gusto,"* it pleases me, and the conversation continues in its merry way on the porch by the blooming flowers as his foot suppurates inside his shoe and the wait for the bus goes on and on until the time it should end.

A child with a set of plastic Mickey Mouse ears on its tiny head crosses a dirt yard, a child of perhaps two pulling a wagon while vaqueros drive the steers into the mesquite corral. The moon hangs over León, the heart of the *problema,* and I sip the mezcal while Alfonso dreams and what I see is. . . the child in perfect silhouette, the black ears dancing above its little blue jumpsuit. There was a dance a week ago over at the village school, the small building named after Benito Juárez. A rock band came out from town and set up huge speakers (the school has electricity) and hundreds of people gathered. A school-teacher came out from town, a woman famous for flirting with all the men, who, of course, as the dance cranked up were drunk. One vaquero became inflamed with passion, pulled out a pistol, and kidnapped the schoolteacher. But he had no horse, no car, no truck. The villagers disarmed him and he went back to his bottle. For weeks, he will fuel a lilt of good humor in the talk of the people.

In a few hours, the dawn will seep from behind a pyramid-shaped peak where the villagers say the water is poisonous because of radiation in the stone. The day will begin very early, before first light, with Don Pedro milking his scrawny cows, Doña Flora feeding the wood stove and making murderous coffee, Panchita staring out the window for something in the world to happen on the dirt lane of León. But for now, Alfonso sleeps and dreams.

Not the bad dreams, not the ones that stalked him for years as he hunted for the next bottle. In those dreams, an old man sits in a wicker chair, his face covered with stubble, and he winks and then grins at Al who sprawls helpless and drunk on a bed. Or Al's head is severed from his body, his head sits on a machine that sustains his life and men with white coats circulate around him, their faces calm and passive behind their clean spectacles. Family and friends arrive, knocking at the door of the laboratory, and Al shouts, "No! No! Don't let them see me this way." The men in the white coats always say, "But we must for your mental health." And then they let his father and mother, his sisters and brother, his wife and children come streaming in.

Those dreams, they are almost gone, sunk back into the pit called the past. Now earlier dreams come, earlier smells, hungers, hopes, and loves. They come here in León where the marijuana has been harvested and waits in stash houses up and down the valley for that moment when a voice will say, "Take them

north, drive those tons to market, *compañeros!"* Now the dreams
have wonderful colors.

The paint in the moon and other parts of the village in Alfonso's picture, the paint is thick and fat. Over León the sky is a rich
blue and a white streak squirms across it like a worm. The yellow
of the moon in Alfonso's dream is deep, almost an orange, the
orange yellow you find in cheap margarine when you are down
on your luck and hungry for a loaf, some baloney, and the thick
oleo spreading off your knife, all in the hopes of stopping the
shakes. But of course you will soon vomit the meal and seek a
bottle instead. In the painting, the crescent rises up above dark
brown mountains that sketch chocolate peaks against the horizon. The houses are slightly irregular white rectangles, the windows brooding eyes, the doorways lack any thick doors to keep
the night out. All this in the painting rests on an oval, a platter of
warm brown, the soft polished brown of the Indian's face as she
stands before you mute, her eyes sealed forever from your hunts
and questions. On the edge of the oval, so lonely and determined,
grows a pale, blue-green agave, spikes waving in the night winds
that I can feel rushing across the hairs on the back of my neck.
Then suddenly a square frames this scene but it cannot contain
León, the mountains punch right through and above them rides
a purple heaven. The warm brown earth of the oval gives way to
soil thick, ground the color of an ox's blood. Then the ox blood
escapes again, pushing past the effort to contain it and now it is a
warm orange, an orange singed and darkened by smoke. Finally,
a wall is thrown up, the thing must end, and a wooden frame
dripping with ox blood sets the limits to the village's wanderings.
That is the moon over León in Alfonso's dream. The one that
never exists to the eye but steals through the night and seeps into
the mind.

Al was never quite as open and innocent as Alfonso. He is nine
years old and he reads about Van Gogh, Gauguin—the painters

of a dying Europe—and he notices all they seem to do is never work for anyone and lay around and smoke and drink. And he wants to be a painter. The rest is decades interrupted by drink. When he is thirteen his father brings the family north, leery of the fact that Al is becoming Mexicanized. But it is too late, the trap has already been sprung. When he is sixteen he flees the desert, goes to ground in Texas, and takes a job on a farm. The neighboring guy is a black preacher, the kids dirt poor. Al buys a chicken to cook, drinks and forgets about it. When he remembers, it has gone bad. So he pitches it out in the trash. The preacher's kids find it, take it home, and their mother cooks it up. Stockton. The tales continue. He is in the service, drunk in Germany, tossed in various jails. He is in San Antonio working at a military hospital where they bring those blown up by stray bombs, seared by unexpected fires. He stands for hours over armless or legless or faceless people, a scissors in his hand, as he carefully snips rotten flesh from their bodies, picks out little gleaming fragments of bone buried in their muscles. The smell is very powerful. Of course, every story is just a brief interruption in the bottle. His is a very old story. He is on a plane across the United States when he starts a fight on a commercial flight. The pilot puts down in Atlanta and the police come and it gets very bad. Then there were the days he painted for a drink. There is this bar in San Antonio and Al did the mural on the wall. He put all the regular drunks of the bar in the painting and by God, business just boomed. The juicers loved looking up at themselves on the wall as they sat on the stools getting drunk.

He thinks back to those times once in a while.

"I don't regret one day of my drinking," he says.

No one does when they survive it. He is a boy on the farm, Jesús is twenty-three and he wants a woman and he is drinking. Jesús is the foreman, but tonight he is a bravo, a bronco, and full of juices he must use. He goes to the man's house to take his fifteen-year-old daughter. The man sees that Jesús is standing in the night with a long knife in one hand, the kind of cheap knife you buy in border towns with elaborate scenes etched on the chrome blade, and there is drunkenness sketched across his darkened face. The father climbs through a window, gets behind Jesús, and swings against the back of his head with a stout piece of mesquite. He is in a coma for two days, his eyes open and rolled back in his head. When Al looks down at him his eyes are blood red, nothing but blood red. No one regrets a day of their drinking.

I am ready to go back to the hut. I have emptied my cup of mezcal. The moon, she just rides there. The white houses are not so white, the earth is not a rich brown or ox-blood red. The sierra is a dark shadow, not inviting piles of chocolate. I look off but cannot penetrate the night, cannot see the house—there, that one right there—where the man sleeps tonight, the man who did four years in an American federal prison. Finally, he earned some slack thanks to good behavior and was transferred to Safford in southern Arizona where the good cons go and there are no walls. He walked off into the desert and hiked back south to León. Near him are similar small houses, some with fine stables made of blocks, stables much larger than the homes. And much, much newer. The *problema*.

But then, problems are everywhere. Here, at least they are concrete, hard, and when the hand reaches out they can be felt. There are no theories here, there are many practices, some good, some not so good. The girl who brought me here, she is dead and now survives as a smear of paint that tumbled out of Alfonso's head one day. It was a painting that triggered me. As soon as I saw her, I knew I must go find her. But I do not know how to reach her. I think of her story—the marriage to the drug dealer she did not love, the trips he would make, trips such as are necessary for a man in the life. In the beginning, the drug dealer finds her in this valley, perhaps on a night much like this with the moon soaring over the land, and he takes her for his own. She is probably fifteen then, that is the time here when a woman is ready for a man. There is something in their eyes beginning about their twelfth year, a child's eyes wide open to the world and yet overflowing with a kind of knowing that is a much rarer thing to the north. I think men see this look and that is what makes them act. They want those eyes under their roof. I can understand this desire.

Anyway, this time the drug dealer is a man with a present and a future in a place where most men possess only a past. But something does not work, she cannot forget her true love—how I love the sound of those words, "true love"—and slowly? suddenly? somehow she begins to go for the food she must have. Perhaps, she looks out one of those windows of León, the ones lacking glass that stay open to flies and God all day long, and then at night crude wooden shutters are swung shut and the house faces the darkness with blank eyes. But she is standing at the window right now, looking out, and the sun is up, just up, and he goes riding by on his horse, the saddle old, the Levis worn and tight, his straw hat square on his head, the belt on his small waist cinched so fiercely you would think it is supporting a knight's sword. And he glances over. His lips form a firm line, but his eyes give away everything. She sees the eyes.

There is that house out in the desert, I must find it. The one where they finally begin to meet. Alfonso asks no questions about the matter. It is not safe to probe anywhere on the edges of the *problema*. But I am patient, I will listen for hours and finally without warning or reason the right moment will come and I will ask. This is my hope. In my dream, Doña Flora will glance over with those dark eyes barely visible, just two craters in the faint glow of the lamp, and I will ask. She will talk to the floor, a low mumble. Yes, it will happen, some day, some night. If only in a dream, it will happen.

Alfonso writes a poem about the woman and the drug dealer and the lover (he cannot ask questions, he is not that way, so he writes), a poem that circles his painting like a child's scrawl on a wall. His writing book insists, "This is a good poem, every phrase is in three words." He scratches out these things at first in a heavy leather-bound old ledger book, each thing dated and signed as he slowly trudges into the territory ahead. In his poem, the flowers on the woman's grave are blue, and the woman is weeping because her lover has now moved beyond the touch of her hands.

Now the woman is dressed in a long white dress, her eyes are closed, the lips a faint red, a red that surely will fade fast, hour by hour. Alfonso makes a note on the execution of the painting: "The sun slowly faded the flowers to a mystical shade of blue that almost matched the sky."

It will be a painting with a certain charm. When I first see the image, it is hanging at a show in a very expensive resort in Tucson, the kind of resort where people pay $600 a day in order to lose a few pounds of fat off their useless hips. I remember three women sitting on a sofa at the show, their faces masks, the smiles tight, the skin so taut that I think with one more face-lift the skin will tear and blow away like dry paper in the wind. Their loins are dry, anyone can see that at a glance. They are very pale, creatures that do not seek the sun. Their bodies are rigid, the arms stiff, the torsos tight, bodies you will need a crowbar to pry apart. You will never touch them, your hand will freeze before you will ever do such a thing. The eyes are hard, almost cruel, eyes very angry at the trick life has played on them by giving them everything they wanted and never permitting them one real night of love.

No one bought the painting at the show. Maybe it was the child's hand scrawling the poem around the frame, maybe the dead woman staring up at the desert sky does not go well with the couch and the drapes back at the home with the electronic alarm system. I really don't know, it just didn't sell.

Tomorrow, or the next day, or the day after—some day I will find the house in León where it happened. It should not be hard, there is one in every neighborhood. I have a need for visiting the battlefields of love.

I get up early, at first light, but no matter how early I rise in León I am always behind the pace of the village. Don Pedro is at his cows, bent down squeezing the teats over a bucket. There is no way to cool or keep milk here. See that ocotillo-walled shack with the roof of Johnson grass? Well, in there is the dairy room. Every two days the old man makes four kilos of white cheese, about nine pounds. This he sells for the equivalent of, say, nine bucks. Let's make the take twenty-five bucks a week—you must subtract the cheese the family eats. That is the cash flow.

And we do eat the cheese. We are at breakfast now, the room smoky from the wood stove and on my plate are two fried eggs— the hens live locked up in an ocotillo warren where they are sometimes safe from the legions of coyotes. I have some *frijoles*, refried beans, and there on the table steams a stack of warm flour tortillas patted out by Doña Flora this very morning while I still slept. Of course, there is also salsa picante and cups of that bitter black coffee laced generously with sugar. There is an old Indian woman in the village, a crone of almost a hundred years, with smooth apple-like cheeks that sparkle in the sunlight, and this old woman fries the coffee beans for the people of León.

Doña Flora flutters about like a bird and sits against the wall on a chair with Panchita while the men eat. She smokes a ciga- rette and listens to the talk. I do not know how she stays alive—I have never seen her eat. Outside four starving dogs sleep in the winter sun, heaped up, eyes open but blank, sides neat rows of bones. They do not lift their heads when I pass and no matter how often I encounter them, they will never wag their tails. They are seldom if ever fed.

"What are the dogs for?" I ask.

"To keep the coyotes back from the house," Doña Flora explains. Then she pauses and adds, "It does not work."

A lot of things don't work here. In the last ten years or so, the villagers say about half the people have left León looking for jobs. They remain part of the village but only the mind's eye can see them. Don Pedro and Doña Flora have eight or ten kids, now all grown, and all but one scattered. The girl, she got an education and lives in town where she is a bank clerk. Her husband works in Nogales, Arizona, in a microchip factory, driving home each weekend. Alberto lives in Tucson where he has gotten a green card and mows lawns and hauls away trash. The others have similar stories. One son, in his fifties, lives at home, a man who has never married, and he drives the rickety village bus that the old man with the pickaxe hole in his foot was waiting for.

They are all out there but in some ways they are all here. They come back all the time bringing old washing machines, a few bucks, some food. They come to sit and drink and dance and smell the mesquite smoke rising off the valley floor. Nothing about this fact is new. Don Pedro was gone for forty years, working as a vaquero on the ranches of northern Sonora and southern Arizona for what would be in modern money about eighty cents a day. His family stayed in León and he would come back when he could—often enough to father a large family. He is old enough to pre-date the modern border. Until about 1930 it was a line on a map, not on the earth, and Don Pedro remembers cattle drives from the valley up to Tubac in Arizona. The same kind of border the Yaquis knew and crossed in their endless comings and goings for refuge and guns and bullets.

For these people at some level it is all a piece of ground and the ground is absolutely connected. This is not a political view, or even a thought in many ways. It simply is. The people live in the desert and so they move across the desert. The fences merely cause slight delays. In Spanish the term for the United States

is *Estados Unidos*. In northern Sonora, this is sometimes said
Estamos Unidos, we are united. Alfonso has a story that neatly
plays with this fact. He lives in a barrio in Tucson and he has this
Mexican woman come in once a week and clean it up a bit. One
day she saw he was getting ready to go south to León and she
said, "Will you take me to Altar so I can see my family?" He said
yes, the town is right on the way in Sonora. They arrive at her
family's home after dark, and of course Alfonso must stay and
eat. So he sits and works his way through a meal. Then the father
says, "You cannot go on in the night, you must sleep here," and
he shows Alfonso the bedroom he normally shares with his wife.
He says, "Here, you must honor me by sleeping here."

Alfonso gives in. Then he and the family sit in the living room
while the father shows photo albums. In the pictures the family
members and their friends are all out on the porch. And everyone in the pictures is holding a gun. *La vida.* Alfonso begins to
feel edgy. Then out of the darkness a flatbed truck pulls up and
men dressed in camouflage pile out and enter the house. Each
man cradles an automatic weapon in his arms. The father greets
them warmly—*"¡Compañeros!"*—and the newly arrived guests
and the family go out on the porch to visit.

Alfonso takes the woman aside and asks, "What have you gotten me into?"

"Ah," she says, "do not worry. I have spoken to my father,
everything is all right."

The men with the guns? Well, they sit on the hillsides around
the fields and guard them lest someone get greedy and try to
harvest a crop he has not planted. Some crops are very valu-
able and not to be shared. In the morning, the woman says,
"Let's go to Tubutama. I have more friends there." But Alfonso
has had enough, he says that he is a day late for his expected
arrival in León and he must press on to the village. So he goes
to ground.

In León, of course, the same night could occur, depending upon the house. The same coming and going. There is all this talk about the border, talk that so involves statesmen. The men with guns leaping off a flatbed truck in the darkness with automatic weapons, those men know the border exists but this is not a wall in their life. All this armament in a village where when the men still go into the sierra to hunt deer they take twenty-two rifles and maybe one or two cartridges. A village where Don Pedro was born, seeing his first automobile one fine day in 1928 while visiting a nearby town. There is little crime in this village, no rapes. No one here uses drugs much, unless you count cigarettes, mezcal, and that murderous coffee.

So we all have breakfast. Out the window I see men on horseback ride by to drive cattle into the fields where they will graze on the stubble left by the corn and beans. Don Pedro sits against the wall, his hands rough and bent from arthritis. He says, "Even if these hands turn into claws or hooks, I will still use them."

A sideboard in the kitchen holds an electric clock, and an electric clock radio. There is no electricity in the house. There is a huge set of kitchen cabinets, nice stained wood, inset with a stainless-steel double sink. Alfonso hauled the thing down from the States. Since there is no running water, the water is hauled up by the bucketful from a well near the corrals. Doña Flora and Panchita fill the sink when necessary and do the dishes. A plastic pipe drains the water off to the flowers and herbs growing in the bare dirt front yard. Each evening, a man mounts a horse, ties the rope to his pommel that trails back into the darkness of the well, and pulls up water bucket-by-bucket while another man empties it into a trough for the stock. This takes place up and down the valley at dusk and eats up about an hour.

Estamos Unidos is so very near in miles—forty or fifty miles as the raven flies—but very far for some. In 1935, Doña Flora made her first trip to Nogales, Arizona. She went shopping. For this journey, she got a passport complete with seals and stamps and photograph of herself, a young woman of twenty-five. Her next visit was fifty-one years later in 1986. Her old passport was in perfect condition, she had kept it well and wanted to keep it forever. But the man at U.S. Customs grabbed it, saying, "You have no use for this." Perhaps, it went to some museum of rare historical documents. Doña Flora was saddened, she wished to retain the photograph of her as a woman of twenty-five, a woman in her prime.

I look out the kitchen window, past the sink, past the faucets that do not work, and see a man ride past on a fine horse covered with a red quilt. A flock of children follow the man, who sits well in the saddle and holds a riding crop. The horse is the fruit of the *problema* and some of the villagers make a little money exercising the animals won by players in the life. León is famous for horse racing, straightaway match races held in the desert on a big airstrip just above the fields. So it is natural for her sons to cash in their success with new stables and hot-blooded animals. I have had enough coffee.

Animals are life here. Chapo, the woodcutter, leaves before dawn every day or two for town riding on a wagon full of cut mesquite, the whole thing drawn by burros. One day a dog attacked one of his donkeys and made a deep slash on the throat. Chapo stirred up a thick concoction made from creosote, plugged the wound, and he and his animals went back about their business.

The sun blazes in the yard, the plastic Virgin of Guadalupe in the window is a berserk statue of acrylic colors. And about then the crazy one arrives. His name is Miguel, but everyone in the village calls him crazy behind his back. He talks very loudly, is wild-eyed, and is about thirty years old. He is famous for doing dangerous work—breaking the horse other men do not choose to ride, digging out the deep well with soft sides. He lives with his father and, from time to time, Miguel gets drunk and beats the old man up. He is a man without fear, a fool. His eyes are blackened this morning from a recent visit to Magdalena. He walked all the way over the sierra to the town so that he could have a proper fight. He wears a baseball cap that says in English, "The Worst Day Golfing is Better than the Best Day Working." During the season, he toils as a trimmer in the marijuana fields. He wants to do some business with Alfonso. He has found some old beams, ancient pieces of mesquite worked by *la gente* in earlier years, in the hard days before they could buy milled lumber and sit at tables covered with fine gleaming Formica. Alfonso buys and sells such weathered things.

We drive the truck north, cross the Arroyo León, a steep banked cut into the soil of the valley, move slowly past the fields, and then climb back up on the bajada to the east. On the nearby hill is the huge new house and behind it stretch long stables, also newly made. The Man lives here. The mesquite have been chained out and bulldozed for about a thousand acres and fine grass now grows. The man is a native of the village and he has done very well in the life. Power poles dance around his big brick house like candy canes. There are men up there with guns, in the day and the night, if you wish to find such things. Across the valley up against the sierra I can make out the faint white smudge of a cross on the cliffs and below it the looming white shrine to the Virgin of Guadalupe. The shrine cost several million pesos. The man who lives in the new brick house with the fine stables trailing behind, he paid for the shrine.

Miguel has a sack filled with green chilis and a huge squash rides on the truck floor. There, there, he says, take that dirt track off into the trees. Alfonso balks, this is exactly where he does not want to go. Ever. But Miguel is insistent, he is digging a well there and he promised to deliver the chilis and the squash. The machine grinds down the rutted road, swings around a grove of trees, and then in a bare patch of earth a little ranch sits white in the sun. Out back under some low trees, three beehives hum. Hungry dogs laze in the yard, and the house has a row of car batteries lined up against the wall, a cable snaking through the window to the television. A big picture of the Virgin of Guadalupe has been taped to the front window. There are also sacks of crushed Tecate beer cans. And nearby, a small white hill made of hundreds of cattle skulls, the horns a twisted tangle in the morning light. This is a stash house, where the bales are stacked and stored until that voice says to take it north.

The place is very silent and no one comes out. Miguel walks up, disappears inside, and returns without his sack or squash. He is increasingly embarrassed by his blackened eyes so Alfonso gives him a pair of sunglasses. He puts them on with delight, and becomes the movie star.

The other small ranchos we visit are much the same, all nestled back in the trees without running water or electricity. But sometimes the trucks are quite new and always the eyes are quite cold. Miguel cannot shut up, he is not a fool for nothing—"Aiiiiiyah," he shouts, "over there is a fine field of marijuana, there tucked down in that fold of the land, that house, ooh, that house has five tons in it right now, and up there is more, and those folks? Mafiosos!!" He roars on and on.

I look over and see the cross on the mountain. In Alfonso's painting the woman in the white dress is lying very dead in a box in the earth. She is not happy, I think. There is something I can see in her face and her hands, some resistance to the blackness flowing over her forever. The sun in the painting peeks over the shoulder of huge cumulus clouds, billowing towers of white. The child's scrawl of the poem marches slowly like the movements of pallbearers down the aisle of a dirt-floored church.

There is money in the morning breeze, lots of money as Alfonso's old truck rumbles down the rough dirt roads. I can see small coins fall from the sky and create a line of car batteries, the cable

snaking through an open window into the small house. A pile
of crushed Tecate cans. Fine horses, their coats glistening from
brushing, their heads proud, big hot veins throbbing on their
heads.

She was so close, that dead woman, so very close. If only she
could have absorbed the lessons in time. Maybe it was something
in the way her old lover's hips looked on the horse as he pranced
past her home in the morning. I do not know. I can feel it, but I
cannot know for sure. She made a choice, a sound one in many
ways, when she married the man in the life. Heaven was so near.

It is late at night and Doña Flora talks to the floor about the
problema. *"Mal dar,"* she says, bad give. Her many children have
been told. They may never again cross her doorway if they have
anything to do with this evil-giving business. Nothing good
can come of it, the old woman insists, her face weathered and
wrinkled and ghostly in the light of the kerosene lamp. Her children, what do they do? Who knows. Doña Flora is very old, she
will soon die, and her life is a tapestry that trails behind her. The
children are in the midst of their life, they are hungry, and who
will refuse a way out of a trap? Three sons are famous for being
badasses, men to be feared. Another son is a small legend in
the valley. Once in Caborca when he was drunk, a cop tried to
arrest him. He picked the cop up—a Mexican cop!—and threw
him over a car. This act is not what the legend springs from. It is
rather this: he threw a Mexican cop over a car and lived.

That son married a woman from Caborca and a few months
ago there was this incident. There are often incidents. Alfonso
has walked out of his hut into the morning light of León and
seen camouflaged helicopter gunships move up the valley like
angels of death. Flying for whom? The Mexican police, the CIA,
the men who are in the life? Who knows. If you are in your mesquite corral bent over and squeezing milk out of the teats of your
scrawny cows, in what way does the answer matter to you?

But the incident in Caborca was different, it made the newspapers on both sides of the line. In the papers, there was some kind of bombing and shootout in the town and buildings mysteriously exploded and men died. The village tells a different tale. The son who married the woman from Caborca, well, her people lived next to the houses of some Mafiosos. At night *beladores,* candle tenders, keep guard on the street. These are men who build fires at night and stand by them through the dark hours with machine guns in their arms lest some harm come to their *patrons.* This day as people sat out in front of their homes a man came up the street, an ordinary man in ordinary dress. He told them to go back into their houses and stay there. They did. Then they blew up the houses and their guns barked and they roared away in cars. The fleeing cars drove past the army base, past the police headquarters, past the big church Father Kino launched centuries ago, drove out into the desert where a chopper waited. There they burned the cars and flew away. *Mal dar.*

The sun is warm, the small houses white and inviting, always the Virgin of Guadalupe taped to a window, a small statue on a shelf, housed in a crude shrine in the yard. By the door, a cross made from herbs tied with ribbon and hung from the wall. The roof is dirt and grass grows from it. Children look up and smile shyly. The yard is scratched clean and then the desert begins and sweeps away until the sky touches down. The cottonwoods lining the wash are golden now, the fields clean and orderly, the cattle with heads bent plod silently across the stubble. A few miles away in a real town, right across from a small grocery store, is a big building of stone and cement. The roof line is lavender, then a long high window, then marble facing ending in a ribbon of dark stucco. This is the *Casino Ejectivo,* the Executive Club. It was built by a local man, a good businessman who is said to have tens of millions in the life. He now sits in jail in Tucson, his millions in homes and cars seized, the indictment against him long and full of alleged business deals that are normal in the life. His is a name that no one says out loud in this valley. The club, well, he built that so he and others in the life would have a place to go in the night. Down the street at the meat market, flies buzz around the strips of red flesh and the butcher sells steerhide *reatas,* ropes made from a strand carved in one continuous strip from a single hide and woven by hand. Only a few old men can still do this craft, and the butcher wants $80 American for a single *reata.* Too much, but then the money has changed many things here.

There were many bad killings that people say lead to the drug lord's door. This may be hard to discover. His bond is enormous and so he sits in a cage, but still the witnesses against him seem to be vanishing. There is the young boy, a local boy, said to have perished because of him. The villagers refer to the dead boy as *pobrecito,* the poor little one. But this act is unlikely to be proven in the American courts of law. Or any other courts.

I swear, if you had a camera, you would be snapping pictures like crazy—the valley below looks like some careful painting by Grant Wood, the little ranchos are handmade pieces of folk art, the faces of the men are weathered and chiseled and seem carved from some strange kind of warm stone. There are always flowers growing in the bare yards, a struggling honeysuckle, a rose bush, a blooming mum braving the winter air. The rooms are full of old secondhand furniture kept immaculately clean, the faces of the children glow like candles. There is no end of wonderful pictures. And stories. And cups of black coffee laced with sugar. The pictures would not be false, not at all. They would tell what the eye can see. Perhaps, there is no drug problem here, just a business kept out of sight. There are problems, there have always been problems. But this drug problem, it is a phrase for politicians. Before the phrase came into vogue, life was hard and beautiful. It still is. When the phrase falls from fashion, life will still be good. In Alfonso's painting of the dead woman, past the grave, past the *capilla,* far back against the mountain, I can see a faint white trail against the sierra leading up to a cross on the mountain and the peace that symbol offers.

We roll into Zanahoria. The school is naturally named after Benito Juárez, the cantina is called the garden, and the plaza sports a few concrete benches and barren flower boxes. People here are noted for their ability to gouge large troughs out of hard mesquite logs. And for the life. This village is said to be deep in the life. A man works a hand forge, a small boy cranking the bellows as the man beats out the end of an iron rod. We pull up to a tumble-down house with mesquite corrals in back, a saddled horse staring at us. An old man comes out, he is about five feet five inches, his jeans faded and held together with coarse thread, the knees and seats different-colored patches. His hands are gnarled, the skin a rich coffee brown. He is very good with the wood and Alfonso has dealt with him often. Calves drink from a trough that was made from a single mesquite beam, a huge log carved out with an adze. The thing was created at least a century ago. Thirty dollars. A beam is being used as the post for a stable door. Yes, that too. And those ancient beams lying in steer shit out back, the ones thrown away when good lumber became available for your home. We will take them also. The items will all probably wind up in Sante Fe where adobe and red tile floors and Mexican geegaws have become a new religion for monied people detoxing from their wealth by fanning piñon smoke into their nostrils.

The men are standing under a tree watching a young vaquero shoe a horse, the women are doing the wash in a galvanized tub and on a scrub board, a goat browses, and everyone watches us with veiled but curious eyes. After all, there is no telling what gringos will buy. Miguel is in full flower, braying to the wind. He says loudly, "The guy who lives here, my God, does his wife have a big ass!" But no one takes notice of the remark; after all, Miguel's role in the valley is to be the fool.

We go on, the old man climbs in, and we head into the bajada. Winding dirt tracks, little ranchos glancing off our eyes as we crawl past. Sullen dogs too weak to rise up from the dirt, and flies. The old man motions with his hand—Miguel is now sitting in back on the truck bed—right here, left there, on and on as we thread our way through a maze of trails fingering between mesquites. Suddenly the rancho appears, a trim white mud house with a stout fence of metal surrounding it. The man of the house is gone, off in the brush searching for a missing steer. One steer matters. The woman is young and fresh, her hips firm beneath her tight Levis, a small child clinging to her knee. Her face is lovely, the eyes dark and suspicious, the lips full. A small dachshund, or a dog mostly dachshund, stands by her feet. He is fat, the first fat animal sighted in the valley. This is another stash house. Somewhere off there in the brush, the bales wait for the message to go north. The old man and Miguel start wrestling up hand-hewn beams, things tossed aside by these people and seen as dry rot from a past that is to be left behind as soon as possible. From the house music floats, music from a tape player probably living off another row of car batteries. I lean out the window and hear, a carol, "Santa Claus is coming to town."

Alfonso is growing nervous. This is the part he does not like. There are no good dreams here for him. He has enough bad dreams already. He remembers drinking and his mother is going to hold a party and he knows there will be lots of beer, cases of beer. He drives near her home, parks, and turns off the lights. He steals up, goes out to the shed where he knows the beer will be stacked, and he carries off cases one by one. It is terrible beer, Schmidt's beer, he thinks, and he remembers it had ducks on the can. He is appalled by the look of the cans he is stealing. He goes home and for days drinks the cases. Christmas is coming and he must celebrate.

He has lots of bad memories. That is why the angels are so necessary. They drift into his paintings like strangers looking for the bus stop. But that is not unusual in his paintings. No one in them ever looks quite comfortable with their role, there is always this feel of disturbance even in the good dreams. The angels can be huge, maybe five feet high, and they will have full breasts, swollen full breasts with the nipples fighting to escape the fabric. The eyes will be open full and rich with memories and musk. The hair will look as if a man has buried his fist in it and hung on. Sometimes the angels are naked.

But this rancho is too much, so Alfonso leaves. He wants the wood, not the life. We go back to Zanahoria and let the old man off. He has made good money from this visit. Miguel, too, has garnered his few bucks commission, enough to finance a couple of bottles of mezcal. The vaquero is still standing there in leather chaps shoeing the horse, the goat still browses, and a black-and-white rooster scratches in the dirt street like a god who can face any possibility. The Virgin of Guadalupe stares from every window. Take any village you want, they are all there huddled in the desert. See drug country. See campesinos. See Virgins. Some boys ride down the street happy to have horseflesh under their small bodies. Take a photograph. Eight months ago some boys ride down the street happy to have horseflesh under their small bodies—and the boy in front fell and the others, before they could gain control of their animals, trampled him to death. *Pobrecito.* A funeral. Blue flowers fading in the desert sun.

It is afternoon, the light is strong, and we enter the small house, *"con permiso?"* On the wall a radio plays—the house has electricity. The man is a shadow in the kitchen, a wraith of a man in tight Levis, the faded shirt, the customary stubble beard. He is *enfermo,* dying of cancer. He says he has an ulcer, that is what the dying always say here. He has been a vaquero all of his life, and now he is the merest shadow of the man he was but six months before. He lives with his unmarried sister and brother and for years there has been bawdy talk all over the village about them. That will soon be behind him. On the wall are two framed black-and-white photographs. One shows a grizzled man with a worn Levis jacket, cowboy hat, three-day beard, rope, and a cigarette dangling from his lips. The image is his father—for forty-five years a vaquero on the huge Alamos ranch in Sonora. This is the pattern of life in León. For decades the old man who is now dying worked on a ranch just north of Tucson, one called Willow Springs. Like his father before him he left to make money to keep his family and the village going. Now the younger men leave seeking money on their forays into the days and the nights. The other photo is of a simple stucco house in Los Angeles where one of his sisters lives. The old man talks in a low monotone while bougainvillea in big five-gallon cans bloom shyly on the edge of his porch. He has seen his last spring.

Off under a mesquite tree, the village idiot, a man full grown with a child's grin and his pants hitched high above his hips, plays in the sand with a bucket. He wanders León and wherever he is in the valley at night people take him and feed him and give him a bed.

There, moving like a ghost under the tree, see the old bent man? He is Juan de Dios, the richest man in the village, a man glutted with cattle. His house has no electricity. He lives with no woman. He spends little. He is the necessary miser.

Down the road there is work around a hole. The house is stucco, the paint faded, grass growing on the dirt roof. The doorway is open and inside an old woman peers out like a ghost, a *rebozo* wrapped around her ancient head. The toil at the well absorbs the two men and two boys. One man stands on a fragile platform hung down the hole, a rickety thing held by old hemp ropes. Flattened pieces of a fifty-five-gallon drum serve as the forms for walling the well. A boy mixes cement in a car hood lying on the ground, each bucketful lowered down on nice yellow nylon ropes. The boy's cap says "On a Quiet Day in Ford Country You Can Hear a Chevy Rust." Alfonso sighs, "You can always hear the rust in León." Behind the well an old, old man bends and looks down. He is at least ninety—when Don Pedro was a small boy, this man was a man—and glances at me and asks, "Do you have any little sisters?"

I say no.

He laughs and says, "I still like you."

Once, Alfonso was back in the desert when the old man suddenly rode up on horseback dragging five mesquite posts along on the end of his lariat. He stopped his horse, took his rope and tied the posts to a tree. He said, "I am going to pray to God that those posts will follow me home tonight."

And then he rode off.

Take a picture. Black. Or white.

We get home before dark. A front is moving in, the air has gone raw, the blue sky is crowded with cirrus wafting fast across the heavens. Dinner is much the same, beans, coffee, tortillas, some soup with a small piece of meat floating in the broth. On the wall is a print, an old religious print bought more than fifty years before by Doña Flora at the annual festival at Magdalena, the town where Kino's bones lie. Each October the Indians and Mexicans of the desert gather there for days to drink and gamble and make love and fight and celebrate *San Francisco,* Saint Francis. The frame of the picture has gold gilt that is falling off, the glass is cracked, and on one side are stickers from various Mexican states where family members have no doubt traveled. The print itself is a straightforward vision of heaven and hell on Judgment Day. Doña Flora watches my eye get lost in the images. In the corner, a bandit prepares to slit the throat of a priest, the bag of gold spilled on the rock, the flames of hell licking up just before the face of the murderer. Christ is in the background hanging from his cross, his eyes and lips saying clearly his father has forsaken him. Here a line of people begins to fork. Down a wide path comes the miser clutching his bags of money, the lying lawyer his arms cradling books and papers to trick the poor with, the European in his funny khaki clothes, a pith helmet on his addled head, a gun strapped over one shoulder, a bottle of booze held up to his licentious lips, his other arm through the arm of a half-naked African woman. Then come the clowns, the Gypsies—the woman's breasts wantonly on display, the rich man in his tuxedo with two harlots of wealth on his arms, the thief with his bag of loot, the false priest with his cross. The Arab sultan and his seraglio. And then the dragons with open mouths, flames spitting out from between their fangs. Finally, the flames with devils grabbing the new arrivals and dragging them off for roasting in the eternally burning pits. There is a man facing forward, hips seared by fire, his expression one of horror. His every hair is blond. The group heading for heaven is less interesting: nuns, the gallant officer, the newlyweds, *niños,* a bishop, the convict in his shackles reading some paper—perhaps a prayer? All heading for a wonderful city with a great domed church, fine homes, full well-leafed trees, and weather that never varies, never fails *la gente.*

Doña Flora asks if I like the picture.

I say, "For me, it is a mirror, Señora."

She smiles and gives it to me.

"De nada," she says.

The old woman is a warm wall. Inviting, friendly, kind, bawdy, wrinkled, clucking, smoking, draining cup after cup of strong black coffee. But a wall. The other side is not my country and never can be. The *problema,* a matter not to be discussed. Merely new language for old things, a reality as constant as heaven and hell. A year ago after a lifetime of toil, the dirt floors in her small home were replaced with cement. *Así la vida.* That's life. Down that dirt lane a ways is a huge house, the porches swirling around its second floor like verandas and painted a passionate pink. The house is ten times as large, twenty times as large as the biggest house in the village. Glass in every window, tiled this and that, new furniture, fancy cars parked before it, an expanse of brick blotting out the blue sky. The *problema.*

Things not said, things close, oh so close. Some think the local drug lord made one killing too many. He took the boy, the *pobrecito.* The boy—his years are hard to pin down, perhaps twelve years old in the American newspapers, more a young man in the eyes of the village—the boy who accidentally spoke of something he should not have spoken of. Let slip a few careless words. They came to the boy's house in the nearby town—it is still there, you can go see it if you desire—and left with him. They put ice picks through his eyes. They castrated him. They did many things. And then killed him. He was Doña Flora's kin.

Pobrecito. Mal dar.

Things not said. Caro Quintero's people came to the village hiring men to work an orchard, apples they said. No one believed this but money is money. Many went from León, going is part of the fabric of life here, or there will be no León to return to. They wind up in Chihuahua at a huge plantation, endless fields, all wonderfully irrigated, all lush and green, all marijuana. They work hard and are guarded like slaves, lest anyone leave. Here accounts differ. It is said in the newspapers that American authorities got wind of this big plantation, this blob of green in the desert so large it was an affront, an enormous slab of lush growth in a plain of brown earth, perhaps the whole enterprise bouncing off the lens of the satellites spinning across the heavens. And they demanded it be shut down. So the Mexican army came and, the official accounts say, they found nothing but peasants whom they freed from a kind of slavery. All the big shots had disappeared. The peasants were liberated, the dark region shut down. End of story. *La gente* in León have a different tell-ing. The army came in firing, slaughtering peasants, fifty or sixty men died. León wept for its dead. One boy from the village fled, escaped into the sierra, was taken in by families, worked his way slowly through the encircling lines of soldiers sweeping the area, and made it back to León where he lives this very night. What does it matter. Caro Quintero? What of him? The authorities say he now sits in a Mexico City prison for his crimes, a caged animal. No one in León believes this. Perhaps, few even wish it. They say the man in the cell in Mexico City is a double, a look-alike hired to satisfy the absurd demands of the Americans. Caro Quintero himself, they say, has been seen at parties in nearby Caborca. Ask anyone. He is free, free as a bird. Besides, he is not all bad. Did he not pay for an orphanage in Caborca? Men have written plays about him, movies have celebrated his life story. Have you not heard *corridos* singing of his feats?

> Born in Sinaloa
> The kind that are not born every day
> And that don't give up.
> For killing a policeman. . . .
> Today he is found arraigned
> They say they want to judge him,
> The Americans over there in their lairs.
> They take him to make our souls sweat.

There is something about the eyes. Alfonso notices it espe-cially in the young girls, eyes capable of innocence yet full, over-brimming with a kind of knowing. He has spent years trying to get those eyes into his paintings and now they have crept in and stake out places on the faces of everyone his brush touches. They are almond-shaped eyes and wide open and the corneas are blue or black and rich and full. And they have no pupils. None. He can see these eyes especially in the young girls. Look at Chapo's daughters, they are standing there in the doorway, twelve and thirteen years old. They are very dark, very Indio, but then so is their father. When they walk the village during the day they must carry parasols lest they grow darker, get more *prieta*, more Indio.

Alfonso says, "They have this look, God, this knowing—that is what I put into my paintings, that is why I paint."

They are small girls, breasts just beginning, bright clean clothes, perfect teeth, eyes like saucers, black sealed saucers. Alfonso is in love with them. He feels he is lucky to sit and want something as badly as he wants them. He does not want to possess them, he wants to feel such a deep hunger. Yes, he says this, knowing it is a jumble of words, that they are girls and when they hit fifteen they will instantly be women and when they are sixteen there will be a baby sucking at their breasts. One daughter is already gone, married at fifteen into Magdalena. Another slice of the pie.

But the eyes, they do show up. They can be found on the street, they lurk on the flat surfaces of the paintings. The dead woman, Hermelinda, they are on her face even though her eyes are closed. You can feel them, that knowing. Not acceptance, but the knowing. Look closely at the painting. Her fists are clenched. She is not happy in her coffin with the blue flowers fading at her graveside. The childlike scrawl swirls around the corpse.

Night has fallen, the village is disappearing into small cells of adobe, here and there yellow eyes peer out from the windows. There is no moon, I am sure of it. No moon at all. I do not need the painting for this scene. She is anxious, her hips are loose, her crotch is moist. The coyotes cry out on the evening breeze, the dogs bark back with shudders running up and down their spines. In the sierra, the lions swing down hoping for that stray calf to make into more bones—the nerves at the roots of their fine sharp teeth are tingling with desires and excitement. The blood, the blood will spill down their hot lips, splash against their anxious tongues, and a deep purr will rumble from their throats. She stands before the open window, the shutters swung back, the black winds playing with her clean long hair. He will mount her on the dirt floor with the crude beams and carrizo grass of the ceiling staring down on her warm brown body. Yes.

She checks the stars. It is time.

The horse is calm, it does not like the night, but it is calm. It knows the way through the creosote and ironwood, through the saguaro and palo verde, the prickly pear and mesquite, past the fangs of cholla, the bearded ancient heads of the senita, the scattered bones of the steers so careless and sloppy in their deaths. The dogs of the village do not bark as he passes, they recognize the local smells. The hooves clop softly on the brown earth, the land rolls as she climbs. The rancho, who knows what it looks like?—an abandoned thing for sure, the stucco falling off in plates, the raw blocks crumbling and strands of straw tasting the wind. The roof sags but still holds, the door remains but hangs a bit crooked on the tired hinges. She is wearing a scent perhaps. This is possible. Doña Flora is the Avon lady of León and purveys many strong potions for love-hungry *cabelleros* and *mujeres*. The vaqueros will come in from weeks or months in the line camps where they have been left with steers, a pile of food for their bellies, and an axe for building their huts. They will come in with their Levis fat with pesos and buy cologne, pay eight to ten dollars American so that they will smell sweet and macho and ready when they go to town finally for the *baile* or their turn with whores. Surely, a woman as hungry as this will not hesitate to splash some scent against her throat.

The man who comes this night does no less. He is her first love, her *novio*. His horse also moves softly through the desert. He thinks of her breasts, the dark nipples against the lighter flesh, the tits hard from the cool air. Her tongue in his mouth.

They arrive separately, each leaving the horse free to browse near the small building out on the parched ground. They lie on an old bed, a metal cot such as armies use, the springs broken here and there are repaired with old wire, the grid of the metal smoothed and softened by a blanket. She bites his lip, the tiny trickle of sweet blood. Sounds seep out the open window into the darkness where nighthawks bank and arc as they hunt.

Someone is waiting out there, of course. For the village to exist, to function, to have a past, a present, and a future, for the deep well from which the campesinos draw up their *corridos* in buckets to never run dry, for all these things and reasons, he has always been waiting out there. It is just that tonight he has finally arrived. He has learned and returned from his work in the life. He creeps quietly forward, gathers up the horses noiselessly, and leads them off. The couple does not hear him, they are not really listening as they buck and sweat. Now they lie there, side by side, his cock throbbing and slowly subsiding, her crotch, her *panocha*, wet and warm and rich with musk. Finally, after the silence, after the talk, the rush of hurried, slurred words, they dress and go out the door into the blackness. The stars glimmer above their heads, cold stones stingy with their light.

The animals are gone. They crouch, strike matches, detect tracks, follow them arm-in-arm into the thorn bushes and cactus. Twenty, fifty, perhaps a hundred yards off from the hut they stop as the bullets cut through them. He dies. She lives a while and gets to think or feel. The funeral is sad, they always are, women weep and wear black. The man disappears. He will be gone for a while. Partly he has his work in the life. And blood feuds are to be avoided, they are so open ended and relentless.

They finally put her in a hole and slop dry dirt over her face. That I think is a certain fact. But Alfonso cannot see it that way. He has her in her coffin, to be sure, and the coffin in a grave nicely surrounded by an iron fence. In the background the sierra stands dark brown, around the grave the earth is the warm brown of a woman's breast when glimpsed in the early morning light. A saguaro blooms with white flowers. There is this huge white cross with her name on it and a garland of blue flowers, fading very fast. Three more big blue flowers spring from the dry earth. The fists give her away. She is determined not to be dead, she is not walking down those generous paths that lead to heaven and hell in Doña Flora's picture. Her eyes, too, refuse to join eternal sleep. They are closed, that is true, but almost clinched shut as if she will not accept this new reality. A trail, a white very clear trail, winds up the distant sierra toward the sky and white cross. But she seems reluctant to get up and follow it. Alfonso admitted some of this in his brief note: "the sun slowly faded the flowers to a mystical shade. . . ."

The killer, he may become a *corrido* sung in the ranchos and bars, a few verses bouncing off the walls of the whorehouses. She will be whispers among the villagers and then perhaps forgotten. Or she may become a ghost, a Weeping Woman, walking the dirt lanes at night, her loins hungry for the probe of a man. Her needs will be endless, her conquests terrifying, her tongue a subject of much talk late in the night when the globe on the lamp grows sooty and coyotes face down the dogs and take over the hours which they clot with their songs. The story is not new. It keeps happening everywhere. In time, the desert will swallow it all and grind it to a fine dust. But it may take centuries. The bones linger here, just look at Padre Kino still staring up at the faithful with that odd button on his chest. The grin is exquisite. But he lacks the eyes, lacks those knowing eyes, and his fists are not clenched, not clenched at all. Of course, he wore a hair shirt, used no spices or herbs in his food, liked to be flogged, and according to all reports did not lie with women or crave their warm loins. This last part I doubt, the part about not craving women, the crack of the whip into his pale skin sings with an unmistakable message.

Love is very hard to deny. I have tried often. The desert is a hard mistress. To the quick eye it is ugly, to the studied eye it is empty, to the greedy eye it is to be taken, used up, and then discarded so that some thing that is better, some place that is better may flow into life and caress the skin. There are no easy bowers of flowers to lie under, the coyotes do not truly bark but scream and whine on the night wind. The cattle stare hungry and lean and always you are finding moist bones out under mesquite where a tooth has ripped them apart or, in the dry years, the hot winds have tortured them until their black tongues swell with thirst and they give up and become quick rot, or mummies. *Pobrecitos.*

The drugs, those ice picks in the eyes, the rat-a-tat-tat of machine guns at Caro Quintero's plantation, these are but recent versions of very old things. Back behind the village of León stretches the Rancho Huerta. When Don Pedro was a boy, even then the rancho was an ancient place. The mausoleum there is like a small house, think of it, a building with nothing but the bones of *ricos.* The *ejido* has always been at war with the rancho over the land in the area. Now the rancho is owned by a woman and she is never there, she lives elsewhere and just takes the income. In the night, men come and cut her fences. The village runs its cattle in and grazes on her land, uses her water. The fences go back up. They are cut again. The huge *tombe* with the bones has been robbed again and again.

These moments are about what everything is about here: the land. The killings, they come and go. The *patrons,* they seem to be forever. You are riding by in a truck with Don Pedro and over there, just at the lip of the rise, you see the fresh mesquite posts, the new wire, all put in to replace what villagers have sacked in the night. Don Pedro's old face is passive but the eyes they are knowing, you can see little teeth there that will gnaw at the bones of the hacienda forever. Don Pedro points out to the sierra and he says León's lands extend to the other side of the mountain. The Rancho Huerta stands in the way of the communal lands. No doubt his father and grandfather worked at the rancho as peons, keeping a family and cornfield in the village below. No doubt the rancho kept encroaching on the ancient holdings. No doubt Don Pedro spent his decades as a vaquero on a rancho very much like this grand Rancho Huerta. It is all in his black eyes.

He says the woman apparently has had enough. She is dickering to sell the ranch to a Mafioso. She seems to believe such a man can keep what she finds difficult to retain. If that takes place, the sale, then the fences will be watched by men with Uzis. Perhaps, things will calm down for a while. Time runs long here. Since only God seems to know the beginning of León, only God can glimpse its ending.

As he says these things the huge image of the Virgin of Guadalupe stares down from the cliffs, that preposterous visitation in 1531 when a brown Indian, Juan Diego, came to the bishop in Mexico City clutching an armful of fresh red roses in the dead of winter, the sign to the Spaniards that God smiled upon their conquest, the signal to the Indians that the Virgin with her brown skin and black hair was one of them. When the drug dealer of the valley spent his millions of pesos for the image on the cliff, when he had this thing fabricated and it was finally finished, that morning one of Don Pedro's sons got up before dawn and left the house with a bouquet of flowers in his hand and walked the many miles across the desert and up into the sierra and laid his offering at her feet. It will go on a long time.

Or will it? The desert, perhaps, but this combat over hard land? This scramble for food, this rich scent of women on the night wind? The village, logically, the village will vanish into the city, the fields will fall back into desert, the small mud houses will melt into the earth from which they were made. The drugs will go away whenever rich Americans and poor Americans grow bored with this particular variety of life. Doña Flora, Don Pedro, the smiling children, the girls with hungry hips, the starving cattle, the mild cow cheese, all these thing will vanish from memory. As will Charlie Keating with his pyramid of junk bonds, real estate flips and twists and contortions, foreign currency plays, and donations to the church. The Seri will cut down the last ironwood tree, slaughter the last turtle, pull up the last fish, and vanish into the puddle of our European culture. Kino will dissolve into dust, blow away one afternoon in the wind, the button on his breast surviving longer than his memory. The petals will fall, one by one, from every last bloom in the flower world. The sacred deer will stop talking to us and go away and fall down tired and eagerly rot. The magic tree will no longer give us messages. The last cat will be slaughtered in the sierra, the tingling teeth grow still, the tongue stop groping and slopping for that sweet slurp of hot blood. The dead woman clenching her pale fists in the open grave with the blue flowers fading above her hungry lips, she will surrender and become dirt, sweet-smelling dirt when the winter rains drift slowly across the desert floor. Alfonso's paintings will age, pigment flake off, and become blanks. The damn guitars will grow still, the whores with their fat hips, and red lips—and when I get to the room and they pull off their simple dresses their nipples glow darkly in the kerosene light—those fat whores will disappear also along with the cursed shrines to the Virgin of Guadalupe that always stare serenely by the creaking bed. I will drive down the avenues and the traffic will be gone, piled up by the side like wooly mammoths, the stoplights will be dark, the tall buildings felled like redwoods, their blocks scattered across the intersections. Literacy will fall away, tongues will be ripped out, words will stop cluttering our heads. A bird will soar overhead with a cruelly sharp beak. Logically, we are all fucked, as is everything, even the baby searching fiercely for the mother's swollen breast.

I am told that even the sun will someday die.

But not a one of us believes it. When Doña Flora gives me the cheap print of heaven and hell she got at the fiesta in Magdalena fifty years before, she insists I wrap it carefully in my jacket. Her face is very wrinkled and, given her years, she will be dead soon, as dead surely as the boy is who had ice picks driven through his eyes and then the knife descended to his crotch. No more children will slide down her loins, and she will not be another slice of the pie. I wrap it very carefully. She apologizes for the cracked glass. *De nada.*

We go out in the yard, one of the half-starved cats has killed a woodpecker, the feathers, bold black-and-white fletched feathers, are scattered by the doorway. But there is no meat left, not a clue of the head, not even the beak. She walks off with two sticks and gathers broken pieces of cholla, drops them one by one around her few flowers and herbs. Lest the cats feed there also.

I think for my needs, for my blood, for my life, for the moon swinging over León, Hermelinda will last just long enough. True, the blue flowers fade. But they keep throwing down seeds and I can see them growing in the brown hot soil. I put my hand down and the flesh heaves, the nipples grow hard, my hand slips lower.

Desierto, the word rolls off my clumsy lips.

I find night at last on the bed of saguaro ribs hung off the crude ironwood posts. Alfonso lies on his cot by the fire. He makes beautiful things. Getting sober had taken a lot of time out of his life. He had tried to dry out, of course, and might go, say, three months without a bottle and everything would be fine and then that day would come. He would lose it, but he had been losing for so long it seemed natural. His voice tells me the tales of his struggle, the voice is a pure thing, flat yet with feeling, a kind of flute floating across the smoky blackness of the hut with the leaky fireplace, smoke seeping from the chimney Don Pedro is convinced would work if he could just find that bird's nest. Ah, that it would be that simple. Then, Al recalls, one holiday, things came to a head. Christmas was coming and this feeling came over him, something stronger by far than his feelings for his wife and his children. And he broke out all the windows in this crummy house he was renting. The cold winter air flowed in. The rest cannot be remembered. He wound up in this county drunk tank. Out back they had a check-in center in a small trailer that was surrounded by chain-link fence and concertina wire. He looked at it under the bright beams of the spotlights and was convinced it was a gas chamber. He ran for freedom, and scaled the fence before two cops pulled him down. They took him to the hospital where he was shot full of drugs and then brought back for lockdown.

He woke up in a barracks. There were bunk beds and drunks sat on the edge of each and vomited out their guts. Al did the same for a day or two. The cages were on the Mexican side of town, deep in the barrios. Finally, he began to straighten out, the shakes were not so bad, the sour taste in his mouth not so frightening. This old drunk came out of the shadows and eyed him.

"Do you think," the old juicer asked, "this is a movie set? Do you think this is not real? Don't you know that you're a type? Do you think this place was built just for you? Don't you realize that they built this place before you were born, before you existed? You're a type."

That was Christmas Day. Al was twenty-nine.

He called his wife and said he would never drink again. But those were words everyone had heard before.

He was working on a painting at the time which had this huge tree covered with leaves. At first, Alfonso could paint but one leaf a day. It was hard to even manage that. But he stuck with it, leaf by leaf. That is the story flowing through the night air as the mesquite fire backflushes from the mud fireplace and the moon rides over León. Alfonso has not had a drink since that Christmas and now by the calendar he is forty-one years of age.

He paints these images that many mock, images of a strange Mexican village, and some say such a place does not exist. I can understand this hostility to his work. The eyes, for example, the knowing eyes that lack pupils, who sees such eyes? Show me the photograph. I can find perfect photographs of desert sunsets with the sky blood red, the cactus silhouetted against the sky, each needle, each tiny needle backlit and glowing like a promise of life and love. I can find books filled with the sweat rolling as shimmering droplets through the canyon of a woman's cleavage, the warm sun on her bare ass, the glow of the leaves on the cottonwoods hugging the banks of a rock-hard canyon. The thin lips on a drug dealer's face as he faces the camera and says, "So what?"

But blue flowers fading by a young Mexican woman's grave, ah, my God, that hot brown skin and her teeth biting the lip, flowers fading until they match the sky? *Pobrecito.* That nerve, that forgotten nerve, tingling, triggering some little synapse in the ganglia, probing, searching for the space between the vertebrae.

Out there. Don't you understand that this place existed, that this place was ready before you were born, before you were a thought? Don't you understand that you are a type? Do you really think this is a movie set?

Let us be sensitive, it is our task, is it not? One of Doña Flora's relatives is driving back to *El Norte*, to *Estamos Unidos.* He is a young man, a Mexicano, but one who works and makes his money north of the line that human beings have drawn across the desert. Do not be alarmed by the line, it is all right, such divisions have been drawn and warred over forever, by plants, by animals. By us. He is driving—see him there, all cocky and happy and dreaming of a girl, a cold bottle of beer, her smile, his hands on her hips—when he hits the Mexican army roadblock. They search the vehicle, a waste you say, yes? With a Mexicano, what can he possibly pay? But he is from the north, the money drips off him. They find a joint. He is not spoken for, he is not in the life. He does not grow, he does not pay, he does not deliver, he does not risk, he lacks the appropriate rights. They give him a *calientada,* a warming over. A soldier breaks his jaw with the butt of his rifle. As the bone breaks, the night breeze flows like love across the arm of the saguaro, the coyote howls, and the blue flowers grow yet paler.

Don't you realize this place existed before you were born?

We awaken before dawn, smell the smoke of the fire in Doña Flora's wood stove, trudge through the desert to her table and pour down the black coffee. The plates are cold and beans steam into my face, the tortilla warm in my hand. Don Pedro has finished milking his cows and sits waiting. The metal detector has arrived from *Estamos Unidos,* a thing picked up by a son at a swap meet. For days, the old man has been abuzz about the imminent arrival of the device. There is gold in the sierra, everyone knows this to be a fact, gold left by the Yaquis as they fled nōrth behind the village, the long dresses of their women rustling softly as they padded through the desert. At night, sometimes the gold glows, truly, the villagers often see these glowing sores on the stone cliffs. Twenty-five years ago, a man of León drove his cows back against the face of the sierra for better grazing. He set up a camp there, built a little cheese house out of ocotillo. Every few days, he would come down with his cheeses for sale in the neighboring towns. Soon he had worn a regular path in the brown soil. Where he cut through one gully, he noticed a smooth-sided thing emerging from the cut bank. He thought, that must be a buried tree trunk. With time, more of the form emerged and he realized the surface was perfectly flat, an object that had to come from the hand of a man. So he took a shovel and pickaxe back and dug. The chest was very old, and inside were heaps of gold coins.

This is not so surprising in a country where for centuries the banks either did not exist or could not be trusted, in a valley where for centuries human beings buried their hoards under the dirt floors of their houses or back in the secret nooks and crannies of the desert. They glow at night on the sierra. No one doubts such glows. One night Doña Flora and Don Pedro and some friends were sitting out when they saw a strong persistent glow up on the mountain. Gold. They piled in a truck and drove off into the darkness, and as they approached the peaks the glow got stronger and stronger and stronger. Their excitement charged the air with an electrical fury. They found an old man and boy huddled around a wood fire under the huge shrine to the Virgin of Guadalupe. They had been hired by the drug lord to create the blessed image.

Now Don Pedro is very anxious to be moving. There is one hitch—the instructions for the metal detector are written in English. Translation will be necessary, *por favor.* I thumb through the yellow booklet, the cover showing a prospector panning a desert stream, his burro tied behind him, the sierra ghostly on the horizon. The troubleshooter section begins,

Q: I heard of an account of an operator who located an old rifle ball, embedded in the ground, with his instrument and as he dug it up he noticed some white bones. Digging further, he uncovered a skeleton of a man. Is it possible?

A: Yes, this was also reported to us on one of our trips back from the wonderful land of Mexico. . . . We also received a report where a skeleton was found, in a suit of armor, in Arizona. One never knows what he may find.

We stuff the machine with batteries, check the meters, but nothing will get it to cough up that hum through the speakers that means metal can be announced. Finally, we give up. Don Pedro is a little disappointed. The machine lies on the table like a corpse and men from the village drop in to admire it and run their hands along it.

Don Pedro climbs in the truck—we have shovels, picks, and lots of water. He will not enter the desert without lots of water. Last year he was up against the sierra when his horse threw him and ran off and the old man of eighty had to walk out, walk out dry. We grind slowly up the dirt road, snake past the school, the small *tienda,* around various ranchos tucked away in the brush, and minute by minute the sierra comes closer. The Virgin begins to take shape, her outlines grow hard, the colors faintly flicker. The robe is red, the cape green, the cement slab harsh white. Up on the white corner someone has stuck a red flag that is held in place with a section off a chrome bumper. Paper flowers in vases fade at Our Lady's feet, a colored piece of cement shaped like a heart has little stones glued to it spelling Ave Maria. Don Pedro scampers past the Virgin and in a moment the old man is boulder-hopping high above my head. He snaps limbs off some Sangre de Cristo and comes back with an armload. Good for a cough, he says.

Down below León spreads like a quaint painting with little fields and houses and the arroyo is a green snake writhing down the valley. If one tracks a direct line from the Virgin's eyes to the valley floor it seems to lead to the big house of the drug lord, the man who paid millions of pesos for the creation of the shrine.

Blue flowers fading by an uneasy grave.

Don Pedro says the little basin below the Virgin is rife with the javelina, a wild pig-like animal. Last time he was up here he saw two skins hung out to dry on a tree. He says when the Yaquis fled north, they often camped right here in this little basin. And, of course, they buried gold, lots of gold. We descend, drop down into a wash, and the old man begins to shovel gravels, search the soil with his hands for a trace of mineral, almost twitch his nose for a whiff of gold. The handle of his shovel is broken; no matter, he makes do.

Pitahaya and saguaro tower over the old man. He moves like a cat, an old cat but still a cat. He is lost in his work, reaching that point everyone craves where you stop thinking and become an animal, an organism that is, rather than one that contemplates someday being. All the interior dialogues that we kill time with suddenly stop, all the day-to-day concerns vanish, all the little speeches that ruin the moment by dismissing the scent on the wind, all these things end. The eyes, those are the eyes that Alfonso loves to paint. Ancient eyes, young eyes, open eyes full of knowing. Eyes that have sunk to a place past thinking and do not mourn the loss. Alfonso is convinced that in the village there are far more of those eyes than in the city. Perhaps he is right. Don Pedro glows now with those eyes.

We never find gold, not even a trace. Perhaps tonight there will be fire on the sierra, a fire where no man camps, a fire in a place where Yaquis padded north with guns on their shoulders and the flower world reeking of perfume in their heads. We will go up there, and truly, the fire will persist, the glow from the rock, the passion burning in the earth. We will dig and there will be the golden chalice, or the strongbox full of coins, the shimmering candlestick, the raw ore of a mother lode. It has happened before.

Alfonso believes strongly now in guardian angels, in auras, in many things, but especially in guardian angels. He paints them with a fervor that is sensual. The breasts are huge, the eyes deranged, the hair a mess, the nipples hard, the hips full. The face will not let you go. The angel has just slept with you. You can feel her sweat against your body. This is against the rules, but it cannot be helped.

Alfonso's angel says, "I'm not supposed to love you, not the way I do."

And with one glance you know what she means. Alfonso has always wanted to make love to an angel, to pour his body in hers. The angel holds red roses in her hands, a dove flies against her skirt.

She says, "Each night when you are sleeping, I give you moonbeams from the sky. Then I softly touch your body, and it always makes me cry."

* * *

They tell a story in León and they believe the story. Sometimes I tell this story to the people in the States, and they often say they do not understand what it means. I never explain it because I cannot believe anyone fails to understand it, that the only issue is whether or not one admits to understanding this story. It is about the danger of darkness in the desert. For example, recently Chapo and his wife walked to Magdalena to visit their fifteen-year-old daughter who had married. On the way back across the desert, night fell on the lonely dirt road. During the daytime if a car approached or a truck, they would hitch a ride. Everyone here takes rides or gives rides. But at night when they saw headlights they fled into the desert until the car had passed. Many of the villagers are now reluctant to be out at night if they are afoot.

The story is very simple. A black man and a white woman, both Americans, are riding around this area on a motorcycle. They roar down the dirt roads, the air streaming through their hair. The white woman is blond, the black man is large. They ride at night, always at night. They are hunting. When they find a child, they kill it and drain the blood. This blood they sell to AIDS patients in the United States. Always they leave the child's corpse right by the road; to the chest they pin lots of money for the parents.

The story makes perfect sense. Of course, the gringos have need for the blood of our pure and clean *niños.* Consider the gringos' soulless faces, their bestial ways, the things they do to each other and call love. The men loving the men. They must come here, to León, if they want strong blood, rich blood, pure blood. And filth that they are, they would trade our beloved children's lives for money.

They are out there right now, riding the desert at night looking for the blood of *la gente.*

7

Pacific air sweeps across the sands near the saltworks of Guerrero Negro in Baja California. The small plane lands on a dirt strip by the sea, the runway a glaze of clay surrounded by small dunes of sand. An old man stumbles out of a shed as she climbs from the pilot's seat. I walk over and ask for aviation fuel and he scurries away like a crab dragging the heavy black hose, and pushing before him a small little metal platform for reaching the tanks in the wings. She ambles away in her tight Levis and black leather bomber jacket, her long black hair blowing in the wind. The old man looks up at me, his face a wasteland of gray stubble, the teeth rotten and dark.

He asks, "Is she good to fuck?" Right away it is out in the open, the reason a person comes to Mexico, or the thing that quickly drives a person away. I remember a moment a couple of months back, down at Cabo on the tip of the peninsula. We'd landed the plane and I walked into the air terminal and this guy says to me, "You want some coke?" and I think, I'm getting out of here. So we fly north to a farm town on the Pacific side named Todos Santos, All Saints, and land on a little road in the garbage dump. The plane gets stuck, and a bunch of guys show up out of the garbage and push us out. We hitch a ride into town, have a couple of beers, she's high as a kite from the landing in the garbage, and then we find this lodging called Hotel California right across from the local pool hall. The whole town is based on sugar cane, *panocha,* and they make nice flat cakes of the syrup. I couldn't be happier, *panocha* is Mexican slang for pussy. We walk along the dirt streets and come to this restaurant that is like a giant ramada, thatched top resting on columns and a low concrete wall circling. The whole thing nestles in a depression with vines and trees staging a tropical riot. The table is metal and naked light bulbs hang down and we order platters of shrimp and some more beers, and then I notice her staring over my shoulder, her eyes locked on this table where this Mexican couple, the guy in his forties, the woman past thirty, are locked in a moment. The man is talking endlessly, his head bent down toward the table top, talking that stream of sadness and worldliness that Mexican men like to dish out to their women. She sits there, her abundant body about to burst out of her clothes, her flesh reeking with desires, and nods her head carefully. Her blouse is unbuttoned and huge breasts promise to topple forward and go splat on the cool metal table top. The man keeps his low rumble of words going. This goes on for an hour and he never stops and she never skips a beat in doling out her attention, or ceases to exude this musk.

When the woman leaves, I look hard and long at her hips. Outside I can hear the faint sound of the Pacific swells crashing into the curve of clean sand beach. Then we walk back to our hotel, buying a six-pack of Tecate on the way, and strip and lie on the bed with the window open. It is hot and there is no cooling system and for hours we fight and grow sullen and I sit on the side of the bed and look through the window and see the night wash across the trees and vines and hear people's voices laughing and smell that musk, and the beers are warm now and taste bitter in my mouth. Sometimes, I love this country.

The town of Guerrero Negro, the Black Warrior, is ugly, a company town for the largest saltworks on earth, one now owned by the Japanese. Huge pans have been carved out of the sand, the sea floods in, is trapped, evaporates, and the white blaze of salt stares up. Then it is loaded on barges, hauled out miles across the ocean to Isla Cedros, loaded on big freighters, and disappears into the maw of Japanese life. The wind never stops blowing here, the sand is always in the air, the streets moving walls of dust, the shops and houses forlorn out on the barren sands. The desert is just a happenstance, a platform where looting takes place, a thing ignored in the frenzy of capturing the salt. The desert ends here, surrenders to the big waters.

I have come to see the whales, the Pacific grays that plunge down the coast from Alaska to calve in Scammon's Lagoon, the site of the saltworks. Whales and barges somehow negotiate around each other. Longer than we know, the cows have come here to drop their young in the lagoon while the bulls patrolled outside its mouth like warships. It is like the salt, like everything in the desert, something that could go on forever, until we discovered it. They arrive around January and some linger into March. No one knew they came here until a captain stumbled upon them in the mid-nineteenth century. He found the entrance to the hidden lagoon and the rest was blood in the water and strange cries.

Now, people come to watch, pay to go out in small boats and touch. For the time being we are busy murdering the oil beds and the whales get a break until their turn comes up again. From the plane window, they are shadows in the green water, the huge cow, the small young, two pods nestled against each other in a gigantic nursery. Scientists and tour guides run the lagoon, and while the saltworks still grinds away day and night, those seeking nature and nature's ways flee their jobs and come here to look into eyes the size of pizzas. I am no different.

I'm in this cafe tackling a fish dinner when I notice a guy sitting at another table mainlining *cervezas* in the heat of the afternoon. He drinks three Coronas fast but picks at his *pulpo coctele*. The beard is trimmed, the shirt white with blue stripes, the slacks tan. He looks across the cafe and asks, "How do you say 'times time'?"

He translates for the Japanese who own that hefty chunk of the salt. He is the Mexican intellectual, the Marxist, the man who has written articles, done time in the intense conversations of Mexico City. His grandfather was a captain with Pancho Villa—and died before a firing squad. This is a common background of horror that every Mexican can produce when the occasion warrants it. Now he is back in the desert, back to his native town, this hellish outpost of salt. He says, "I love Baja."

He tells me I must stay to see the sunset.

Why, I ask? The town stares out to sea at an almost permanent fog bank brewing just off the coast, a dull morass of swirls.

"For the grays," he explains, "all the grays."

He continues on about his pueblo. Ah, of course, he must touch on the drugs. Have you heard of Caro Quintero? he asks. Well, he has several ranchos near here out in the desert, places well guarded with buried oil tanks by secret airfields. The life. He does not seem disturbed by this fact and I know what he will say if I ask about it. He will tell me that if Americans wish to kill themselves with this vile poison it is not his affair or that of his country. That they are very poor, and have deep problems, that they are two nations, European and Indian, trying to heal ancient wounds, a festering memory of a rape. Besides, the desert is good, Baja is home, and these other matters, whether *narcotrafi-cantes* or capitalists lusting for salt, these other matters cannot touch the deeper life, the one that holds him in its thrall. I agree. Not because I believe this argument, this act of faith actually, but because I am living it. I am watching ruin, and yet savoring life. I am complete. At one time, I thought such a state would require solutions, or at least absolution. But now I realize all it requires is hunger, the hunger to belong to something that is worth giving my bones to.

Two or three years ago, the man in the cafe tells me, his brother was the town doctor. A man was found dead in the desert and there was nothing left of this man except for some bones and a few bottles of American medicine. A man, I suspect, like myself, someone who had gone into the desert for reasons he could not really explain or deny. All this, the bones, the pill bottles, was brought to his brother in a plastic garbage bag. The remains told nothing and the American consulate discovered nothing. No one missed the man in the garbage bag. Finally, he and his brother took the bag of bones down to the sea where the desert tasted the salt water and they cast the remains upon the waves.

"We gave him," he says almost wistfully, "a faraway."

I have never heard a mountain lion bawling over the fate of his soul.

—Edward Abbey, introduction to *Desert Solitaire*

ABOUT THE AUTHOR

Author of many acclaimed books about the American Southwest and US-Mexico border issues, CHARLES BOWDEN (1945–2014) was a contributing editor for *GQ, Harper's, Esquire,* and *Mother Jones* and also wrote for the *New York Times Book Review, High Country News,* and *Aperture.* His honors included a PEN First Amendment Award, Lannan Literary Award for Nonfiction, and the Sidney Hillman Award for outstanding journalism that fosters social and economic justice.

ABOUT THE AUTHOR OF THE FOREWORD

WILLIAM DEBUYS is the author of nine books, which range from memoir and biography to environmental history and studies of place. His books include *The Last Unicorn,* named one of *Christian Science Monitor*'s 10 best nonfiction books of 2015 and *A Great Aridness: Climate Change and the Future of the American Southwest,* which won the Weber-Clements Prize for best book on the Southwest in 2011. *River of Traps* was one of three finalists for the Pulitzer Prize in General Nonfiction in 1991. He lives on the farm he has tended since 1976 in the remote village of El Valle in northern New Mexico.